The Prior of the Knights Hospitaller in Late Medieval England

The Prior of the Knights Hospitaller played a major role not only within the Order, but also in the wider arena of English – and indeed European – politics. This role, and its changes between 1272 and 1540, are the focus of this new book, which draws extensively on archival material both in the United Kingdom and in the Hospitaller archives in Malta. It argues that the Prior's allegiance to the crown was as important as his allegiance to his order, that the relationship between crown and priory was generally cordial and that usually there was no contradiction between service to the crown and to the Convent. The book demonstrates a general expansion in the public roles of the Hospitaller Prior, not just under the most politically important Priors. It analyses the Priors' interactions with financially important merchants and the terms that three Priors served as treasurers of England. Finally, by revealing how the order lost political control of its estates, it contributes to the broader themes of secularism and emerging nationalism.

Dr SIMON PHILLIPS is Research Fellow at the University of Winchester.

The Prior of the Knights Hospitaller in Late Medieval England

Simon Phillips

THE BOYDELL PRESS

First published 2009
The Boydell Press, Woodbridge

ISBN 978-1-84383-437-3

The Boydell Press is an imprint of Boydell & Brewer Ltd
PO Box 9, Woodbridge, Suffolk IP12 3DF, UK
and of Boydell & Brewer Inc.
668 Mt Hope Avenue, Rochester, NY 14620, USA
website: www.boydellandbrewer.com

The publisher has no responsibility for the continued existence or accuracy of URLs
for external or third-party internet websites referred to in this book, and does not
guarantee that any content on such websites is, or will remain,
accurate or appropriate.

A CIP record for this book is available
from the British Library

This publication is printed on acid-free paper

Printed in Great Britain by
CPI Antony Rowe, Chippenham, Wiltshire

In memory of my mother
Gwendoline Tanswell
and my cousin
Thomas Tanswell

Contents

Figures

Acknowledgements

Recognition is due to many people who offered their expertise during the production of this book. Firstly, I wholeheartedly thank Professor Michael Hicks for sharing with me his extensive knowledge of late medieval England and for commenting on the manuscript. Further thanks are owed to Dr Helen Nicholson for her helpful suggestions on the work and to Professor Anne Curry and Dr Stella Fletcher for their counsel on Chapter 4. Professors Thomas Beaumont James and Barbara Yorke provided a general perspective on the text. I am indebted to Dr Anthony Luttrell for his advice on the Malta archives. Thanks are also offered to the anonymous reviewers of the manuscript. I wish to express my deepest gratitude to Victoria Tanswell for proofreading the final version. All the above helped to improve the text. Any errors are entirely my own.

Appreciation is also owed to the staff of the Institute of Historical Research, the Warburg Institute Library, the British Library and to Pamela Willis of the Museum and Library of the Venerable Order of St John. Special credit is owed to the staff at the National Archives, Kew, and the National Library of Malta for making me welcome and for efficient service. I thank the staff at Boydell & Brewer for their assistance and Phillip Judge for drawing the map on p. xiv. I am grateful to the Research and Knowledge Transfer Centre of the University of Winchester for providing me with a bursary to visit the National Library of Malta.

Thanks also to Dr Richard Brown and Dr Winifred Harwood for general advice, to my sisters, Louise, Cristal, Denise, my father, Geoff Phillips, and my uncle, Brian Tanswell, for their interest and emotional support. I am thankful to Dr Julia Boorman who sparked my interest in the Crusades and military orders. Finally, I would like to thank Dr Maria Mina, both for her advice on database construction, used to analyse the Hospitaller lease books in Chapter 6, and for all her love and encouragement.

Abbreviations

1338 Survey	*The Knights Hospitaller in England: Being the Report of Prior Philip de Thame to the Grand Master Elyan de Villanova for AD 1338*, ed. L. B. Larking, Camden Society, LXV, 1857
Annales Monastici	*Annales Monastici*, 5 vols, ed. H. R. Luard, Rolls Series, London, 1864–1869
Bekynton Correspondence	*Official Correspondence of Thomas Bekynton, Secretary to Henry VI and Bishop of Bath and Wells*, 2 vols, ed. G. Williams, Rolls Series, 1872
BIHR	*Bulletin of the Institute of Historical Research*
BL	British Library
Cartulaire Général	*Cartulaire Général de l'Ordre des Hospitaliers de S. Jean de Jérusalem (1100–1310)*, 4 vols, ed. J. Delaville le Roulx, Paris, 1894–1905
CCR	*Calendar of Close Rolls preserved in the Public Record Office, 1288–1509*, 45 vols, London, 1904–63
Cely Letters	*The Cely Letters 1472–1488*, ed. A. Hanham, The Early English Text Society, CCLXXIII, London, 1975
CFR	*Calendar of Fine Rolls preserved in the Public Record Office, 1272–1509*, 22 vols, London, 1911–62
Clerkenwell Excavations	B. Sloane and G. Malcolm, eds, *Excavations at the Priory of the Order of the Hospital of St John of Jerusalem, Clerkenwell, London*, Museum of London Archaeology Service Monograph XX, London, 2004
CMSP	*Calendar of State Papers and Manuscripts, existing in the Archives and Collections of Milan 1385–1618*, ed. A. B. Hinds, London, 1912
CPL	*Calendar of the Entries in the Papal Registers relating to Great Britain and Ireland: Papal Letters, 1198–1492*, 15 vols, London, 1893–1960
CPR	*Calendar of Patent Rolls preserved in the Public Record Office, 1281–1509*, 47 vols, London, 1893–1916
CVSP	*Calendar of State Papers and Manuscripts relating to English Affairs existing in the Archives and Collections of Venice and in other Libraries of Northern Italy, 1202–1674*, vols 1–6, ed. R. Brown and H. F. Brown, London, 1864–84
Death and Dissent	*Death and Dissent: Two Fifteenth Century Chronicles. The Dethe of the Kynge of Scotis and Warkworth's Chronicle*, ed. L. M. Matheson, Woodbridge, 1999

EHD	*English Historical Documents*, 12 vols, ed. D. C. Douglas, London, 1953–77
EHR	*English Historical Review*
English Diplomacy	J. Ferguson, *English Diplomacy, 1422–1461*, Oxford, 1972
Fasti Ecclesiae Anglicanae	J. Le Neve, *Fasti Ecclesiae Anglicanae, 1300–1541*, 12 vols, ed. H. King, London, 1962–7
Feudal Aids	*Inquisitions and Assessments Relating to Feudal Aids, with Other Analogous Documents Preserved in the Public Record Office, A.D. 1284–1431*, 6 vols, London, 1899–1920
Foedera, London	*Foedera, conventiones, literæ, et cujuscunque generis acta publica, inter reges Angliæ, et alios quosvis Imperatores, Regis, Pontifices, Principes, vel communitates, ab ineunte sæculo duodecimo, viz. ab anno 1101, ad nostra usque tempora, habita aut tractata*, 2nd edn, 20 vols, ed. T. Rymer, London, 1727–35
Foedera, Hague	*Foedera, conventiones, literae, et cujuscunque generis acta publica: inter reges Angliae et alios quosvis imperatores, reges, pontifices, principes, vel communitates, ab ineunte saeculo duodecimo, viz. ab anno 1101. ad nostra usque tempora, habita aut tractata: ex autographis, infra secretiores archivorum regiorum thesaurarias per multa saecula reconditis, fideliter exscripta*, 3rd edn, 10 vols, ed. T. Rymer, Hague, 1739–45
Forey, *Military Orders*	A. Forey, *The Military Orders: From the Twelfth to the Early Fourteenth Centuries*, Basingstoke, 1992
HBC	E. B. Fryde, D. E. Greenway, S. Porter and I. Roy, eds, *Handbook of British Chronology*, 3rd edn, London, 1986
JEH	*Journal of Ecclesiastical History*
JMH	*Journal of Medieval History*
King, *Knights of St John*	E. J. King and H. Luke, *The Knights of St John in the British Realm*, London, 1967
L&P HVIII	*Letters and Papers, Foreign and Domestic of the Reign of Henry VIII*, 22 vols in 37 parts, London, 1864–1929
Lords Journals	*Journals of the House of Lords*, 171+ vols, London, 1802–
Medieval Religious Houses	D. Knowles and R. N. Hadcock, *Medieval Religious Houses: England and Wales*, 2nd edn, London, 1971
Nicholson, *Knights Hospitaller*	H. Nicholson, *The Knights Hospitaller*, Woodbridge, 2001
NLM	National Library of Malta, Valletta
O'Malley, *English Knights Hospitaller*	G. J. O'Malley, *The Knights Hospitaller of the English Langue, 1460–1565*, Oxford, 2005
Parchment and People	L. Clark, ed., *Parchment and People: Parliament in the Middle Ages, Parliamentary History*, XXIII, Special Issue, 2004
Parliamentary Writs	*The Parliamentary Writs and Writs of Military Summons, together with the records and muniments relating to the suit and service due and performed to the King's High Court of Parliament and the Councils of the Realm, or affording evidence of attendance given at Parliaments and Councils*, 2 vols, ed. F. Palgrave, Record Commission, London, 1827–34

POPC	*Proceedings and Ordinances of the Privy Council of England*, 7 vols, ed. N. H. Nicolas, Record Commission, London, 1834–37
Profit, Piety and Professions	M. A. Hicks, ed., *Profit, Piety and the Professions in Later Medieval England*, Gloucester, 1990
RDP	*Reports of the Lords Committees Touching the Dignity of a Peer of the Realm*, 5 vols, London, 1820
Rot. Lit. Claus.	*Rotuli Litterarum Clausarum in Turri Londinensi*, 2 vols, ed. T. D. Hardy, London, 1833–4
Rot. Parl.	*Rotuli Parliamentorum ut et Petitiones et Placita in Parliamento*, 6 vols, ed. J. Strachey, London, 1767–77
Rot. Scot.	*Rotuli Scotiæ in Turri Londinensi et in Domo Capitulari Westmonasteriensi Asservat*, 2 vols, Record Commission, London, 1814–19
Sacra Militia	*Sacra Militia: Rivista di storia degli Ordini militari*, 2 vols, Genoa, 2000–1
Sarnowsky, 'Kings and Priors'	J. Sarnowsky, 'Kings and Priors: the Hospitaller Priory of England in the Later Fifteenth Century', in *Mendicants, Military Orders, and Regionalism in Medieval Europe*, ed. J. Sarnowsky, Aldershot, 1999, 83–102
Sire, *Knights of Malta*	H. H. A. Sire, *The Knights of Malta*, New Haven, CT, and London, 1994
SR	*Statutes of the Realm 1278–1714*, 9 vols, Record Commission, London, 1810–28
Taxatio	*Taxatio Ecclesiastica Angliae et Walliae auctoritate P. Nicholai IV circa AD 1291*, Record Commission, London, 1802
TNA	The National Archives, Public Record Office, Kew
Tyerman, *England and Crusades*	C. Tyerman, *England and the Crusades 1095–1588*, Chicago and London, 1988
Valor	*Valor Ecclesiasticus*, 6 vols, Record Commission, London, 1810–1834
VCH	*The Victoria History of the Counties of England*, 200+ vols, London, 1899–

Commanderies of the English Priory, 1300–1540.

1

Introduction

Late medieval England was still a crusading country. The greatest military order after 1312, the Knights Hospitaller, also called the Order of St John of Jerusalem, held extensive English estates and supplied the crusading war effort with both money and manpower into the Tudor age. Their head, the Prior of St John, had his headquarters at Clerkenwell, just outside the city of London. This book focuses on the role of the Prior of St John in service to the crown between 1273 and 1540. Developments within both the crusading movement and England make this an appropriate starting point. In November 1272, Henry III of England died. The Lord Edward, at that time on crusade in the Holy Land, succeeded him, and appointed Joseph Chauncy, Hospitaller treasurer at Acre, as treasurer of England. Thus, a tangible link developed between the crusading movement and the realm of England, with the former offering service to the crown, and the latter promising support for future crusading campaigns. The later thirteenth century is also a suitable place to begin because the changes in the Prior's role in England can in part be explained by the perceived failings in the crusading movement that led to the loss of Acre in 1291. It is from 1295, for example, that the Prior started to receive regular summonses to parliament. A state of almost constant war from the 1290s with either Scotland or France also had a significant effect on the Prior's role. In 1540, the suppression of the English Priory took effect alongside the general dissolution of the religious houses.

It is the contention of this book that there was a sudden increase of participation by the English Prior in English royal affairs from a routine level, such as on courts of oyer and terminer, to high-profile political and diplomatic service. Although this development can be traced to the latter half of the fourteenth century, it was not until the mid-fifteenth century that the Prior started to serve on a regular basis. That this increased frequency occurred simultaneously for both king's council and diplomatic missions suggests that there was a common reason. This involvement in English public affairs continued until the eve of the English Reformation.

The primary aim of this book is to investigate the unique political role of the Prior of St John in England with reference to parliament, royal council and foreign affairs. The investigation of parliament includes full parliaments, great councils and colloquia. The royal council includes the king's council and its associated committees. Foreign affairs cover the Prior's diplomatic and military roles. The book will investigate changes in the Prior's public role over time, with reference to particular moments when individual Priors were senior political figures. Secondly, the study examines changes in the English Priory to see how they influenced the development of the Prior's role. The Prior was never as independent or as active a crusader as is normally supposed, but neither did his office quite become a royal sinecure. This book will investigate alterations in the degree and balance of service between crown and Hospitaller duties rather than complete changes. Related aims include investigation of the effect of events in the eastern Mediterranean on the policy of the central chapter of the Order and the ensuing consequences for the Order and Prior of England, and exploration of the loss of the Order's political control of its estates to local aristocrats.

The Hospitaller Order

The Hospitallers originated in a hospice for pilgrims at Jerusalem in about 1070. They were formally recognised as a religious order in 1113, in the bull *Pie postulation voluntatis*, by Pope Paschal II (1099–1118). They quickly developed a military role in the first half of the twelfth century, at first by providing safe conduct to pilgrims and later by taking on the responsibility for protecting Christian strongholds in the Holy Land. After the fall of Jerusalem in 1187, the Hospitaller headquarters (the Convent) was moved to their castle at Margat, in the county of Tripoli, before settling in Acre in 1192, where they remained until the fall of the city in 1291. During the period covered by this book, the Hospitallers had their headquarters firstly at Acre, then Limassol on Cyprus (1292–1309), Rhodes (1309–1522) and finally, after temporary residences in Viterbo (1523–27) and Nice (1527–29), on Malta from 1530. Unlike the other military orders, such as the Teutonic Knights, who were active mainly in Eastern Europe, the Hospitallers remained a truly international order throughout the period of this study.

The Hospitaller brethren fell into three categories, knights, sergeants and chaplains, all of whom took vows of poverty, chastity and obedience. They had a strict hierarchy.[1] At their head was the Grand Master, who was elected for life by the brethren in the Convent, where the Grand Master usually resided, although during the Great Schism, as Tipton has noted, he often resided at Avignon.[2] The Grand Master was assisted by other important officials of the Convent; the grand commander acted as the Grand Master's lieutenant; the marshal was responsible for military affairs; the turcopolier, who originally commanded the light cavalry, was in charge of coastal defences on Rhodes and Malta; the treasurer dealt with finances; the hospitaller was in charge of the hospital; the draper in charge of clothing; and the prior of the Convent dealt with spiritual matters. The position of

---

[1] For greater detail see A. Luttrell, 'The Hospitallers at Rhodes, 1306–1421', in *A History of the Crusades*, III, ed. H. W. Hazard, Madison, WI, and London, 1975, 278–339; Sire, *Knights of Malta*, 25–39; A. Luttrell, 'The Military Orders, 1312–1798', in *The Oxford Illustrated History of the Crusades*, ed. J. Riley-Smith, Oxford, 1995, 326–64; Nicholson, *Knights Hospitaller*, 68–97.

[2] C. L. Tipton, 'The English Hospitallers during the Great Schism', *Studies in Medieval and Renaissance History*, IV, 1967, 91–124, at 104.

admiral developed after the move to Cyprus, a consequence of their transformation from a land-based to a sea-based force. Whereas the military brethren in the Holy Land had lived together in one large *auberge* (inn), while on Cyprus they started to live in smaller units called *langues* or 'tongues' that were based on linguistic or 'national' lines. These were in existence from at least 1295, when there were seven tongues, which in order of precedence were Provence, Auvergne, France, Spain, Italy, England, and Germany.[3] The head of each tongue held one of the important offices mentioned above.

The most senior member of the English tongue held the office of turcopolier, at least from 1330. Although the turcopolier was technically head of the English tongue, the Prior of England was the position to which English brethren ultimately aspired: they stepped down from the turcopoliership in order to gain it. The other dignities of the English tongue were the prior of Ireland and, from the fifteenth century, the bailiff of Eagle. The Hospitallers never officially recognised a prior or priory in Scotland, only the commandery of Torphichen, under which all Scottish lands of the Order fell. However, from the later fifteenth century the Scottish crown sometimes referred to the commander of Torphichen as the Scottish prior or 'Lord of St Johns', the same title used by the Prior of England at that time.

In Western Europe, the Hospitallers were organised into provinces known as priories, again based on the 'national' boundaries that determined the tongues. The English Grand Priory, which included Ireland, Scotland and Wales, had its head-quarters at Clerkenwell on the outskirts of London, where the Prior of England, who was head of the Grand Priory, resided. The Hospitallers' lands were organised into houses called commanderies or preceptories, each headed by a commander/preceptor.[4] These commanderies consisted of manors granted by patrons to the Hospitallers. Typically, commanderies were staffed by no more than two or three brethren, which meant that communal life was virtually non-existent. However, non-brethren such as servants and *confratres* (lay men and women who made a dona-tion or annual gift) also lived in the commanderies. Commanders who were not on service in the East were expected to attend the annual chapters of the Priory, which were normally held at Clerkenwell. The Prior of England presided over these chap-ters, at which were discussed, amongst other things, leases of land, the reception of new recruits, promotions, discipline and the revenues, known as responsions, that were sent to the Convent. Priors of England were elected by the English brethren and then confirmed by the Grand Master and the Pope. Although the election was meant to be free from lay interference, in practice Priors, as feudal lords, needed the acceptance of the local king and were required to swear fealty to him. Thus the Prior of England, as for the priors in other provinces, had duties not only to the Order, but also to the crown. The purpose of this study is to explore this service to the English crown, which until now has not received detailed attention.

---

[3] Nicholson, *Knights Hospitaller*, 73; Sire, *Knights of Malta*, 32.

[4] As Helen Nicholson has observed, because some of the Hospitallers' records were written in French and some in Latin, one finds references to the head of a house in one document as *commandeur* (French) and in another as *preceptor* (Latin), Nicholson, *Knights Hospitaller*, 73, 78.

The State of the Order in England, 1300–1540

By way of a prologue to the role of the Prior, a brief account of the English Priory before 1300 is necessary. More detailed histories can be found by King, Rees, Cowan et al. and more recently by Sire.[5] The exact date of the foundation of the Order in England is unknown. Henry I (1100–35) founded the Hospitaller commandery of Villedieu in Normandy, but he does not appear to have granted any lands to the Order in England, saving his patronage for other religious orders, such as the Cluniacs.[6] The first English lands were granted to the Order in Clerkenwell c. 1142–44 by the Bricett family, when the first Prior, Walter, was recorded. These were contemporary with other grants by Sybil de Raynes and the earl of Gloucester (Shingay c. 1144), Agnes de Lacy (Quenington c. 1144–62), Ralph fitz Stephen (Waingrove c. 1147), the Percy family (Mount St John c. 1148), Ranulf, earl of Chester (Maltby c. 1153), Gilbert de Clare, the earl of Hertford (Standon c. 1154), and William, archbishop of York (Ossington c. 1154). Henry II also favoured the Order, as the benefactor of Battisford (1154), and his brother, Henry of Blois the bishop of Winchester, may have founded Godsfield (c. 1167).[7] By 1154 the Order had nine commanderies in England and Torphichen in Scotland.[8] At this time, the English Priory was still subordinate to the priory of Saint-Gilles, remaining so until at least 1184, and then came under the control of the priory of France in 1189. It is probable that soon after this the English Priory gained independence, perhaps due to the prominence of English brethren such as Robert l'Anglais, who was grand commander of the Order between 1195 and 1201, and later Prior of England between 1204 and 1214, but also due to the crusading activities of Richard I.[9] By 1199, the number of commanderies had increased to between 28 and 32. In that year, a royal tax exacted £500 from the Order in England, only half the amount that the Templars paid, but still a sizeable amount, suggesting that the Hospitallers had acquired substantial wealth by the end of the twelfth century.[10] Further commanderies were founded in the thirteenth century taking the total to 43, but the majority dated from the previous century.

The English Priory reached the zenith of its acquisition after the transfer of the belongings of the suppressed Order of the Temple (see Figure 1). It did so with some difficulty, as those who had been awarded custody of the Templar lands during their trial between 1308 and 1312 were unwilling to cede them. The Pope had expressed his wish as early as 1309 that revenues from Templar lands should be used in aid of

[5] King, *Knights of St John*; W. Rees, *A History of the Order of St John of Jerusalem in Wales and on the Welsh Border*, Cardiff, 1947; I. B. Cowan, P. H. R. Mackay and A. Macquarrie, *The Knights of St John of Jerusalem in Scotland*, Edinburgh, 1983; Sire, *Knights of Malta*.

[6] Sire, *Knights of Malta*, 176; J. A. Green, *Henry I: King of England and Duke of Normandy*, Cambridge, 2006, 170–2, 201, 277–83.

[7] *Medieval Religious Houses*, 298–309.

[8] Sire, *Knights of Malta*, 176; *Medieval Religious Houses*, 494.

[9] Sire, *Knights of Malta*, 177; *Cartulaire du Prieuré de Saint Gilles de l'Hôpital de Saint Jean de Jérusalem (1129–1210)*, ed. D. le Blévec and A. Venturini, Paris, 1997, *passim*.

[10] Sire, *Knights of Malta*, 177.

the Holy Land, and thus by implication that the Hospitallers should assume their administration.[11] However, very little passed immediately into Hospitaller custody, and only a few Templar properties were gained after the formal suppression of the Templars and allocation of their possessions to the Hospitallers in 1313. The king appears to have given up those that were in his possession by 1320.[12]

It took the statute of 1324 to revive the process of redistribution to the Hospitallers. Unfortunately for the Hospitallers, the statute also allowed the right of appeal, and there were many claims against them, so much so that by 1328 only £458-worth of Templar revenues was in Hospitaller hands.[13] By the time of the 1338 Hospitaller survey, the situation had changed, so that some £2,489 gross, and £1,711 net of Templar possessions were in Hospitaller hands, due principally to the efforts of Prior Leonard de Tibertis, formerly prior of Venice, who had been overseer of the transfer of Templar lands in the West since 1312, and had actually been present at the formal transfer of English Templar lands by the crown to the Hospitallers in 1313.[14] However, some significant possessions of the Templars remained beyond Hospitaller control, such as Guiting and Bradewell (£133), Hurst and Newsam (£120) and Faxfleet (£100), totalling over £776 altogether. Those holding these possessions were people of influence, such as Ralph Neville, the earls of Arundel, Gloucester and Warenne, the countess of Pembroke and the king's physician and financier Pancio de Controno.[15] At this stage, the Hospitallers still had hopes of regaining these possessions, and they were mentioned in the 1338 Survey. Indeed, the total sum of all the Hospitallers' revenues, £6,389, includes the £776 not yet received, and the responsions, set at £2,280 (a third of the income), included these unrealised revenues.[16] This strongly suggests that the Hospitallers were fairly confident of recovering these possessions, although this turned out to be a drawn-out process. In the case of Saddlescombe in Sussex, they only gained possession in 1397. Some properties, such as Bisham (Berks.) and Denny (Cambs.), were never recovered and were used to found other ecclesiastical establishments.[17] Nevertheless, the Priory of England had, by 1338, turned round its perilous financial position of a decade earlier.

The income of the Order in England in 1338 and 1535 is given in Figure 2. The *Valor Ecclesiasticus* of 1535 does not give as much detail as the 1338 Hospitaller survey, so a complete comparison of the state of the English Order in 1338 and 1535 unfortunately cannot be undertaken. Nonetheless two key areas can be tackled, those being the income of the English Priory, and the number of houses. In comparison to the 1338 income of anywhere from £4,602 to £7,406 and expenses of £1,388, in 1535 the English Priory had a net income of about £5,705, with expenses of £496. One obvious difference is the reduced number of independent commanderies and

---

[11] *CPL 1305–1342*, 64.
[12] *Ibid.*, 198.
[13] *Rot. Parl.*, II, 21, 41–2; 1338 Survey, 217.
[14] TNA E 135/1/25.
[15] 1338 Survey, 212–13.
[16] *Ibid.*
[17] S. D. Phillips, 'The Recycling of Monastic Wealth in Medieval Southern England, 1300–1530', *Southern History: A Review of the History of Southern England*, XXII, 2000, 45–71 at 47–8.

therefore the amount of income that had come under the control of Clerkenwell. By 1535, Clerkenwell had almost 42 per cent the gross income for the whole of the English Priory. One question that needs to be asked is why the Prior came to gain control of possessions throughout the country (other than those associated with his office) that one would expect to have been distributed to the regional commanderies. Was it due to a lack of brethren to supervise these houses, or was the Prior inducing closures to create wealth for himself? A further explanation may lie in the closure or amalgamation of commanderies. It is difficult to know the exact number of commanderies, for either 1338 or 1535, but an approximate number would be between 37 and 53 for 1338, and 19 or 20 plus Clerkenwell in 1535. The disparity in the earlier survey is caused by the categorisation of houses into commanderies, *camerae*, and ex-Templar houses. Some Hospitaller houses, such as Standon in Essex and Sutton-at-Hone in Kent, were listed as commanderies in 1338, but, as they had no brothers resident, they can have been little more than manors under the custody of a chaplain or bailiff. Others appear to have had only one brother, but if one takes into account that some brethren were commanders of more than one house, then these too cannot be considered as separate functioning commanderies. Such was the case with Clanfield in Oxfordshire in 1338, where the only brother listed was the commander Michael Macy, who was also the commander of the more populous house of Quenington in Gloucestershire, where he probably resided. The same is true for John de Caunville, who was commander of both Hardwick and the larger house of Melchbourne in Bedfordshire.

The situation is different when one looks at the *camerae* and acquired Templar houses. Whereas most commanderies had at least one brother resident, of the 29 *camerae* only three, Hampton, Harefield and Wynkebourne, had one brother present as custodian in 1338. Out of 65 Templar properties, only 12 are listed as having resident brethren. One of these, Upleadon in Herefordshire, had only one brother, Robert Cort, who was also commander of the Temple Bruer and Eagle houses in Lincolnshire. Given these amalgamations, one can calculate that of a possible 53 houses in 1338, only 37 (eight of which were ex-Templar) at the most could have formed a religious community, 11 others having only one brother, and a further five having no brethren.[18] Of the 37 'active' commanderies in 1338, 21 houses had two brothers, 13 had three brothers, and only three houses had six or more brethren (out of about 113 brethren in total for the English Priory), Buckland commandery (six), Chippenham (10, six of whom were in the infirmary), and Clerkenwell (seven, plus the Prior).[19] The average commandery was thus a small unit, with even the Hospitaller nunnery of Minchin Buckland, which reportedly had 50 sisters in 1338, now thought to have been much smaller.[20] This suggests a concentration of power and activity at Clerkenwell, even at the beginning of the period studied, and substantiates the portrayal of the Order as a highly centralised international unit.

In the case of the 1535 *Valor Ecclesiasticus*, brethren are not listed, so this method

---

[18] *Camerae* have not been included in these calculations.

[19] 1338 Survey, 19. The Survey says that there were 119 brethren (page 214), but some of the names are duplicated.

[20] A. Luttrell, 'Addenda et Corrigenda', XXV, 1–7 in A. Luttrell, *Studies on the Hospitallers after 1306: Rhodes and the West*, Aldershot, 2007, 4.

cannot be used to calculate the number of commanderies. Many commanderies appear to have been absorbed by Clerkenwell. As the number of new Hospitaller recruits was strictly controlled, these mergers were probably done deliberately to maintain, or perhaps increase, the income of the Prior. However, those that had not become part of Clerkenwell are given separate entries and from this we can calculate that there were approximately 21 houses including Clerkenwell. The 1535 valuation makes it clear that Clerkenwell was not the only commandery to accumulate other houses, as all those commanderies that remained open had increased in value; the lowest net income given is £52, but most were nearly double this, and in the case of Dalby as much as £231.

What is striking in this comparison between 1338 and 1535 is that the expenses incurred seem to have been drastically reduced. This is because the *Valor* underestimates the actual expenses of the Order in a way the 1338 Survey did not. The *Valor* only allowed obligatory expenses and taxes. Voluntary expenses, such as alms and pensions, included in 1338, were not counted in 1535. For example, in 1338 Clerkenwell had expenses of over £421 and the rest of the English Priory £967. In 1535, Clerkenwell's expenses appear to have dropped to £205 and the other commanderies to £291. For Newland commandery, the *Valor* states that the responsions paid to the English brethren on Malta in 1535 was £88 per year, yet the net amount is given as £129 and thus £41 is unaccounted for. Again, for Mount St John, the net value was £102, but only £47 was paid in responsions, a shortfall of £55. Finally, Ribston had a clear profit of £207, but only £82 was paid in responsions, a shortfall of £125.[21]

Although the *Valor* did not account for all expenses, it is likely that the Hospitallers followed the same trend as monastic houses during the later Middle Ages and traditional Hospitaller services, such as hospitality and alms giving, were reduced or withdrawn.[22] For example Slebech, a commandery renowned for such acts, had reduced its expenses from £135 in 1338 to just £27 in 1535. This represents a drop in spending from 43 per cent of that commandery's total income to 12 per cent. The trend towards the withdrawal of hospitality is further indicated by a Hospitaller visitation to the English Priory in 1479, which reported that Prior Weston was not maintaining hospitality at Clerkenwell.[23] However, that report was compiled by the turcopolier, John Kendal, a rival of Prior Weston and keen to point out his faults. Small wonder, then, if Weston was not keen to offer *him* hospitality! Nevertheless, the Hospitallers' spending on charity was higher than the 5 per cent that has been estimated for monastic houses from the twelfth to the fifteenth century.[24] The paying out of pensions and corrodies of various kinds was, in comparison, a major outlay for the Priory.

This commitment increased after the transfer of the Templar lands. On 26 March 1324 sheriffs in England, the bishop of Durham, the earl of Chester, and justices in Wales were informed that the parliament at Westminster had agreed that neither the king nor anyone else had a right to the former lands of the Templars, and that, 'in

---

[21] *Valor*, V, 68, 94–5, 256.
[22] R. H. Snape, *English Monastic Finances in the Later Middle Ages*, Cambridge, 1926, 111–16.
[23] *CPL 1471–1484*, 253.
[24] Snape, *English Monastic Finances*, 116.

as much as the Order of the Hospital of St John of Jerusalem was similarly insti-
tuted and canonised for the defence of Christians and the Holy Church', all lands,
fees and liberties of the Templars would be assigned to the Prior, on condition that
services such as feeding the poor, hospitalities, celebration of divine service and the
defence of the Holy Land were maintained. The parliament agreed that all those
who had come into possession of former Templar lands, whether by hereditary
succession, gift or purchase, would have to give them up. Crown officials were to
publicise the decision so that all tenants knew.[25] Despite this statute, it is likely that
it was in the area of services that costs were cut. The statute also was a cause of
tension, as the only way for Templar patrons to regain lands was to prove that the
Hospitallers were not maintaining services. For example, on 6 July 1335 a commission was called to establish whether the Hospitallers had withdrawn the services
due for the ex-Templar manor of Eagle (Lincs.).[26] In this case they were exonerated,
as on 10 May 1344 the sheriff was ordered to let Prior Thame hold Eagle quit of
alms and other charges, as an ex-Templar property held in frank almoin,[27] and
on 9 February 1377 exemplification of this withdrawal of alms and chantries was
given at Prior Hales' request.[28] In this case, the withdrawal of services had been
legitimised, but this was not always the case. On 1 July 1426, the king's hand was
removed from the manor of Upleadon (Hereford), even though services had not
been maintained since Brother William Roche, knight, had occupied it. It was stated
that three priests should celebrate in the chapel, there should be five sick beds with
two men in each, with meat and raiment, and if one died, he was to be replaced.
Travellers should also be entertained and refreshed with meat and drink.[29]

Withdrawal of services on some manors is understandable given the merging of
properties following the acquisition of the Templars' possessions, as these services
were probably transferred to other places. This excuse, however, cannot be used for
the English headquarters at Clerkenwell in the late fifteenth century. For example,
on 12 December 1479, John Kendal, turcopolier and envoy of the Grand Master to
the papacy, informed the Pope that Prior Weston had not been maintaining hospitality at Clerkenwell, as was customary, and was cutting excess wood and selling it
for his own use. Weston was ordered to re-commence hospitality within two months,
and to stop cutting wood.[30] There is also evidence that some commanderies were
vacant, as on 27 March 1487 papal letters note that the Irish Hospital was so poor
that it could not give hospitality, and that void benefices were to be appropriated
to it.[31] Having said this, it has to be acknowledged that by 1535 some commanderies had been demoted to manorial status. Buckland commandery was leased
out by Prior Kendal to John Verney in 1500, though Verney was responsible for
maintaining hospitality and finding chaplains to perform services in the church

25 *CCR 1323–1327*, 91.
26 *CPR 1334–1338*, 199.
27 *CCR 1343–1346*, 313.
28 *CPR 1374–1377*, 424.
29 *CCR 1422–1429*, 244; Upleadon was part of Dinmore and Garway commandery, which Roche
    had had an association with since 1408 and was still commander of in 1428, NLM 334, f. 105;
    NLM 336, f. 134; NLM 340, ff. 117v–118; NLM 342, f. 131v; NLM 348, ff. 114–114v, 118v.
30 *CPL 1471–1484*, 253.
31 *CPL 1484–1492*, 170.

and related chapels.[32] In 1526, Balsall was leased by Prior Docwra to his kinsman Martin Docwra (who had been seneschal of Balsall since 1511) and discharged to his widow Isabel, also through indenture.[33] Chapter Six provides detailed analysis of this secularisation trend.

What can be inferred from the general history of the Order in England that sheds light on the role of the Prior in England? In conjunction with other sources, the contention that the Prior's integration as lay baron increased over the period seems to be upheld. However, the Prior was involved in the English governmental structure by the thirteenth century at a basic level, serving as a commissioner of oyer and terminer and on the eyre, although by this time the latter was a duty from which the Prior was frequently excused.[34] The skills of Joseph Chauncy, Hospitaller treasurer from 1248 to 1273, were utilised as royal treasurer whilst he was English Prior (1273–81) by Edward I, with whom he had gone on crusade. Chauncy's successors, Priors William de Hanley and Peter de Hagham, acted as royal officials, such as on the king's bench, and in 1295 Hagham was also the first Prior of England to receive regular summonses to the House of Lords.[35]

The Prior occurs regularly in royal records and in the printed chancery calendars. From the details given in the various chancery rolls, a number of roles of the Prior in England are evident in addition to his duties as head of the Hospitallers in the province, and can be categorised as follows. The Prior served as a commissioner on various bodies, such as oyer and terminer, the general eyre, the king's bench, as a commissioner of sewers, and as a commissioner of the peace; he assisted the king militarily and financially; he attended parliaments and colloquia to advise the king, and to act, for example, as a trier of petitions; he also collected and stored for safe-keeping crown subsidies and taxes; he arranged for maintenance for the king's retired servants on Hospitaller estates; he dealt with complaints from foreign merchants and citizens when trading agreements were broken; finally, he acted as the king's ambassador to the Pope, the Grand Master and other monarchs.

Summonses to parliaments and colloquia were constant throughout the period studied. That there were numerically fewer summonses in the fifteenth century was because fewer parliaments were called. The Prior was summoned to all of the 26 parliaments held between 1439 and 1509, and was trier of petitions at 16 of them.[36] Also a constant were commissions, such as of oyer and terminer, relating to the complaints of foreign merchants, and commissions of the peace. Another role that increased in significance was that of holding important offices. In the thirteenth century, Prior Chauncy had been royal treasurer. In the fourteenth century, Prior Hales was admiral of the southern (also called western) fleet in England (as was his successor Prior Radington), royal councillor and royal treasurer. These, however,

---

[32] *Medieval Religious Houses*, 241; BL MS Lansdowne 200, f. 84–84v. The nearby Minchin Buckland nunnery continued as a semi-autonomous Hospitaller house, with Verney responsible for maintaining chaplains to perform divine service at Buckland Prioris and Minchin Buckland.

[33] BL MS Cotton Claudius E VI, ff. 87, 265v–266v; *Valor*, I, 404, 405; TNA C 1/778/30–33.

[34] *CCR 1272–1279*, 565; *CCR 1279–1288*, 41; *CCR 1296–1302*, 293.

[35] *CCR 1288–1296*, 445.

[36] J. C. Wedgwood and A. D. Holt, *History of Parliament: Register of the Ministers and of the Members of Both Houses 1439–1509. Biographies of the Members of the Commons House*, 2 vols, London, 1936–38, II, *passim*.

were isolated examples. It was only from the priorship of Robert Botyll onward that crown appointments became more consistent. These appointments indicate the further integration of the Prior into English politics and society.

Of course, the Prior still had duties to perform as head of the English Priory. As the senior provincial representative of the Order, he had to ensure the smooth running of the Order's affairs in England, Scotland, Wales and, in collaboration with the prior of Ireland, in Ireland.[37] This involved all manner of tasks including land dealings, such as alienations of manors, advowsons, maintenance of services and hospitality, ensuring ancient rights and liberties were upheld, recruitment, entertaining foreign brethren, financial dealings with foreign merchants, as well as being the Grand Master's ambassador in England and elsewhere. Later Priors, such as John Kendal, acted as the Grand Master's ambassador to the Pope. Before his appointment as Prior of England, Kendal (then turcopolier) was the Hospitallers' resident ambassador in Rome. In September 1487, he was both the Grand Master's and the Pope's nuncio to France concerning the custody negotiations for Djem, the Ottoman sultan's brother.[38]

In reality, the Prior alone could not perform all tasks for the Order and the king. He appointed attorneys, most of whom were commanders, who in turn had power to appoint other attorneys. The increasing number of attorneys appointed in the fourteenth century (two in 1302, 12 in 1354, and 18 in 1398) indicates that the Prior's tasks appear to have become more onerous.[39] These attorneys served in all courts in England, including the king's bench. In addition, the Prior occasionally sent a proctor to parliament, unless he was ordered to appear in person. Another indication of the increasing number of tasks the Prior was burdened with is the number of commissions he was appointed to. Although preceptor Hildebrand Inge (in 1381) and Prior Malory (in 1434) were both commissioned once, the commission of the peace was a duty for the Prior that started with Robert Botyll in the first year of Edward IV's reign.[40] Between 1485 and 1507, the Prior was regularly appointed as a commissioner of the peace, mainly in Middlesex and Essex, but also in Cambridgeshire, Derbyshire, Hertfordshire, Huntingdonshire, Norfolk and Warwickshire, though it is not certain if he personally attended proceedings.[41]

As mentioned above, the move towards greater involvement in governmental affairs appears to have taken place in the 1440s, under the priorship of Robert Botyll. Furthermore, this is contemporary with the closure, from the 1430s, of a number of commanderies and their allocation to the Prior (see Figure 3). Before this date, apart from some amalgamations in the twelfth century, the only significant merging of commanderies took place in the 1330s, at a time when the acquisition of the Templars' wealth required a major reorganisation, and only a few were allocated to the Prior. In contrast, the majority of closures after 1430 were granted to

---

[37] The provincial order of seniority was, English Prior, Irish prior, bailiff of Eagle (Aquila). All were subordinate to the turcopolier, at least in the Convent on Rhodes, who held the highest position in the English tongue.

[38] *CVSP 1202–1509*, 166–8.

[39] The fifteenth-century English state rolls do not record the appointment of Priors' attorneys.

[40] *CPR 1381–1385*, 84; *CPR 1429–1436*, 408; *CPR 1461–1467*, 567.

[41] For instance see *CPR 1485–1494*, 493.

the Prior. Although the number of English brethren was never large, allocation of commanderies to the Prior was not due to a lack of knights to run the commanderies. The Convent carefully restricted the number of recruits to ensure there were not too many. It is more likely that allocation to the Prior indicated the increasing prestige that the Prior had attained, or the higher social status of the later Priors, and thus the need for them to have an income to match the lifestyle. Alternatively, it might indicate that the value of Hospitaller lands was falling, and mergers were necessary to maintain living standards.

The monetary value of the commanderies allocated to Clerkenwell in the first years of Botyll's priorship amounts to approximately £548, and the three allocations between 1470 and 1489 added a further £499, giving a total value to Clerkenwell of about £1,686.[42] This meant that the Prior had an income rivalling, and often surpassing, other magnates. Such a view is confirmed by correspondence of the later fifteenth century, such as the Cely letters, that, for example, note in 1480 that Richard Cely junior was one of the many retainers in Prior John Weston's service.[43] This increase in status is likely to have started much earlier. Figure 3 shows that the acquisition of Hospitaller commanderies by the Prior began in the early 1430s, when William Hulles was Prior. That Hulles was regarded highly is indicated by the fact that he accompanied Henry Beaufort, bishop of Winchester and uncle of Henry V, for part of his intended journey to the Holy Land.[44] Furthermore, orders to London customs officials on 3 August 1419 suggest that Hulles travelled with a considerable entourage numbering at least 54. He was allowed to take abroad, without tax, 34 parti-coloured gowns of green and red (colours that matched his coat of arms), embroidered for his gentlemen, yeomen and grooms, one gown for a chaplain and 20 gowns for himself and his brethren of England.[45] The facts that Hulles had a large household and that his servants wore his livery, indicate that he was an important lord.

From the middle of the fifteenth century, the Prior became more alienated from the Order's headquarters on Rhodes. Prior Botyll and his successors did not spend the lengthy periods out of England in service to their order that Prior Radington and Prior Grendon had. If they were out of the country, it was usually on diplomatic duty for the crown. The failure of the Prior to depart for the defence of Rhodes in the years preceding 1522, the year the Hospitallers lost the island, is an apt illustration of this. The Order's position on Rhodes in these final years was a precarious one. As early as October 1509, the Grand Master had asked Henry VIII to allow Prior Docwra to join them. Instead, in May 1510 Docwra went to France as an ambassador to ratify the Anglo-French treaty.[46] The request for the Prior and other brethren to go to Rhodes was repeated almost every time the Grand Master wrote to Henry VIII, but Docwra remained in England or on crown duties on the continent, and was not present at the 1522 siege of Rhodes.[47] However, as

---

[42] *Medieval Religious Houses*, 300–1.
[43] *Cely Letters*, 83–4.
[44] *CPL 1417–1431*, 6.
[45] *CCR 1419–1422*, 18.
[46] *L&P HVIII 1509–1513*, I, 282, 299, 302.
[47] *Ibid.*, 98, 282; *L&P HVIII 1521–1523*, III, 1191–93.

a veteran of the 1480 siege, Docwra must have been too old for active combat in 1522 anyway. English brethren, such as Thomas Newport, Thomas Sheffield, turco-polier John Bothe and future Prior William Weston were on Rhodes and fought in its final defence. It is difficult to ascertain whether Henry VIII was unsympathetic to the Order, or whether misinformation led to an underestimate of the danger that Rhodes faced. Correspondence of the period seems to give confusing and conflicting reports of the situation in the eastern Mediterranean, so it is possible that the Turkish threat was believed to be under control. Despite the retention of Docwra, Henry VIII had allowed Newport and Sheffield to travel to Rhodes as early as 1513, in response to the Grand Master's plea of April that year that the Prior and all commanders be allowed to go to Rhodes. Newport, the bailiff of Eagle, and Sheffield, commander of Shingay and treasurer of the Order in England, were senior members of the English Priory, and so fell within the category of those required.[48] Finally, the entries in the *Valor* for Newland and Mount St John comman-deries suggest that as late as 1535 the king allowed responsions to be paid to Malta.[49] This suggests that the portrayal of Henry as unsympathetic to the Order of which he was honorary protector, and later keen for their dissolution, to be an exaggera-tion.[50] That Henry VIII considered using the English Hospitallers for the defence of Calais after the fall of Rhodes was no different from the use of the Order by other monarchs for their own means. The king of Castile used the prior of Castile to regain Toledo in 1521, and the king of Portugal imposed his brother as prior of Crato in 1528, although the latter did have to pay the Order for its consent.[51]

Priors of England 1300–1540

Between 1297 and 1540, there were 19 Priors of England, excluding Sir Richard Woodville, whom Edward IV tried to impose on the Order in 1468, but who did not take up his appointment. Appointments to all positions within the Order were based on seniority, the main criterion being length of service. On admission to the Order, brethren had to go to the Convent and perform military service for five years. Only when this was completed were they eligible for a commandery. A brother had to wait, however, for a commandery to become vacant and this could take many years. Commanderies themselves were ranked in order of importance, according to value, and brethren had to work their way up to one of the senior commanderies. To become Prior, or hold other senior office, it was not enough for preceptors to successfully manage their preceptories; they needed to serve their order in other roles. The most successful were awarded significant positions, such as turcopolier or bailiff of Eagle, which brought with them the wealthiest comman-deries. A further qualification (from 1344) to become a prior, was that a brother needed to have been a member of the Order for 20 years and a member of that

---

[48] *L&P HVIII 1513–1514*, I, 1081; *L&P HVIII 1509–1513*, I, 804.
[49] *Valor*, V, 68, 94–5.
[50] See King. *Knights of St John*.
[51] Sire, *Knights of Malta*, 151.

particular priory for five years.[52] Consequently, brethren became priors towards the end of their lives, and tended to have fairly short terms of office (see Figure 4), such as Prior Archer, who was described as old and weak in 1329.[53] Unfortunately, we only have the exact ages of a couple of Priors. Langstrother was 52 when Prior Botyll died in 1468 and John Weston was 45 when he took up office in 1476.[54] There could be considerable competition between brethren for promotion to Prior, one case being the apparent animosity between John Weston and John Kendal. Kendal seems to have been fiercely competitive with Weston. He supported the election of Robert Multon as Prior, possibly to prevent Weston becoming Prior, even though Multon had only been a member of the Order since 1463 and a preceptor since 1470. Quite clearly, Multon had not served long enough as a Hospitaller or as a commander to be considered suitable as Prior. Then a few years later, Kendal seemed keen to report that Weston was not maintaining hospitality at Clerkenwell, as if hoping Weston's position as Prior would not be confirmed.[55] Appointment as Prior was initially for a period of ten years, after which a decision was made on whether to extend his tenure. For example, in February 1307, ten years after he was first mentioned as Prior, Prior Tothale took a letter of support from Edward I to the Grand Master, which asked for Tothale to be confirmed as Prior of England.[56] In 1331, Prior Tibertis was confirmed as English Prior for ten years, although he had been acting as such for some time.[57] Similarly, Philip Thame was confirmed as Prior in September 1335 for ten years.[58]

Although, unfortunately, little exists to tell us of the character of individual Priors and most of what does relates to the later fifteenth century, it still provides a glimpse into Priors' personalities and pastimes. Priors enjoyed hunting. In August 1237, Prior Nussa was granted limited hunting rights with hounds in the king's forests.[59] In January 1253, the king granted Prior Mauneby, on his retirement, the right to hunt with his own dogs for hare, fox and cat in any forest in various counties for life.[60] Later Priors also enjoyed hunting. John Weston liked to go hawking with servants such as Richard Cely (junior), though as the Cely letters indicate, he did not always take good care of his companion's hawks, one dying in his possession![61] Weston felt guilty for this mishap, offered to pay for another, and the following year (1479) was asking Richard to bring his hawk to him (though the Prior did have his own hawk), as there were many fowl around.[62] Priors had to have good interpersonal skills in order to gain the cooperation of other brethren. Edward I's letter to the Grand Master in 1307 mentions Tothale's suitability to continue as Prior, not only for his many services to the king, but also because of the great affection that the English

---

52 Nicholson, *Knights Hospitaller*, 72.
53 *Foedera*, Hague, II, III, 22.
54 NLM 352, ff. 128v–131; NLM 73, f. 86; *CPL 1484–1492*, 16, 19.
55 *CCR 1468–1476*, 380; NLM 374, 139–139v; NLM 379, 142v–143; *CPL 1471–1484*, 253.
56 *CCR 1302–1307*, 525.
57 NLM 280, ff. 1, 2v.
58 *Ibid.*, f. 33v.
59 *CPR 1232–1247*, 194.
60 *CPR 1247–1258*, 170.
61 *Cely Letters*, 33.
62 *Ibid.*, 35–8, 65–6, 122–5.

brethren had for him 'by reason of his friendly behaviour and befitting conversations'.[63] Etiquette was also important in maintaining good relations with members of the lay society, especially when the Prior needed a favour. For example, on 10 July 1479 John Weston wrote a polite letter from Balsall to Sir William Stonor, member of a long-established merchant family, asking him and the Prior's solicitor to resolve a dispute between two priests, both of whom Weston had, apparently, presented to Chipping Ilsley church (Berks.).[64] Weston was happy to recompense whichever priest resigned his office and was no doubt keen not to have his stay at Balsall interrupted. Weston always sent his greetings to members of the Cely family, also merchants, and when, as in 1488, he suspected that he or his brethren might have offended them in some way, he was quick to write to resolve any issue.[65] Prior Docwra's nepotism also shows that he looked after his kin (see Chapter 6). However, the closest we get to the personal side of a Prior is in the two letters that Prior Kendal wrote to the Plumpton and Paston families. In the letter to Sir Robert Plumpton on 3 September (1500 or before), Kendal shows us he was a man who cared for his family, looking after the interests of his nephew Brother John Tong while the latter was serving the Order on Rhodes.[66] The most moving letter is the one written to Sir John Paston on 1 June (1500 or before) concerning a marriage between his cousin (Clippesby) and Paston's niece. At first, he thought it wiser for his cousin to marry someone in the London area, perhaps betraying his initial objection to the marriage. Once he knew the love that was between them and their wish to marry each other, he then agreed to the marriage and wished Paston to do the same.[67] Clearly, Clippesby, who was taking the letter to Paston, had gone to see the Prior and successfully pleaded for his acceptance.

Historiography of the English Priors

It must be admitted that, with a few exceptions, the Priors are hardly referred to in the histories of late medieval England. When they are mentioned, it is only in passing and rarely consumes more than a sentence.[68] Comments on the Prior's role are only offered in the literature on the crusades and military orders. A main source for the Hospitallers in England is Edwin King's 1924 work *The Grand Priory of the*

[63] *CCR 1302–1307*, 525.

[64] *Kingsford's Stonor Letters and Papers 1290–1483*, ed. C. Carpenter, Cambridge, 1996, II, 38; *Cely Letters*, 54–5.

[65] *Cely Letters*, 241–3.

[66] Kirby says it was some time before 1501. It was likely to be in either 1495 or 1496, in which years the Prior held provincial chapters near London, and when Tong wrote a similar letter of thanks to Plumpton: *The Plumpton Letters and Papers*, ed. J. Kirby, Camden 5th Series, VIII, 1996, 115–16.

[67] A provincial chapter was held at Clerkenwell in June 1492. Clippesby may well have been the son of William (esquire) and Katherine Clippesby, of Clippesby, Norfolk. *Paston Letters and Papers of the Fifteenth Century*, ed. N. Davis, 2 vols, Oxford, 1971–6, II, 480; *CPR 1494–1509*, 127.

[68] Exceptions include J. Ferguson, *English Diplomacy, 1422–1461*, Oxford, 1972 and M. A. Hicks, *False Fleeting Perjur'd Clarence. George, Duke of Clarence 1449–78*, 2nd edn, Bangor, 1992.

Order of the Hospital of St John of Jerusalem in England. Despite a corrected reprint in
1934 and a second edition under the title *The Knights of St John in the British Realm*
in 1967, few revisions were made in relation to the role of the English Prior. This
standard work, to which later histories refer, relies mainly on secondary sources,
with a few references to printed primary sources. Those familiar with the Hospitaller archive on Malta will recognise from where the information was obtained,
but, unfortunately, it is not referenced. Furthermore, the sources used are limited to
works specifically related to the Hospitallers. This predisposes King to view Anglo-
Hospitaller relations from the viewpoint of the Hospitaller Convent and in a nega-
tive light.

More recently, the contribution of the Hospitallers and those involved in the
crusading movement from the British Isles is covered in Luttrell's many articles,
especially 'English Contributions to the Hospitaller Castle at Bodrum in Turkey:
1407–1437', Tipton's 'The English Hospitallers during the Great Schism', Tyerman's *England and the Crusades, 1095–1588*, Lloyd's *English Society and the Crusade,
1216–1307*, Macquarrie's *Scotland and the Crusades, 1095–1560*, and O'Malley's *The
Knights Hospitaller of the English Langue, 1460–1565*.[69] Although Riley-Smith wrote
a history of the Hospitallers from their origins until 1310 in 1967, it is only relatively recently that works have been published covering the whole history of the
Hospitallers.[70] The first of these was Henry Sire's *The Knights of Malta* (1994), which
has a separate section on the English tongue, spanning from its origins up until
the eighteenth century, including the formation of the Anglo-Bavarian tongue.[71]
This was followed by Riley-Smith's *Hospitallers: The History of the Order of St John*
(1999), which contains succinct coverage of the Priory of England until the late
fourteenth century, focusing on the commanderies and brethren before and after the
acquisition of the Templars' lands, but also mentioning the king's treasurer Priors,
Chauncy and Hales.[72] Nicholson's *The Knights Hospitaller* (2001) contains an astute
chapter on the Hospitaller relations with the rest of Christendom, which mentions
the English Priory and some of the English Priors.[73] Nicholson has also written two
valuable articles relating to the English Hospitallers; one on relations between the
military orders and the English crown in the twelfth and thirteenth centuries and
the other concerning the lack of English Hospitaller participation in the Order's
affairs in the east during the fourteenth century.[74] Archaeological knowledge of

---

[69] A. Luttrell, 'English Contributions to the Hospitaller Castle at Bodrum in Turkey: 1407–1437',
      in his *Studies on the Hospitallers after 1306*, Aldershot, 2007, 163–72; Tipton, 'English Hosp-
      itallers'; Tyerman, *England and Crusades*; S. Lloyd, *English Society and the Crusade, 1216–1307*,
      Oxford, 1988; A. Macquarrie *Scotland and the Crusades, 1095–1560*, 2nd edn, Edinburgh, 1997;
      O'Malley, *English Knights Hospitaller*.

[70] Riley-Smith, *Knights of St John*.

[71] Sire, *Knights of Malta*, 176–89.

[72] J. Riley-Smith, *Hospitallers: The History of the Order of St John*, London, 1999, 79–81.

[73] As Nicholson's preface states, the aim of her book is not to give a detailed history of the Order
      in Europe, but there is a thorough bibliography for that section; Nicholson, *Knights Hospitaller*.

[74] H. Nicholson, 'The Military Orders and the Kings of England in the Twelfth and Thirteenth
      Centuries', in *From Clermont to Jerusalem: The Crusades and Crusader Societies 1095–1500. Select
      Proceedings of the International Medieval Congress, University of Leeds, 10–13 July 1995*, ed. A. V.
      Murray, Turnhout, 1998, 203–18; H. Nicholson, 'The Hospitallers in England, the Kings of
      England and Relations with Rhodes in the Fourteenth Century', in *Sacra Militia* II, 25–45.

the English Hospitaller Priory at Clerkenwell has been enriched by Sloane and Malcolm's publication.[75]

Very little has been written specifically on the Priors of England and what has is limited to short studies of individual Priors or to brief comments on their role in single events or their family context.[76] They are also mainly limited to studies of the Priors from the mid- to the late fifteenth century. The first of these is Peter Field's 1977 essay on Prior Malory (1432–40).[77] Field commences with an account of Prior Malory's career as Prior and then continues with a discussion of his family origins. While the detail concerning Malory is thorough and the genealogical links made are clever, the introductory remarks on the role of Prior of England in the late Middle Ages are assumed. It is worth dwelling on these assumptions, for they are misapprehensions that are common in crusading and Hospitaller histories.

The Prior is described as 'one of the great magnates of the kingdom, given power, money and access to the king by his rich priory based at Clerkenwell, the five commanderies his office entitled him to and his places in the upper house of parliament and the royal council'.[78] Although some of these observations are correct for Prior Malory and those priors who followed him, this description needs qualification. Certainly the Prior of England had power and money. He did not, however, have automatic or regular access to the king. This book demonstrates that, although some kings patronised the Order and visited Clerkenwell, the Prior's direct access to the king was limited. Prior Chauncy (1273–81), who appears to have had a close relationship with Edward I dating back to the latter's crusade as the Lord Edward (1270–72), was made treasurer of England, and they corresponded after Chauncy's resignation as treasurer and return to the Holy Land. Similarly, Prior Botyll (1440–68) attended on Henry VI at Windsor with the bishop of Winchester during and immediately after the king's incapacity in the 1450s, which also gives the impression of intimacy, though the king's council appointed them to perform this task. These, however, are the exceptions rather than the rule, and most Priors' access was limited to attendance at parliament or great council. It is also imprecise to mention the Prior's places in the Lords or 'royal council' in a manner that gives the impression that these were longstanding, certain or recurrent. In contrast, this book shows that it was only from 1295 that the Prior started to receive anything like a regular summons to parliament. Consequently, it was also at this time that he started to receive regular summonses to great council. Before this, summons to both was irregular. This is not to demean the importance of the Prior, for the development of his summons to great council and parliament matches the development

75 *Clerkenwell Excavations.*

76 The series of St John pamphlets should be consulted with caution. They are transcripts of short communications, literally a couple of pages, which are not annotated, so that the accuracy of the details is difficult to confirm, L. Butler, 'The Order of St John and the Peasants' Revolt', *St John Historical Society Pamphlets*, I, 1981; S. Dyer, 'The Weston Family and the Order of St John', *St John Historical Society Newsletter*, September 1983; P. R. Coss, 'Knights, Esquires and the Origins of Social Gradation in England', *Transactions of the Royal Historical Society*, 6th Series, V, 1995, 155–78 (the Archer family is discussed on pp. 174–6).

77 P. J. C. Field, 'Sir Robert Malory, Prior of the Hospital of St John of Jerusalem in England (1432–1439/40)', *JEH*, XXVIII, 1977, 249–64.

78 *Ibid.*, 249.

of the English parliament itself, the form of which was still developing until the later fourteenth century. This privilege, then, was acquired gradually and was not in existence from the formation of the English Priory in the 1140s. Finally, there is the reference to the 'royal council'. The examples that Field gives in his article refer to the great council, rather than the king's continual or 'privy' council. Attendance at great council was, however, assured for all the lords long before Prior Malory's time, and thus implied no more influence than attending parliament. Attendance at the council appointed by the king, on the other hand, indicated a deeper level of involvement and choice. This book demonstrates that, with the exception of Prior Hales during Richard II's minority and Prior Grendon during Henry V's absence from England in 1415 (both exceptional cases), it was not until the mid-fifteenth century that the Prior started to appear regularly at the king's council. The assumption that the Prior always had these rights is thus unfounded.

The second study of the English Priors is by Jürgen Sarnowsky (1999), who examined the relationship between the English Prior and the crown between 1440 and 1501.[79] It provides a concise discussion of the Prior's role in English politics, though the role of Prior John Weston (1476–89) in English politics and diplomacy is not covered.[80] The article then concentrates on the election of English Priors and the perceived attempts by the crown to influence these elections. Thus from the beginning, a theme of conflict between the Order and the crown is created. However, the periods of conflict between the crown and the Hospital were relatively few. Certainly, there were occasional tussles, such as when Prior Thame wished to send responsions to the Convent in the 1330s or if a new Prior found himself temporarily excluded from the Priory by the crown, as was the case with Prior Kendal between 1489 and 1492.[81] However, for the majority of the time, there was not only peaceful coexistence, but also co-operation, with strained relations usually explicable due to international factors or perceived breaches of the royal prerogative. It is understandable that the king would be wary of large sums leaving the realm in the late 1330s when England was at war with France. It is also natural that Henry VII expected Kendal to follow the traditional procedure of election for an English Prior. It was only Prior Langstrother, personally, who was in dispute with Edward IV over his right to the English Priory, and this was due to his association with Warwick. It was not a power struggle between the king and the Hospitallers. Even so, after excluding him for a year, Edward did finally admit Langstrother to the Priory in 1469, which he would not have done if he had considered him a great threat at that point.

Finally, Gregory O'Malley's book *The Knights Hospitaller of the English Langue, 1460–1565* (2005) mentions the English Priors from Botyll onwards.[82] As O'Malley's main aims are to explore the Order's 'organisation and character' in the British Isles between 1460 and 1564 and activities of the members of the English *langue* in the Mediterranean during the same timeframe, he looks at their activities from within

---

[79] Sarnowsky, 'Kings and Priors', 83–102.

[80] Sarnowsky, 'Kings and Priors', 86, 89; *Rot. Parl.*, VI, 313, 410; *CCR 1476–1485*, 290, 339; *CCR 1485–1500*, 69.

[81] *CCR 1337–1339*, 240–41; O'Malley, *English Knights Hospitaller*, 144–5.

[82] O'Malley, *English Knights Hospitaller, passim*.

the Order, mainly using the extensive Hospitaller archive in Malta.[83] His work is thus complementary with the later period covered by this book, which looks at the Prior's role outside the Order and mainly from UK sources. However, the English Priors are not the focal point of O'Malley's book. In contrast, this book describes in detail and analyses the Prior's role in service to the crown, covering a much wider timespan than other works on the English Priors. It reveals the changing role and details about the Prior in a way that shorter studies do not.

This book contributes to the study of Anglo-Hospitaller relations by looking at the Prior from a new perspective. All the above works consider the Prior's first loyalty to be to his order and only secondly to his king. Those who are acknowledged as becoming involved in crown government, such as Hales or Langstrother, are used as cautionary tales of the dangers in participation in local politics. Crusade historians also view Anglo-Hospitaller relations as mainly one of conflict, though it is acknowledged that the crown allowed contact between the English Hospitallers and the Convent during the Great Schism, even though the English kings supported Rome and the Hospitaller headquarters supported Avignon.[84] Conversely, this work views the Prior as an Englishman first (as all were from the mid-thirteenth century except Prior Tibertis), with his first loyalty to the crown, and a Hospitaller second. This does not mean that the Prior neglected his Hospitaller duties. Indeed, involvement in local politics, and the resultant rewards, were one way of gaining benefits for the Order. Until the fourteenth century, the Prior's duties to the crown were minimal, but during the period of the Hundred Years War they increased until by 1450 the Prior was playing as full a role as any other lay baron. Although this role developed over about 150 years, it was not a gradual process; it developed in short stages at times when particular Priors were mainly based in England. It is possible that this role could have developed earlier if Priors Grendon, Hulles and Malory (Priors between 1395 and 1440) had spent more time in the country, and had thus built up the trust of the crown. It is also argued that, although there were times of discord, the Prior's relations with the crown were mainly cordial. Indeed, this was a prerequisite for the successful management of the Priory.

As implied earlier, the conventional view has been constructed by the use mainly of the Hospitaller central archives in Malta; the English Hospitaller archives are no longer extant. The few English crown archives that have been used, such as those consulted by O'Malley, are specific to the Hospitallers in England and those that are indexed. This book, however, uses the unindexed sources, such as the council and privy seal records (E 28), issue rolls (E 403), warrants for issue (E 404) and the treaty rolls (C 76). This approach helps to redress the balance in the understanding of Anglo-Hospitaller relationships in late medieval England and portrays the development of the English Prior's role in a much more intricate manner. These state sources made this study of the role of the Prior of St John in England between 1273 and 1540 feasible. It was a necessary study because many of the assumptions about the Prior's role in England are based on a universal theory that has been applied to the leading representatives of the military orders in Western Europe: that their main

---

[83] *Ibid.*, 1.
[84] Tipton, 'English Hospitallers', 94; Nicholson, 'The Hospitallers in England', 40–4.

role was to efficiently manage the orders' estates, ensure the transfer of profits to the central Convent, and recruit members when required, and that this led to conflict with the local rulers, especially over the transfer of money abroad. Even some recent studies on Hospitaller–crown relations in other parts of Europe fit into this model; the evidence they have consulted from mainly Hospitaller sources naturally leads them to that conclusion.[85] This study, based mainly on English sources, presents another side to the story. While acknowledging the importance of the Prior's Hospitaller duties, it argues that the fulfilling of these was only possible when the crown did not require the Prior's service. This becomes apparent only after a detailed analysis of the English archival material.

---

[85] C. Barquero Goñi, 'The Hospitallers and the Kings of Navarre in the Fourteenth and Fifteenth Centuries', 349–54, in *The Military Orders: Welfare and Warfare*, ed. H. Nicholson, Aldershot, 1998.

Figure 1: Number of foundations, mergers, and closures of Hospitaller commanderies

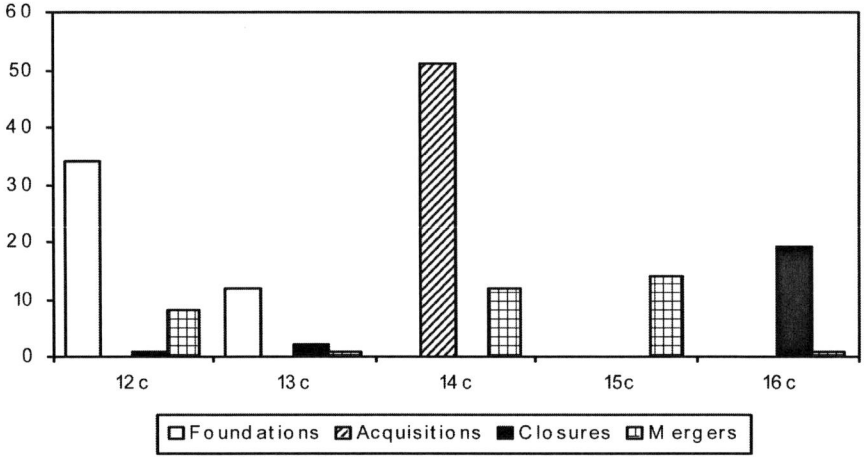

Source: *Medieval Religious Houses*

Figure 2: Approximate incomes of commanderies
of the English Priory[86]

House (1338 subsidiary) (* = commandery in 1535)	County	Value in 1338 Gross	Net	1535 Net
Ansty*	Wilts.	£93 1s. 8d.	£53 1s. 0d.	£81
Battisford*	Suffolk	£93 10s. 8d.	£60 6s. 10d.	£52
Beverley*	Yorks.	£83 17s. 4d.	£40	£164
Bodmiscombe (*with Buckland)	Devon	£50 11s. 0d.	£28 7s. 10d.	
Buckland	Somerset	£124 10s. 4d.	£41 0s. 4d.	£103
Carbrooke*	Norfolk	£192 2s. 4d.	£120 9s. 8d.	£69
Chibburn	Northumb.	£23 18s. 6d.	£6 6s. 8d	
Chippenham	Cambs.	£110 16s. 9d.	£16 0s. 3d.	£33
Clanfield	Oxford	£60 13s. 4d.	£26 4s. 4d.	
Clerkenwell*	London	£400	−£21 11s. 4d.	£2,385
Dalby* (*with Rotherley)	Leics.	£128 15s. 4d.	£61 14s. 1d.	£231
Dingley (*with Battisford)	Northants.	£79 3s. 8d.	£42 3s. 8d.	£108
Dinmore* (*with Garway)	Herefords.	£182 7s. 3d.	£100 5s. 11d.	£96
Eagle*	Lincs.	£122 11s. 10d.	£66 13s. 6d.	£124
Fryer Mayne (*with Baddesley)	Dorset	£96 2s. 10d.	£53 17s. 6d.	
Godsfield, *Baddesley**	Hants.	£67	£36 16s. 4d.	£118
Grafton	Warwicks.	£78 15s. 2d.	£49 0s. 1d.	
Greenham	Berks.	£76 13s. 3d	£42 4s. 7d.	
Halston*	N. Wales	£157 5s. 10d.	£77 18s. 10d.	£160
Hardwick	Beds.	£69 3s. 5d.	£53 13s. 5d.	
Hogshaw	Bucks.	£74 14s. 6d.	£45 18s. 6d.	
Maltby	Lincs.	£116 6s. 8d.	£66 0s. 2d.	£34
Maplestead	Essex	£77 16s. 8d.	£40	
Melchbourne	Beds.	£106 2s. 4d.	£56 4s. 6d.	£241
Mount St John*	Yorks.	£58 8s. 4d.	£33 12s. 8d.	£102
Newland*	Yorks.	£56 5s. 4d.	£25 19s. 4d.	£129
Ossington (*with Newland)	Notts.	£95 0s. 4d.	£17 14s. 0d.	£44
Poling	Sussex	£78 11s. 3d.	£44 11s. 3d.	
Quenington*	Glos.	£179 8s. 4d.	£122 1s. 7d.	£137
Ribston (*with Kilmainham)	Yorks.	£167 10s. 8d.	£101 1s. 10d	£207
Shingay*	Cambs.	£187 12s. 8d.	£126 14s. 0d.	£175
Skirbeck	Lincs.	£84 11s. 8d.	£5 7s. 0d.	
Slebech*	Pembroke	£307 0s. 22d.	£165 19s. 3d.	£184
Standon	Essex	£34 15s. 4d.	£11 15s. 2d.	£23
Sutton-at-Hone	Kent	(Not given)	£40	
Swingfield*	Kent	£82 4s. 4d.	£29 6s. 0d.	£87
Temple Bruer*	Lincs.	£177 6s. 8d.	£93 6s. 6d.	£184
Templecombe*	Somerset	£106 13s.	£40	£107
Trebeigh (*with Ansty)	Cornwall	£75 11s. 3d.	£20 10s. 11d.	£60
Willoughton*	Lincs.	£284 3s. 5d.	£201 12s. 9d.	£174
Yeaveley*	Derby	£95 5s. 8d.	£32	£93

Source: 1338 Survey, Valor, *Medieval Religious Houses*

[86] Torphichen is not included, as in 1338 no value was given due to destruction caused by war, and in 1535 it was not included in the *Valor*.

Figure 3: Numerical reallocation of closed commanderies, 1400–99

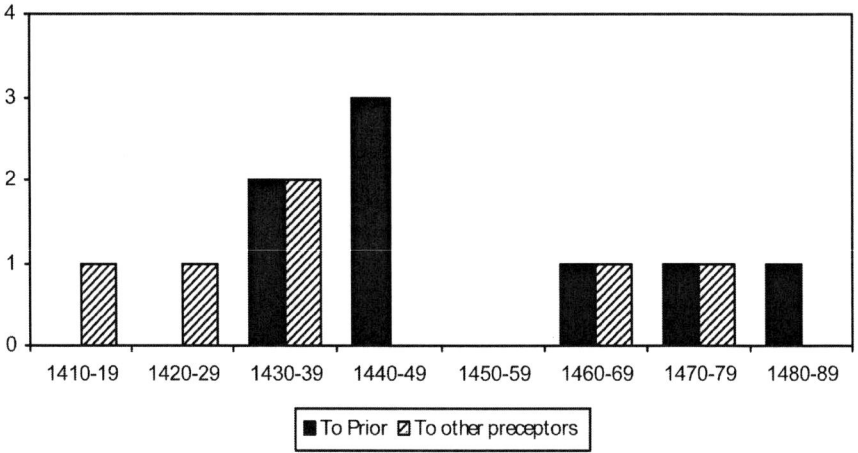

Source: *Medieval Religious Houses*

Figure 4: Priors of England 1300–1540

Number	Name	Year elected	Year died/relieved	Length of tenure (years)
1	William Tothale	1297	1315	18
2	Richard Pavely D	1315	1319	4
3	Thomas Archer	1319	1330	11
4	Leonard de Tibertis♣♦A	1331	1335	4
5	Philip Thame	1335	1353	18
6	John Pavely*	1354	1371	17
7	Robert Hales	1372	1381	9
8	John Radington	1382	1395	13
9	Walter Grendon	1396	1417	21
10	William Hulles♣	1418	1432	14
11	Robert Malory	1432	1440	8
12	Robert Botyll	1440	1468	28
13	John Langstrother T+C♣	1468	1471	3
14	William Tornay T+	1471	1474	3
15	Robert Multon	1474	1476	2
16	John Weston*C+	1476	1489	13
17	John Kendal*♦	1490	1501	11
18	Thomas Docwra*♣	1501	1527	26
19	William Weston*	1527	1540	13

*   Turcopoliers
♣   Previously Prior of other Priory
♦   Grand Master's Proctor General in West
T   Hospitaller treasurer in England
+   Bailiff of Eagle
C   Castellan of Rhodes
A   Alien
D   Draperer

Source: various, including *CPR, CCR, Rot. Parl., Foedera*, Hague, NLM

2

Financier and Treasurer

The Prior of St John's financial role in service to the crown took two forms: as provider and collector of funds and, in three cases, as royal treasurer. This chapter commences with a synopsis of the Priors' previous financial experience within the Hospitallers, to help explain why Priors of St John were chosen for the two roles. It then proceeds to a discussion of the Priors as a source of finance, before analysing in detail the roles of the treasurer Priors, Chauncy, Hales and Langstrother, from the unpublished chancery and exchequer documents in the National Archives.

Financial background of the Hospitaller Priors

Tyerman has noted that the English tongue's chief contribution to the Crusades was financial, providing approximately 12.5 per cent of the Order's total European income.[1] The Prior's main role, as far as the Order was concerned, was to oversee the smooth running of the Order's estates within his Priory in order to maximise their profit. It was therefore essential for a prospective Prior to prove his worth before election to the post, and many future English Priors appear to have done this in one way or another. Priors Chauncy, Hales, and Langstrother are given as examples below.

Joseph Chauncy was the Hospitaller treasurer at Acre for some 25 years (from at least 1248) before 1273, when he was elected Prior of England and became Edward I's treasurer. Very little needs to be added to this.[2] To hold a post that long requires developed financial skills and expertise. For example, it was during Chauncy's office as Hospitaller treasurer at Acre that the Order invested heavily in the Latin East to increase their influence, despite facing financial difficulties.[3] Chauncy arranged loans for the Lord Edward while he was on crusade in the Holy Land, as revealed by the issue rolls of the English exchequer, so Edward knew of his financial experience

---

[1] Tyerman, *England and Crusades*, 356.
[2] Chauncy is first mentioned as Hospitaller treasurer at Acre on 7 August 1248, *Cartulaire Général*, II, 675.
[3] J. Bronstein, *The Hospitallers and the Holy Land: Financing the Latin East, 1187–1274*, Woodbridge, 2005, 28.

before his accession. One can understand why Edward wanted Chauncy as his own treasurer to ground his reign on a sound economic basis.[4] Whereas Edward waited until after his coronation (19 August 1274) before appointing the new chancellor and keeper of the wardrobe, Chauncy was deemed important enough to be placed in office a year earlier (2 October 1273).[5] Within a few days of taking office, he set about establishing the financial state of the realm and maximising crown income. For instance, on 5 October, he ordered the sheriff of Herefordshire to take Dilwin manor into the king's hands, because Edmund, the king's brother, had alienated it without licence. On 12 October, he sent out a writ for the late sheriff of Wiltshire to answer for issues whilst he was in office, and the same day, he ordered the constable of Windsor castle to ensure that all wasteland in Windsor forest was cultivated.[6] These examples indicate that Chauncy was keen to maintain the king's estate from any abuses whilst Edward was abroad, as well as wishing to maximise the profits from lands, something the Hospitallers did well for their own estates. In addition, it was important that he was seen to act fairly, as indicated when he ordered the arrest of goods of merchants from Flanders in Newcastle, and granted a third part to the burgesses of that town until they had gained compensation for plunder by the men of Flanders.[7] These qualities of careful scrutiny of the king's estate, efficiency and fair-handedness were attributes a king desired in a treasurer.

As for Robert Hales, it is more difficult to determine what financial talents he had that suggested his suitability as treasurer. There is no mention of his being a receiver of the common treasury in England or receiver of responsions, as was the case with some of his contemporaries, such as Brothers Nicholas Hales and Richard Overton.[8] His only financial and administrative experience seems to have been as a commander, a position he held from at least 1358, although he also served as one of the Prior's attorneys in 1362 and 1370.[9] Such posts required financial and administrative competence, but they do not indicate any special talent that a treas-urer might require. Unlike Chauncy, who became Prior and king's treasurer almost simultaneously, Hales had already been Prior for nine years before he became king's treasurer and thus had a chance to show his financial ability in that capacity, such as by resolving the problems of receiving responsions from Scotland.[10] Nevertheless, there is little evidence to explain Hales' rise to the treasurership in either English or Hospitaller records. It is possible, given the political climate early in 1381, that he obtained the post because no one else wanted it! Whether Hales was gullible, or whether he had sound reasons for accepting the treasurership, will be discussed in the conclusion of this chapter.

More evidence, from both English and Hospitaller sources, is available to explain why Langstrother was considered a good candidate for treasurer. Langstrother, a

---

[4]   Prestwich's assertion that Chauncy was no more than 'competent' seems to have been made without the knowledge that Chauncy had been Hospitaller treasurer in Acre or arranged loans for him, see M. C. Prestwich, *Edward I*, London, 1988, 231.

[5]   *Ibid*, 92.

[6]   *CFR 1272–1307*, 11–12.

[7]   *Ibid.*, 12.

[8]   NLM 316, f. 198v (1358); NLM 319, f. 179 (1365).

[9]   NLM 316, f. 198; *CPR 1361–1364*, 233; *CPR 1370–1374*, 4, 8.

[10]   NLM 321, f. 145.

member of the Order since 1434, was lieutenant turcopolier by 1444, and as such dealt with the receipt of responsions.[11] He was Hospitaller receiver for the common treasury in England in 1446, a position he still held in 1449 when he and Prior Botyll had orders to discipline the Irish Prior for non-payment of responsions.[12] He was receiver for both England and Ireland the following year and in 1452 was receiver of English responsions on Rhodes.[13] In 1454 he was one of those trusted to collect the indulgence money in England, granted for the protection of Rhodes after the fall of Constantinople.[14] In November 1461 the English government gave him and other senior Hospitallers licence to carry out a visitation of the English Priory, on orders from the Grand Master.[15] Throughout his Hospitaller career before becoming Prior, Langstrother was involved in financial management that singled him out as a possible treasurer.

Priors as financiers, 1300–1540

There were three main ways in which the Prior of St John was involved in crown finances. Firstly, through direct personal loans to the king and parliamentary taxes. Secondly, through negotiating loans and taxes for the crown with foreign merchants and parliamentary approved taxes with members of the clergy and laity. Thirdly by assessing, collecting and storing the revenues of these loans and taxes.

Direct loans

The Prior never lent very large amounts of money to the crown to rival that lent by the Italian merchant companies, but he was a consistent lender throughout the later Middle Ages, as were the Templars until their dissolution.[16] The various state rolls are full of examples of these loans and only a few can be mentioned here in illustration. Loans were usually trade-offs for privileges or exemptions. For example, in June 1306, the Prior and Hospitallers were released from the twentieth and thirtieth for knighting the future Edward II because the Prior had lent the king £200, a loan still outstanding two years later.[17] Sums lent to the crown were often much larger such as the £2,664 to Edward I (d. 1307), still owed in 1315, for which the English Prior, brethren and their villeins were to be free of tallage on goods proper.[18] Edward II's Scottish wars also required the Prior, in common with other

---

[11] NLM 351, f. 135; NLM 356, ff. 141–142.
[12] NLM 358, f. 229; NLM 361, f. 237–237v, ff. 246v–247v; NLM 362, ff. 121–123v, 126v–127.
[13] *Ibid.*, f. 127v; NLM 363, f. 157–157v.
[14] TNA E 28/85/8; *CPL 1447–1455*, 261–2.
[15] *CPR 1461–1467*, 52.
[16] J. L. Bolton, *The Medieval English Economy 1150–1500*, London, 1980, 338.
[17] *CPR 1301–1307*, 443; *CCR 1307–1313*, 79.
[18] *Rot. Parl.* I, 298–9; *CCR 1313–1318*, 184.

lords, to contribute loans, such as the 500 marks lent in 1316, which came with a promise of repayment.[19]

In general, though, there were no large financial exactions from the Prior in the first half of the fourteenth century before the start of the Hundred Years War. This was for two reasons. Firstly, the English Priory was still heavily in debt to foreign merchants for its part in the conquest of Rhodes and, secondly, it was not until the 1330s that the English Hospitallers gained control of the majority of Templar possessions. After sound financial governance in the 1330s by Priors Tibertis and Thame, helped by the acquisition of the Templars' possessions, the crown felt able to start exacting loans again, and the beginning of the Hundred Years War meant that these loans were more frequent and larger. Responsions of 1,041 marks were sequestered in November 1337, with a promise of repayment, but these were still outstanding in January 1339.[20] On top of this, the Prior had to pay a war tax of 200 marks in September 1338, with another 300 marks to follow, and he was burdened with a tax on wool early the following year.[21] Although the Hospitallers became exempt from ecclesiastical jurisdiction and taxation as a consequence of the papal bulls in their favour from 1113 and throughout the twelfth century, they still had to contribute to lay taxation unless the crown granted them an exemption.[22] However, exemptions, such as that of 1347, were only temporary.[23] These exactions put the English Prior in a difficult position, caught between loyalty to the crown and to the Grand Master, and led in Prior Thame's case to his being disciplined by Edward III for sending, and by Hélion de Villeneuve for not sending, responsions.[24]

The temporary collapse of the Italian banking system in the mid-fourteenth century meant that small lenders such as the Prior became of more importance to the crown, and with this came concessions. Prior Thame lent the king 2,000 florins in November 1346, and in return he obtained exemption from the fifteenths on the Hospitallers' (and ex-Templar) temporal lands the following year.[25] Such agreements were common throughout the fourteenth century, such as the 300 marks that Prior Pavely gave to the king in July 1370 for the wars; in return he was free from distribution of caps to officers of the exchequer, a long-term financial saving.[26]

The pattern of loans for concessions or with promises of repayments continued into the fifteenth and sixteenth centuries.[27] What is of interest is that the Prior expected repayment of the loans. The concessions were not to replace repayment,

[19] *CPR 1313–1317*, 521; Edward was also raiding the crusade tenth to finance war with Scotland, *ibid.*, 548.

[20] *CPR 1334–1338*, 549; *CCR 1337–1339*, 632.

[21] *Ibid.*, 500, 535, 633.

[22] *CPL 1305–1342*, 191; See Nicholson, *Knights Hospitaller*, 4–7, for a concise account of these privileges.

[23] *Cambridgeshire and the Isle of Ely Lay Subsidy for the Year 1327*, ed. J. J. Muskett and C. H. Evelyn-White, London, 1900, 44; *Rot. Parl.*, II, 175.

[24] *CCR 1337–1339*, 240–1; *CPR 1340–1343*, 203; *CCR 1343–1346*, 219.

[25] *CFR 1337–1347*, 489; *Rot. Parl.*, II, 175.

[26] *CPR 1367–1370*, 456.

[27] *CPR 1377–1381*, 617, 635; *CFR 1405–1413*, 94; *Rot. Parl.*, V, 419; *CPR 1429–1436*, 60; *CPR 1446–1452*, 298; *CCR 1485–1500*, 234; *CCR 1500–1509*, 255; *L&P HVIII 1521–1523*, III, 1047, 1051; *L&P HVIII 1531–1532*, V, 437.

but appear to be compensation for late payment. Occasionally the Prior was repaid directly, but more often he was repaid through other sources by assignment of crown finance. For example, the loan of 2,000 marks that Prior Grendon made in June 1416, originally on the security of the crown jewels, was eventually repaid from the wool tax on various ports in 1421.[28] The Prior was thus repaid in the same way that merchants preferred, of interest considering the Prior's negotiating role with merchants discussed in the next section.

Negotiators

Hospitaller Priors were not just lenders of money to the crown: they would also negotiate on behalf of the crown with the laity and clergy for tax grants, and with foreign merchants for loans. At first, the Prior treated with the Church and later in the fourteenth century with the laity for taxes. In December 1318, the Prior was one of those commissioned to negotiate with the prelates and clergy of Canterbury province for a tax to help finance the Scottish war, agreed in January 1319, after Pope John XXII ordered all prelates, secular and regular, except the Hospitallers, to pay a tenth for one year.[29] Then in November 1322 the Prior, along with 45 abbots, the archbishop of Canterbury, the prior of Lewes, and the master of the Order of Sempringham, were ordered to Lincoln to agree a grant, again to finance the Scottish war.[30]

Although the Prior attended the above convocations, he was not there as a fellow ecclesiastic, but as a lay negotiator on behalf of the king.[31] There does appear to have been some contemporary confusion over the status of the Priors, but the 1370s firmly placed the Prior in the lay camp. In September 1371, the close rolls note that, on petition of the Prior and brethren, they were to be taxed as laymen not as ecclesiastics as they, they claimed, they always had been.[32] Furthermore, in 1379 the parliamentary rolls state that the Prior was to be assessed for the poll tax as a baron, paying 40s.[33] From this point on the Prior no longer negotiated with the clergy for taxation and by the mid-fifteenth century he was dealing with lay taxation. In August 1449, Prior Botyll was one of five distributors of the allowance on a tax in the city of London.[34] In January 1451, he was commissioned to determine who would pay the tax and the amounts to be paid in Middlesex and London, and in July 1453 he was appointed one of the neutral arbitrators of a tax.[35]

---

[28] *Rot. Parl.*, IV, 96; the loan was to be paid from the tax on wool, hides and wool fells from London (500 marks at Christmas and 500 marks at Easter 1421), Kingston on Hull (200 marks at Easter and 300 marks at Christmas 1421), Boston (200 marks at Easter and 200 marks at Christmas) and Lynn (100 marks at Michaelmas 1421), *CPR 1416–1422*, 279.

[29] *CCR 1318–1323*, 112, 121; *CPL 1305–1342*, 191.

[30] *CCR 1318–1323*, 687.

[31] See Riley-Smith, *Knights of St John*, 375–89, for details of the Hospitallers' exemptions from episcopal control.

[32] *CCR 1369–1374*, 251.

[33] *Rot. Parl.*, III, 58.

[34] The others were Thomas Catworth, John Norman, Geoffrey Boleyn and Thomas Billing, *CFR 1446–1452*, 122.

[35] *Ibid.*, 223–4; *CCR 1447–1454*, 450.

Another important negotiating role was with various merchants, especially foreign merchant companies. As is amply illustrated by Chauncy's term as treasurer, Hospitaller and crown finances were often managed by the same merchant companies, such as the Riccardi of Lucca. In the fourteenth century this was continued mainly by the Bardi and Peruzzi and in the fifteenth century by companies such as the Medici. It was entirely natural, then, that Priors would act as guarantors to merchants for crown loans. The triad of crown–merchant–Hospitaller financing in the fourteenth century is illustrated by a number of examples. In some cases, the merchants were overstretched, as when, in December 1320, Edward II wrote to the Grand Master informing him that the English Hospitallers had borrowed large sums from the Bardi but had not repaid it by the agreed date. The king interceded, supposedly as he felt 'bound by the faithful services of the merchants', and asked that the debts were cleared.[36] More likely is that the king needed the money himself. This was certainly the case in October 1337, when Prior Thame was ordered by the king to pay the Peruzzi all debts owed by the Hospitallers immediately, so that the Peruzzi could help the king with his expenses.[37]

Priors could use their merchant contacts, normally reserved for the transfer of responsions, in order to finance crown needs. The Prior's loan of 2,000 florins in November 1346, half from England and half from abroad, suggests the use of foreign merchants.[38] The link is more easily understood when one looks at how the Hospitallers used Italian merchants to transfer funds, using credit notes called letters of exchange rather than cash. For example, on 10 March 1376 the king allowed Prior Hales to send 1,000 marks in responsions on condition that they certify receipt to the king.[39] A week later, the Lombardian merchant, Giovanni Credi, was licensed to receive this amount from Prior Hales and to make letters of exchange for that sum to be paid to the Grand Master by Credi's associates abroad, the Florentine societies of Strozzi and Passini.[40] Given this existing link between the Hospitallers and Italian merchant branches in England, it comes as no surprise to find, in May 1381, that Hales (treasurer at that time) was holding jewels to the value of 2,000 marks, as part security for repayment of the 6,000-mark loan to the king by another Lombardian merchant, Matthew Janin.[41] An order to Hildebrand Inge (head Hospitaller in England during the vacancy) the following October to deliver the jewels to John Philipot, a crown official, suggests that Hales had been acting in his capacity as Hospitaller Prior to broker a loan, in a similar way to Chauncy a century before.[42] A figure such as the Prior, who had the wealth of his order as a guarantee, might be useful in order to persuade merchants to loan money to the crown that may not be seen again for some time, in Janin's case over two years later.[43]

---

[36] *CCR 1318–1323*, 346–7.

[37] *CCR 1337–1339*, 186.

[38] *CPR 1345–1348*, 211; *CFR 1337–1347*, 489.

[39] *CCR 1374–1377*, 297–8.

[40] *Ibid.*, 333.

[41] *CPR 1381–1385*, 7.

[42] *Ibid.*, 46.

[43] It was not until 1383–4 that Janin was asked to return the crown jewels that he had received because the loan had not been repaid by Easter 1382, TNA E 101/400/29.

Bankers

Hospitaller Priors were also responsible for collecting and storing tax revenues, a function they inherited from the Templars. For example on 18 March 1275, when Chauncy was king's treasurer, the (Templar) treasurer of New Temple was ordered to deliver to Thomas Bek, keeper of the king's wardrobe, £80 from the tallage on the Jews deposited there.[44] In November the same year, the treasurer of New Temple was to deliver 200 marks deposited there to Chauncy, and in January the following year the keeper of works at the Tower of London was paid 1,000 marks out of the money deposited at New Temple.[45] It is clear that the Templars, and especially the centrally placed New Temple, were used as a bank for the crown. There are a few instances of the Hospitallers holding valuables for the crown before the Templars' dissolution, although they were not utilised as often as the Templars. For example, on 25 June 1277, the exchequer declared that all the king's jewels formally deposited in the Priory of the Hospital of St John of Jerusalem had been delivered to Chauncy, treasurer, in the presence of Thomas Bek, within the Tower of London.[46] What we see here are jewels that were guarantees for merchant loans being kept at Clerkenwell. That they were deposited at Clerkenwell rather than New Temple may be explained by Chauncy's own role in negotiating the loans with foreign merchants, as described in the next section. A parallel exists a century later, when Prior Hales was Richard II's treasurer, as detailed above in the case of Mathew Janin, merchant of Lombardy.[47]

The Hospitallers, who had their own credit system, were prime targets for loans to the crown. They were landowners and, crucially, their base in England was at Clerkenwell, just outside London. All money remitted from the various estates found its way to Clerkenwell before it was transported to the Hospitaller headquarters in the East. Moreover, if there was a crusade tax, the Hospitallers were normally involved in storing the money, if not collecting it, and some of those funds also found their way to Clerkenwell. Clerkenwell was thus a convenient local storage pot of money for the crown to dip into when needed. It was even more convenient with Chauncy as treasurer, as the 8,000 marks lent in 1274 from the tenth in aid of the Holy Land illustrates.[48] Other ecclesiastical revenues were used to fund temporal activities and Priors sometimes safeguarded these funds. For example, the close rolls for June 1313 reveal that the subsidy of 4d. in every mark from spiritualities was to be delivered to the Prior of St John and the bishop of London: this money was to be used to pay the men-at-arms, who were about to set out for the Scottish marches.[49] It is likely that these two were chosen not only for trustworthiness, but also for their London location.

Another financial use of the Priors was as a provider of foreign exchange. This they did for themselves through merchant contacts in England and at Calais when they went to Rhodes, gaining letters of exchange in England that they converted to

[44] *CPR 1272–1281*, 83.
[45] *Ibid.*, 114; *CCR 1272–1279*, 264.
[46] *CPR 1272–1281*, 215.
[47] *CPR 1381–1385*, 7.
[48] *Ibid.*, 353.
[49] *CCR 1307–1313*, 537.

foreign currency on arrival at Calais.[50] The same method was used when Priors were on crown duties as well. For example, when Prior Weston went as an ambassador to France in 1480, he arranged with the Cely family for Flemish coin to be delivered to him on his arrival from Dover.[51]

Priors as Treasurers

Treasurers were the head of the exchequer, the main royal treasury and accounting department. The underlying problem they had to deal with in the later Middle Ages was an almost continuous state of war, which required the crown to depend on credit, borrowing and anticipation of revenue.[52] Priors knew something of these problems. As members of a military order, they were involved in a permanent state of holy war, which required them to borrow and take out credit. As the lease books for the late fifteenth and early sixteenth centuries show, the Priors and their commanders also anticipated their revenues.

As noted at the beginning of this chapter, financial competence was one of the essential qualities required to hold the position of Prior. If a Prior was perceived to have failed in this respect, as was the case with Thomas Archer, he was replaced. Those Hospitaller brethren aspiring to be Prior had normally to prove their worth in service to the Order, for example as receivers of the common treasury within their Priory or by carrying funds to the Convent. Experience in their order therefore imbued Priors with financial experience that the crown could utilise if required. Indeed, one wonders why so few Priors held the office of treasurer; this will be discussed in the conclusion to the chapter.

Three Priors, Joseph Chauncy, Robert Hales and John Langstrother, were treasurers of England at approximately hundred-year intervals, which conveniently presents us with a snapshot of their financial roles throughout the later Middle Ages. Chauncy was treasurer from 1273 to 1280, Hales between February and June 1381, and Langstrother in 1469 under Edward IV, and again during Henry VI's Readeption. Using the issue rolls of the exchequer, we can provide detailed analysis of the Prior's role and determine whether each used his office to patronise his supporters. Whilst Hales' and Langstrother's terms of office are associated with controversy (Hales with the alleged corrupt government at the end of Edward III's and the beginning of Richard II's reigns, and Langstrother in the power struggle that was the Wars of the Roses), it is important to remember that Chauncy's long term as Edward I's treasurer had no adverse effects for himself or the Hospitallers. This is important because Hales' and Langstrother's experiences are often used as cautionary tales, as if a Hospitaller Prior should only deal with Hospitaller business. One question that requires consideration is how much choice did Priors have to remain aloof from 'national' events, and if they did become involved in government

---

[50] For example, see *Cely Letters*, 107–10, June and July 1481, when Prior Weston and John Kendal requested Flemish, Rhineland and Venetian currency for their journey to Rhodes.

[51] *Cely Letters*, 87.

[52] A. L. Brown, *The Governance of Late Medieval England 1272–1461*, London, 1989, 53.

and politics, was it in the best interests of their order? Were Hales and Langstrother guilty of meddling in business they could have avoided, or were their hands forced by particular circumstances?

Chauncy, treasurer 1273–80

A number of issue rolls exist for Chauncy's seven-year term as treasurer.[53] From the beginning, it is clear that the main priority was to clear the debts due to foreign merchants during the Lord Edward's crusade and leisurely return to England. That Chauncy was chosen to deal with this is not surprising. As Hospitaller treasurer in Acre, he had arranged loans for Edward. He also appears to have travelled back to England ahead of the king, arranging loans en route, such as that from the Templars in Paris.[54] He therefore had first-hand knowledge about the repayments that he was dealing with.

Chauncy took office at the beginning of October 1273 and there are three issue rolls relating to that Michaelmas term.[55] The first roll is interesting, as it starts with a list of ten names of the barons of the exchequer, including Chauncy, the archbishop of York and William Clifford.[56] The size and membership draw parallels with that of the king's council, a reflection of the close relationship between the two departments at this time. The rolls reveal that Chauncy had to manage the two main tasks that faced treasurers throughout the late middle ages, providing funds for the household whilst satisfying crown creditors.[57] All three rolls deal mainly with household finance, but there are significant payments of debts relating to Edward's crusade. For example, on the first roll there are two payments to Luke de Lucca (Lucasio Natale) and his merchant society (the Riccardi of Lucca), one of £406, then another of £450, both in part-payment of two 1,000 mark loans.[58] It is clear that Chauncy was arranging loans for the king before he returned to England and officially became treasurer, as the second issue roll mentions two other part-payments of 1,000 marks each to the same Lucasio, lent overseas to Chauncy, who had negotiated a loan for the king.[59] Another part-payment on this roll to the master of the Temple in Paris confirms that Chauncy was arranging loans for Edward both in the Holy Land and in France.[60] Chauncy, with 25 years' experience as Hospitaller treasurer, was quickly utilised by Edward and earmarked to be his own treasurer. Edward, as Prestwich has pointed out, borrowed heavily to finance his crusade from various merchants

---

[53] TNA E 403/22–44, Michaelmas term 1273 to Michaelmas term 1280.

[54] It is possible that he travelled back with Edward as far as Paris (where Edward stayed from 26 July to 6 August 1273), but was sent on to England while Edward dealt with the problems in Gascony.

[55] TNA E 403/22; TNA E 403/23; TNA E 403/24.

[56] TNA E 403/22.

[57] See G. L. Harriss, 'Marmaduke Lumley and the Exchequer Crisis of 1446–49', in *Aspects of Late Medieval Government and Society: Essays Presented to J R Lander*, ed. J. G. Rowe, Toronto and London, 1986, 143–78 at 153.

[58] *Ibid*. For background on the Riccardi merchants in England, see R. W. Kaeuper, *Bankers to the Crown: The Riccardi of Lucca and Edward I*, Princeton, NJ, 1973.

[59] TNA E 403/23, m. 1, referred to as 'Brother Joseph'.

[60] 2,000 marks of a 26,000 loan, *ibid*.

on security provided by the Hospitallers.[61] Most of the loans from Hospitallers were arranged by Chauncy as Hospitaller treasurer, so it was entirely natural that he should be appointed Edward's treasurer to deal with the repayment of those loans. Perhaps, also, Chauncy was willing to oblige, admiring Edward's commitment to the crusade and, once he had been appointed English Prior, appreciating the advantages for the Hospitallers of having the regular access to the king that a treasurer enjoyed.

The issue rolls for the following year show that Edward continued to rely on foreign merchants, especially the Riccardi, to finance his activities.[62] There are payments to Poncio de Mora, relating to Edward's coronation, and evidence of payments relating to building works at Westminster and the Tower of London, which from then on became major projects.[63] There seems to be very little patronage of religious orders with the exception of the Carthusians, perhaps because of financial constraints.[64] This appears to change in the issue rolls for 1276, when the Templars begin to receive patronage in return for three chaplains to pray for the soul of Henry III in New Temple, London.[65]

In the Easter rolls for 1276, we see the first payments to Chauncy in his role as treasurer for the 'many and arduous negotiations' that he had undertaken.[66] It is possible that this is a reference to Chauncy's part in introducing the customs tax on wool. Gras mentions the possibility that Edward had seen similar taxes whilst in the Holy Land, but tends to think the idea was native to England.[67] Kaeuper and Prestwich (following the Dunstable chronicler) have both credited a Riccardi merchant as the one that concluded the customs agreement and collected the fifteenth on wool in 1275.[68] However, none of them seem aware of Chauncy's previous connection to these same merchants, of his being in the Holy Land at the same time as Edward, or that he had previous experience as Hospitaller treasurer. These factors, added to his tenure of office as treasurer when the customs system was introduced, suggest that his part in the creation of the wool tax has been underplayed.[69] The Dunstable chronicler reports that Chauncy advised the introduction of the wool subsidy, but that one Poncio de Ponto (perhaps Poncio de Mora of the Riccardi) was the originator.[70] This suggests a working relationship between Chauncy and the Riccardi. Even if the original idea was not Chauncy's, it is clear that as treasurer he took

---

[61] Prestwich estimates that the overall cost to the crown was about £100,000, Prestwich, *Edward I*, 80–1.

[62] TNA E 403/27, mm. 2–3; TNA E 403/28, m. 1; TNA E 403/30, mm. 1, 3; TNA E 403/31, mm. 1 2.

[63] For payments to Poncio de Mora, see TNA E 403/25, m. 1; TNA E 403/27, mm. 1, 3; For building works on the tower and other buildings, see TNA E 403/30–31, *passim*.

[64] TNA E 403/25, m. 2; TNA E 403/28, m. 1; TNA E 403/30, m. 3.

[65] TNA E 403/33, m. 1; TNA E 403/34, m. 1.

[66] TNA E 403/33, m. 1. He received three payments of £50, £70 and £6 11s. 4d.; E 403/34, m. 1, the chamberlain's version, shows a further payment to Chauncy of £76 11s. 5d.

[67] N. S. B. Gras, *The Early English Customs System*, Cambridge, 1918, 62.

[68] Kaeuper, *Bankers to the Crown*, 12, suggests it was Lucasio Natale, head of the Riccardi in England 1256–77; Prestwich, *Edward I*, 100, thinks it was Orlando de Pogio.

[69] Chauncy especially negotiated loans with Lucasio Natale, the 'Luke of Lucca' in the issue rolls.

[70] *Annales Monastici*, III, 258.

the overall responsibility for a prominent part in its formulation. In addition, he decided that the Riccardi would collect the subsidy over the country as a whole, but he ensured that he was the chief appraiser and collector in London and Middlesex, and appointed his own deputies.[71]

Chauncy, as treasurer, was also involved in the taxation of the Jews. This was part of a wider policy of raising funds, and the Dunstable chronicler mentions it as part of the business of the 1275 parliament, along with the fifteenth on the temporalities of the church and lay population.[72] The Templars were also involved, as their headquarters at New Temple, London, was used as a repository for the money.[73] On 23 January 1275, Chauncy, John Lovetot and Geoffrey Neuband were ordered diligently and cautiously to enquire if any merchant-usurers were to be found in London or elsewhere, and if so to arrest them and their goods.[74] The crown was happy to profit out of methods it officially condemned (i.e. charging interest). This is indicated by the instruction on 20 May to Chauncy and the justices of the custody of the Jews to allow the payment of usury debts, though it was added that what was paid should be as the treasurer thinks fit and no more, that is not at exorbitant rates.[75] Chauncy was still involved in chasing up these debts two to three years later. For example, on 14 January 1277, Chauncy and others were to inquire if the late Roger Leyburn had been indebted to the Jews, and on 28 June 1278, Chauncy, John Cobham and Philip Willoughby were appointed to levy the arrears of the tax on the Jews first levied in 1274.[76] Furthermore, on 15 July 1278, Chauncy, Cobham, Willoughby and Walter Helyun were appointed to assess a further tax on the goods, chattels and debts of the Jews; as in 1274, those who resisted were to be threatened with exile.[77]

Chauncy is mentioned in the Michaelmas rolls for 1276 because of a 2,000 mark payment to the Prior and the English Hospitallers in satisfaction of the loan made by Chauncy to the king.[78] It is interesting that Chauncy is only referred to as treasurer when he is carrying out the official duties of that office, but that when he comes to receive the repayment of the loan the title is dropped. Given that it was Chauncy, the treasurer, authorising the repayment to Chauncy, the Hospitaller Prior, we can see how conscious Chauncy was himself of his dual role and duties to both king and order. It also indicates his caution to ensure that he was not accused of appropriating funds to himself, and that the payments were legitimate. This strict division is again apparent in the Michaelmas roll for 1277, where Chauncy is referred to as Prior for £11 paid for duties concerning the collection of a tax in Shropshire, but as treasurer for other duties concerning the same tax.[79] That Chauncy had the resources to make large loans to the crown indicates that the pattern of appointing

---

[71] *CCR 1272–1279*, 251.
[72] *Annales Monastici*, **III**, 266.
[73] *CPR 1272–1281*, 83.
[74] *CCR 1272–1279*, 144.
[75] *Ibid.*, 172.
[76] *CPR 1272–1281*, 188, 273.
[77] *Ibid.*, 274.
[78] TNA E 403/36, m. 1.
[79] TNA E 403/37, m. 1.

wealthy men as treasurers in Henry VI's reign, first detected by Steel and confirmed by Clark, goes back to the thirteenth century.[80]

The issue rolls for Chauncy's remaining years as treasurer continue the pattern of expenditure of the previous years. Other than the usual household expenses, the Riccardi (now headed in England by Orlandino de Pogio) continued to be the main financers of the building works, and religious patronage went to the Carthusians and Templars.[81] Chauncy and the Hospitallers seemed to benefit little from the Prior's long term of service. There was apparently no patronage matching that which the Templars secured. Chauncy's aim in accepting his role as king's treasurer seems to have been (at least in part) to stabilise crown finances to ensure the relatively quick repayment of loans made by the Hospitallers to the king, which was achieved during his term as treasurer. Chauncy did enjoy some rewards of office, such as appointing sheriffs, and granting other privileges, like wards of marriages, which may have had hidden advantages, but nothing on the scale of treasurers in the late fourteenth and fifteenth centuries.[82] Perhaps Chauncy took less because he gave less. The receipt rolls show few large loans by the Hospitallers, with Chauncy working mainly as a middleman for loans from others, such as the papacy (through the temporary loan of papal taxation stored at Clerkenwell and New Temple) or merchants.[83]

Hales, treasurer 1381

Prior Robert Hales was only treasurer for four and a half months (1 February to 14 June 1381), his term of office cut short by his murder.[84] In contrast to Chauncy, who was appointed treasurer by a strong king at the start of his reign, Hales came into office during Richard II's minority and was appointed by the council. Some historians have accused Hales of complicity in the supposedly corrupt government at the end of Edward III's reign and the beginning of Richard II's.[85] Some of the discussion in this chapter will comment on any evidence of this alleged corruption by Hales, which the writer thinks is unfounded.

The months before Hales came into office were problematic for the government. In particular there were difficulties collecting the recently granted poll tax. It was the failure of Thomas, bishop of Exeter, to collect the tax that led to Hales' appointment.[86] Hales had previous experience in government service, as admiral of the fleet in 1377, on the third and longest 'continual council' from October 1378 to January 1380 as one of the two bannerets, and as a diplomat in late 1380. It is interesting to

[80] A. B. Steel, *The Receipt of the Exchequer, 1377–1485*, Cambridge, 1954, 330–1; L. Clark, 'The Benefits and Burdens of Office: Henry Bourgchier (1408–83), Viscount Bourgchier and Earl of Essex, and the Treasurership of the Exchequer', in *Profit, Piety and the Professions*, 119–36 at 122.

[81] Orlandino de Pogio replaced Lucasio Natale as the Riccardi's chief representative in England when the latter returned to Lucca, TNA E 403/37–44.

[82] TNA C 81/1; *CFR 1272–1307*, 12–13, 111.

[83] TNA E 401/70–96.

[84] A number of issue rolls exist for Hales term as treasurer, TNA E 403/481–6, Michaelmas term 1380–Easter term 1381.

[85] Tipton, 'English Hospitallers', 96.

[86] TNA E 403/481, m. 18.

note that business was not carried out on a daily basis, but did take up a substantial part of Hales' time. From 6 February (the date of the first entry) until the end of that month, for example, with the exception of Sundays, the treasury apparently met on 13 out of 20 days.[87] It was thus formally taking approximately two-thirds of Hales' time, and one has to add to this time he would spend in council as treasurer. Although he was not always present, it is likely that he was in the treasury on most days. This impinged on time available to attend to his Hospitaller duties. Small wonder, then, that his lieutenant, Brother Hildebrand Inge, was made his general attorney on 11 February, with the power to make other attorneys.[88]

Hales' preoccupation with crown duties did not necessarily mean that he was indifferent to his responsibilities as Prior. Indeed, he may have seen that the Hospitallers' best interests were served by having a man at the centre of government, especially during a minority. The issue rolls show no evidence of the alleged corruption that Hales' name has been associated with. The rolls for Michaelmas term 1380 show only the usual payments to government officials. Although one of these payments was to a nephew of Hales, Sir Thomas Ilderton, this was for Ilderton's official duties as justice of the peace and as one of the wards of Berwick, and the amount of £10 was hardly excessive.[89] The chancery warrants indicate that Hales favoured Ilderton, already a crown official before Hales came to office, appointing him as escheator in Suffolk (1 February), Wiltshire (25 February) and reappointing him to Southampton (7 April).[90] There is also a warrant for the advocation of a John Radington to Bradeford church (Somerset) on 12 February.[91] This indicates favouritism to select Hospitaller kin, but it was the usual patronage expected of a lord and was considered one of the normal perks of the job.[92]

Similarly, the three issue rolls for Easter term 1381 show no signs of dishonesty or undue patronage. What we do see, however, is the Prior acting in the interests of the Hospitallers and favouring other religious. He tended, for example, to ensure the keeping of alien priories to their own priors, rather than to laymen.[93] The previous June (1380), Hales had lent the king 1,000 marks (£660) which the king (i.e. the council) on 26 April (1381) promised to repay to Hales or a successor, which suggests that the money was borrowed from the Hospitallers and not Hales personally.[94] All but £20 of this was retrieved, after privy seal warrant, in payments of £600 on 9 May and £40 on 30 May.[95] Hales had made another large loan to the crown, one of 1,350 marks on 1 January 1381, for which he obtained a warrant

---

[87] *Ibid.*, mm. 19–20.

[88] *CPR 1377–1381*, 596.

[89] TNA E 403/481, m. 25; See *Members of Parliament for Northumberland 1258–1588*, ed. C. H. Hunter Blair, reprint from *Archaeologis Aeliana*, 4th series, X–XII, 1933–35, 70–1, for the relationship between Hales and Ilderton.

[90] TNA C 81/468/54; TNA C 81/469/19; TNA C 81/469/94. He had previously been appointed escheator of Southampton on 20 January 1381, TNA C 81/468/27.

[91] TNA C 81/468/89.

[92] *Profit, Piety and Professions*, 125–6.

[93] See *CFR 1377–1383*, 240, 251.

[94] *Ibid.*, 617.

[95] TNA E 403/484, mm. 2, 6; warrant of 26 April, TNA C 81/470/20.

for repayment on 18 May.[96] There are no signs of excessive payments to Hales, his servants, or the Hospitallers. The only possible sign of patronage (and it is a slim possibility) is that the £600 paid to the Hospitallers on 9 May was by the hands of Sir Thomas Felton, who was Hales' representative.[97] This in itself is not unusual, but we can link it to a reference in the exchequer various accounts of an indenture between the treasurer (Hales) and the executors of Thomas Felton as to soldiers' wages, which implies that Felton had been employed very much as Hales had been in 1377.[98] Rather than seeing this as giving 'jobs to the boys', one could interpret it as Hales choosing people he knew and trusted to carry out his orders, such as Felton, Ilderton and Stephen Hales.[99] The payments to the Hospitallers suggest that Hales accepted the post of treasurer for the same reason as Prior Chauncy, that is to gain preferment at the exchequer to ensure the swift repayment of loans that could then be sent as responsions. This makes his actions consistent with the concessions he gained from the Good Parliament in 1376 regarding the sending of responsions.[100] The loans also indicate that the crown valued Hales, as with Chauncy, as a source of credit, another example of a wealthy man appointed as treasurer.

It was not just monetary gains or the opportunity for patronage that made the treasurership attractive to Hales. He also gained other advantages for his order. On 10 April 1381, for example, at his own request, a warrant of privy seal confirmed that the Prior and Hospitallers would be free from interference of crown officials and confirmed their lands and tenements to them forever.[101] This sort of confirmation was usually given at the beginning of a king's reign, but due to Richard II's minority one would normally expect it to be granted on petition at the first parliament of his majority. As it was going to be a long minority (until May 1389), Hales saw the advantages of a quick confirmation to avoid disputes over Hospitallers' rights in a politically unstable period.

Langstrother, treasurer 1469, 1470–1

John Langstrother served as treasurer twice, firstly under Edward IV from 16 August to 24 October 1469, and then under Henry VI's Readeption, from 20 October 1470 until his execution on 6 May 1471.[102] Langstrother came into office, as both Prior and crown treasurer, at a crucial time in English politics. It was the period in which Warwick had become estranged from Edward IV and was aiming to restrain or replace him. Langstrother's appointment, indeed, was made by privy seal at Warwick Castle on 13 August 1469, where Edward IV was confined, with Lang-

---

[96] TNA C 81/470/94.

[97] TNA E 403/485, m. 3.

[98] TNA E 101/39/15.

[99] Order of 25 February to Ilderton as escheator of Wiltshire, *CFR 1377–1383*, 242; order for Stephen Hales, knight, on a commission of 16 March in Norfolk to ensure the poll tax was assessed and collected properly, *ibid.*, 248.

[100] *CCR 1374–1377*, 297–8.

[101] TNA C 81/469/98.

[102] One issue roll exists for his first term as treasurer, TNA E 403/843; No issue rolls exist for the Readeption.

strother taking up office three days later.[103] There is no doubt that Langstrother became heavily involved in this power struggle, so much so that Edward IV thought him dangerous enough to rescind a pardon after the battle of Tewkesbury in order to execute him.[104]

An assessment based on those receiving payment gives some indication as to whether Langstrother was fulfilling his duties properly. The issue roll shows no payments to those in opposition to Edward other than a mere £13 to Henry Percy, who was in custody in the Tower of London.[105] There is also a payment to Richard, duke of Gloucester (the future Richard III), who until he came of age in 1468 had been part of Warwick's household, although he was later a supporter of Edward IV and took part in the French campaign of 1475, as did Sir John Howard.[106] Indeed, there are a number of routine payments to prominent royal supporters. Apart from Queen Elizabeth, there are payments to Sir John Howard, Richard Illingworth (chief baron of the exchequer), Sir Richard Fowler (chancellor of the exchequer and, from 1471, chancellor of the duchy of Lancaster), and former treasurer Lord Mountjoy.[107] The other payments are to members of the exchequer and the king's servants. The last entry on the roll is to Langstrother himself, with separate amounts paid for his attendance at council (£97), for his post as treasurer (£300), both from 16 August until 25 October 1469, and a further £60 for other duties from 28 August.[108] The advance payment of his wages indicates that by 10 October he had anticipated his dismissal and gained preference at the exchequer to ensure quick payment. Gaining preference at the exchequer was essential to secure payment and as treasurer Langstrother did not have to wait long for his wages, as Prior Botyll had to do in 1449–50, although Botyll was one of the lucky ones to get an assignment for payment from customs.[109] Langstrother's wage payments were much higher than the set rates for treasurers (£66 13s. 4d. per annum) and councillors (£100 per annum for barons), but they were no more than other treasurers took in the 1450s and 1460s and, as has been shown for Viscount Bourgchier, they were considered part of the usual incentives and rewards of that office.[110]

Examination of the fine rolls and warrants for the great seal reveals that Langstrother controlled crown patronage to appoint his own retainers. Within a week of his first term as treasurer, he appointed people to levy and collect the customs

---

[103] TNA C 81/827/80.
[104] *Death and Dissent*, 113.
[105] TNA E 403/843, m. 1.
[106] *Ibid.* For Richard III in Warwick's household, see M. A. Hicks, *Richard III and his Rivals: Magnates and their Motives in the Wars of the Roses*, 2nd edn, Stroud, 2000, 56; See *Edward IV's French Expedition of 1475*, ed. F. P. Barnard, Oxford, 1925, f. 1v, for Richard on the 1475 French campaign, f. 2r for Howard.
[107] TNA E 403/843, m. 1.
[108] *Ibid.*, m. 2.
[109] G. L. Harriss, 'Preference at the Medieval Exchequer', *BIHR*, XXX, 1957, 17–40 at 18, 38; *CPR 1446–1452*, 284, 376–7. Botyll had originally been granted £640 wages for diplomatic duty on 27 April 1449 from the subsidy on tonnage and poundage, but had to wait until after 30 May 1450 for at least £100, as the duke of Buckingham had been granted money for the wages of the Calais troops. Multon, in 1475, was also to receive part-payment of wages through revenues from customs duties, *CPR 1467–1477*, 545.
[110] *Profit, Piety and Professions*, 120–1.

on wool, as well as the customs due from alien merchants, mainly in London, East Anglia and the West Country.[111] Hospitaller kin also benefited: a John Tong was appointed searcher of ships for uncustomed goods in Bristol and a Robert Malory to the same office for London.[112] Similarly at the start of his second term, Langstrother appointed customs officials, many the same as for the first term and again including Hospitaller kin, such as Thomas Tornay (Boston) and John Tong (Hull).[113] The second term, perhaps because it lasted longer, shows more extensive patronage to Hospitaller relatives and servants and a few examples will suffice to illustrate this trend. In early November 1470, a Thomas Babington was made escheator in Nottingham and Derby and Robert Malory in Cambridge and Huntingdon. In late November and early December those with family names associated with the Hospitallers, such as Newdigate and Tunstall, were made keepers of manors for long terms and at reasonable rates. In mid-December, a Richard Pasmere (later a servant of Prior Kendal in the 1490s) was appointed keeper of the king's exchange to foreign parts in England and Calais. At the end of January 1471, Robert Malory was granted the farm of subsidy and aulnage on cloths for sale in five counties and Norwich for seven years.[114] Finally, on 23 February, Langstrother appointed himself for life as one of the two custodians of coin and money in the Tower of London.[115] As with excess payments, these appointments were considered to be part of the rewards of office.[116]

The fine rolls and warrants for the great seal also show that Langstrother was not just working for himself. He was also a servant of the higher nobility and was appointed to facilitate preference to them. For example, George, duke of Clarence was granted the farm of the Forest of Dean for life on 24 November 1470 and was reappointed lieutenant of Ireland on 18 December.[117] On 15 November Warwick was entrusted with the keeping of the seas with authority to order actions under his own seal.[118] The following February the earls of Warwick and Pembroke were granted the keeping of various castles and lordships in Wales and the Welsh marches.[119] Finally, in February 1471 a William Fisher was appointed to levy and collect the wool tax in London after nomination by the queen.[120]

Langstrother, then, appears to be carrying out his duties efficiently and in accordance with the accepted conventions of the office, which allowed him to make large payments to himself and appoint his own retainers to crown offices. There are large payments, but not any comparable to those that the previous treasurer, Lord Ryvers, had made to himself.[121] Although Langstrother had been appointed treasurer whilst

[111] It was in the West Country that Langstrother rallied troops for the queen in 1471, so the appointments had a clear political element to them, *CFR 1461–1471*, 247–50.
[112] Tong was appointed on 23 August and Malory on 30 August, *ibid.*, 251.
[113] *Ibid.*, 269–74.
[114] *Ibid.*, 281–2, 284, 287–8; BL MS Lansdowne 200, ff. 74–74v, 83–83v; *CFR 1461–1471*, 277.
[115] John Delves, esquire, was the other, TNA C 81/781/6.
[116] *Profit, Piety and Professions*, 125–7.
[117] TNA C 81/780/45; TNA C 81/780/62.
[118] TNA C 81/780/35.
[119] *CFR 1461–1471*, 293, 295.
[120] *Ibid.*, 275.
[121] TNA E 403/842.

Edward was in Warwick's custody, that he was not replaced the moment the king was at liberty, and that he was allowed to continue in office until 25 October indicates that Edward, at this stage, replaced him merely to reassert his authority over Warwick, as was expected, by appointing his own man as treasurer (the bishop of Ely), and not because he considered Langstrother a danger.[122] He did, after all, recognise him as Prior. That he wished for an oath of fealty, often portrayed by crusades historians as a humiliation to Langstrother, was to be expected, given the threat to his realm, and was no more than he extracted from others, such as Henry Percy the younger. On the contrary, as Hicks has pointed out, accepting Langstrother's oath of fealty was one of the few concessions that the confederates gained from Edward.[123] Throughout 1469, Warwick himself still officially recognised Edward as king, so Langstrother was bound to tread carefully.

Conclusion

As this book focuses on the political and diplomatic role of the Prior, some aspects of the Prior's financial relations have been omitted, such as the Hospitallers' creditors and debtors in England, including international merchant companies, because they are relevant more to his role as Hospitaller Prior than to his service to the crown. Nevertheless, some may have had an effect on the Prior's role in service to the king. For example, Priors had links with not only foreign but also English merchants, such as the merchant tailors of London, many of whom were tenants of the Prior.[124] Prior John Weston retained members of the Cely family, merchants of the staple at Calais, and there are indications that Prior Tornay may have come from a merchant family of the Calais staple.[125] Prior Docwra had links with both English and Venetian merchants.[126] The close links that existed between the Prior and merchants may well have determined the Prior's role as negotiator for the king in making loans. The links with Calais may also have influenced the Priors' political role, and perhaps determined his allegiance in times of crisis, such as when Warwick had his base at Calais.

In conclusion we have seen that the Priors had two main financial roles, one as financier in various forms and then occasionally as treasurer. Is there a link between these two roles? In Chauncy's case, investigation of the issue rolls suggests that there

---

[122] C. D. Ross, *Edward IV*, 2nd edn, New Haven, CT, and London, 1997, 136; M. A. Hicks, *Warwick the Kingmaker*, Oxford, 1998, 280.

[123] Hicks, *False, Fleeting Perjur'd Clarence*, 43.

[124] This becomes apparent from analysis of the Hospitaller lease books, for example BL MS Cotton Claudius E VI, 86v.

[125] See the many references in *Cely Letters* and A. Hanham, *The Celys and their World: an English Merchant Family of the Fifteenth Century*, Cambridge, 1985.

[126] For Docwra's Venetian links, see R. C. Mueller, *The Venetian Money Market: Banks, Panics, and the Public Debt, 1200–1500*, Baltimore, MD, 1997, 348; For Docwra's links with the English merchant tailors, see the various entries in BL MS Cotton Claudius E VI and H. Miller, 'London and Parliament in the reign of Henry VIII' in *Historical Studies of the English Parliament*, 2 vols, ed. E. B. Fryde and E. Miller, Cambridge, 1970, II, 125–40 at 135.

was. As Hospitaller treasurer at Acre, he had helped arrange loans for Edward and then he became Edward's treasurer to deal with these loans. Chauncy had good reasons to accept the treasurership. It coincided with his appointment as Prior of England, so it suited him to travel back to England with or in advance of Edward in order to tend to the English Priory. He must have been aware of the great debts that Edward had run up during his crusade and that the king needed to fund their repayment. As king's treasurer, he was in a better position to limit the demands on Hospitaller resources to repay crown loans, and could ensure that any Hospitaller loans to the crown for that purpose were repaid in ready money swiftly. Yet Chauncy may also have become treasurer out of a genuine feeling of duty to his king as well as admiration for his crusade enthusiasm. Indeed, the published correspondence between the two men after Chauncy had ceased to be treasurer suggests that Edward's friendship with Chauncy, made on his crusade, was one that, as Prestwich has noted, lasted throughout his reign, Chauncy modestly describing himself as the 'least and lowest' of Edward's servants and Edward referring to Chauncy as his 'faithful secretary'.[127] Both had something to gain from this: Chauncy's letter clearly displays his hope that Edward would return to the Holy Land, enticing him to the prestige of certain victory with reports that there had never been a better time for reconquest than now.[128] Equally, Edward displays his desire to have Chauncy return to his service as soon as possible, perhaps as treasurer.[129] Even after Chauncy ceased to be the king's treasurer, the mutual respect between the two men still aided the English Hospitallers. For example, it has recently been suggested that it may have been Chauncy's close relationship with Edward I that influenced the king's decision in 1284 to cease litigation against the Hospitallers and quitclaim the advowson of Down Ampney church to Prior Hanley and his successors.[130]

There appears to be a link between Hales' role as financier and treasurer, for similar reasons to those Chauncy had, that is securing the repayment of money lent.[131] There may be another parallel in that, just as Chauncy took on the treasurership to protect Hospitaller interests, Hales may have seen his appointment to the exchequer as the best way to uphold Hospitaller privileges at a time of high government taxation. Add to this the instability that accompanies a minority, and there were sound reasons for Hales to become involved in English government for the benefit of his order, despite the obvious dangers of taking the position, though nobody could have foreseen that it would lead to his murder. Hales was not naïve, but saw it as his duty to his order to become involved in English government. Saul has commented that the third continual council (October 1378 to January 1380), which Hales had served on before he was treasurer, aimed at a 'still cleaner break'

[127] Prestwich, *Edward I*, 81; 'Letter from Sir Joseph de Cancy, knight of the Hospital of St John of Jerusalem, to King Edward I (1281)' and 'Letter from King Edward I to Sir Joseph (1282)' tr. W. B. Sanders in *The Library of the Palestine Pilgrims' Text Society*, V, London, 1897, 7, 14–15.

[128] *Ibid*, 13.

[129] *Ibid*, 14–15.

[130] P. Herde, 'The Dispute between the Hospitallers and the Bishop of Worcester about the Church of Down Ampney. An Unpublished Letter of Justice of Pope John XXI (1276)', in *The Hospitallers, the Mediterranean and Europe. Festschrift for Anthony Luttrell*, ed. K. Borchardt, N. Jaspert and H. Nicholson, Aldershot, 2007, 47–55 at 51.

[131] TNA E 403/484, mm. 2, 6; TNA E 403/485, mm. 3, 7.

with the alleged corruption of the past than the first two councils.[132] He further states that Hales had 'no obvious affiliation with anyone'.[133] If this interpretation is correct, it is likely that Hales was appointed to both the continual council and later the treasurership for his perceived neutrality and honesty. The evidence in the issue rolls upholds this opinion.

In the case of Langstrother, no link between financier and treasurer roles is evident, though he had only just been appointed Prior, so had not had time to act as a source of credit for the crown. Although he had plenty of financial experience, his promotion to treasurer was clearly much more political than Chauncy's or Hales' appointments. He was a supporter of Warwick, but it cannot be shown that he used his position as treasurer in 1469 to further Warwick's aims. It may be that Langstrother had little room to manoeuvre just as, as Ross has noted, Warwick had no fund of patronage despite holding the king captive.[134] It seems that Langstrother, both in 1469 and in 1470–1, was following a policy very much as his predecessor Prior Botyll did: to support the faction that he thought could bring the stability necessary for the Hospitallers to perform their duties efficiently. By 1471, however, divisions were so wide that it was not possible to keep on good terms with both sides.

Another question to answer is why there were not more Hospitaller Prior treasurers. There is no concrete answer to this, but a number of possibilities. Firstly, as Priors were part of an international order, they needed to travel abroad regularly, whereas the crown preferred to have its office holders permanently at its disposal. Secondly, there is the question of choice, that at particular times the Priors thought it was in the best interests of their order to intervene in state business, if given the chance: Chauncy when the king was in great debt and in the aftermath of the Baronial revolt of the 1260s, Hales during a minority and a time of political resistance to government taxes and Langstrother during a period of great political and dynastic struggle. Thirdly, as Clark has commented, while the office of treasurer offered many advantages, it had many drawbacks, including unpopularity or even death if the incumbent was thought to act unfairly or be responsible for misgovernance.[135] After the murder of Hales, one can understand why Priors would not wish to be treasurers.

Finally, how does the Prior's financial role, especially that of treasurer, accord with his other roles in service to the crown? An examination of who else held the treasurership from Edward I to Henry VIII helps to answer this question.[136] When Chauncy became treasurer in 1273, it was usual for ecclesiastics to hold that office. Chauncy appears to be a unique example of a lay treasurer, perhaps because of his close association with Edward, and it was not until 1340 that another member of the laity was treasurer. That there was a distinction between Hospitaller Prior treasurers who, although taking holy orders, were still members of the laity, and

[132] N. Saul, *Richard II*, New Haven, CT, and London, 1997, 31.
[133] *Ibid*, 46.
[134] Ross, *Edward IV*, 133.
[135] *Profit, Piety and Professions*, 120, 128.
[136] The following discussion is based on the list of treasurers in *HBC*, 104–7, the chief governors of Ireland and their deputies, 160–7, and Scottish treasurers, 186–9.

the ecclesiastical treasurers is indicated by the way that they were addressed. Both Chauncy and Hales are referred to as *dilectus nobilis in Christo*, whereas ecclesiastics, such as Thomas bishop of Exeter in 1381, were called *venerabilis in Christo*.[137] When Hales entered the treasury, it was still usual for ecclesiastics to hold the position, but there was a noticeable trend towards lay appointments, of which Hales was part, with four others holding the treasurership between 1340 and 1381, starting with Robert Sadington.[138] By the time that Langstrother took office in 1469, it was the norm for a member of the laity to hold the treasurership, with only seven ecclesiastics holding the position since 1400 and none after 1469. What this reflects is an increasing involvement by the laity in government from about the start of the Hundred Years War. This corresponds to the general development of the Prior's role in service to the crown (Chauncy being the exception to the rule), which was occasional in the fourteenth century and regular from the mid-fifteenth century.

---

[137] TNA E 34/1 (not E 34/1A, as the TNA catalogue states), April 1274; TNA E 101/334/20, 1 February 1381.

[138] Robert Sadington, knight, in 1340; Robert Parving, knight, 1341; Richard, Lord Scrope of Bolton, 1371; Robert Ashton, knight, 1375.

3

Defender of the Realm

By the end of the thirteenth century the feudal military summons was no longer an effective means of raising troops. It was incompatible with the almost continuous war with either Scotland or France and often with both. In the early fourteenth century, the feudal summons had been replaced by the contract system but, as Powicke has pointed out, this was done in a way so that 'the king's position as head, and that of the nobles as leaders, remained unimpaired'.[1]

The Prior of St John is one illustration of this change. Although theoretically exempt from any military service to lay rulers, Hospitallers did in fact do some sort of service. At first summoned by feudal writ, as in 1297 to serve against Scotland, from 1339 the Prior was contracted to muster and lead troops for the defence of the realm.[2] This change was not clear-cut and the Prior continued to provide a mixture of feudal and contract service after 1339 up until the cessation of the feudal summons in 1385. Although the 1385 summons was the first since 1327, this did not stop the crown calling lords in between these dates to muster and lead troops by their 'fealty, affection and allegiance' owed in defence of the realm.[3]

This distinction between the different types of service and their implications for the Prior's role in English society has not been fully appreciated by historians of the crusades, who attempt to apply general theories on Hospitaller history to individual Hospitaller priories. For example, it has been implied that Prior Thame was pressured into offering service in 1337, thus setting up the crown versus Hospitaller dialogue common to most literature on the English Hospitallers. Thame's request that the 1337 service should not become a precedent, however, was asking for no more than the usual concession that all English lords gained from the crown, and that it was granted is really of very little relevance. He, like other lords, was expected to serve in future, if required. Furthermore, Thame's sending of men to Scotland

---

[1] M. R. Powicke, *Military Obligation in Medieval England: A Study in Liberty and Duty*, Oxford, 1962, 166.

[2] *Parliamentary Writs*, I, 304 for the 1297 summons; TNA E 101/22/10 for the 1339 account and indenture.

[3] For example, TNA C 76/24, m. 10, 14 May 1347. This request for men-at-arms also went out to the earls of Gloucester, Hereford, Devon and Surrey, Thomas Berkeley and John Segrave, as well as Prior Thame; see also N. B. Lewis, 'The Recruitment and Organisation of a Contract Army, May to November 1337', *BIHR*, XXXVII, 1964, 1–19.

in 1337 and his role as keeper of Southampton in 1339 have been cited as if they were the same type of service, yet as we shall see, they were very different.[4] Such an interpretation is as far as the printed English primary sources and the Hospitaller archive on Malta permit. This chapter, using especially the treaty rolls, accounts various and foreign account rolls in the National Archives, clarifies the military role of the Prior in the fourteenth century. It further comments on the more limited, but still existing, military role of the Prior in late fifteenth-century and early sixteenth-century England.

Background

The fourteenth century saw changes in the way in which armies were raised, with the *servitium debitum* being replaced by the contractual system.[5] This was induced by continual war, firstly with Scotland and then by the start of the Hundred Years War in 1337. The service of the Prior of St John mirrors these military modifications, with the Priors at first called by feudal summons during the Scottish wars, and then from the late 1330s providing a mixture of service owed with military contract. The Prior's military service appears in general to precede his diplomatic commissions. Succinctly, he was called to service in the Scottish wars of the early fourteenth century, was keeper of Southampton in 1339, and admiral of the southern fleet (often referred to as the fleet east and west of the Thames) in 1360, 1377 and 1385–86. In addition, Prior Multon was appointed deputy keeper for seven years of the middle march towards Scotland in 1474 and, after his resignation as Prior (but still Hospitaller commander of Mount St John), he was deputy keeper of the east and middle marches in 1490. Finally, Prior Docwra is noted in the *Chronicle of Calais* as being in the forward of the force that invaded France in 1513. The final two examples suggest that, although most of the records of the Prior's military service survive from the fourteenth century, it was possible for him to be called on to serve militarily throughout the later medieval period. Most of the time this appears to have been a defensive military role, but Docwra's part in the 1513 campaign indicates an offensive role, with the Prior potentially facing French Hospitaller brethren in battle.

The Prior was expected to take up arms against other Christians for his king, but only on the grounds of the defence of the realm. In common with other lords, he was expected to perform secondary military activities such as providing foodstuffs or transportation of equipment, as in 1307 and 1310.[6] The writs of military service show that he was first summoned to do service in 1297 against Scotland, as were the commanders of Mayne and Buckland, and this was repeated in 1300.[7] Again, in 1316, 1317, 1318 and 1322 the writs of military service and close rolls record the Prior's summons, with his retinue, to Newcastle and York respectively to do

4   Nicholson, 'The Hospitallers in England', 38–9.
5   See Powicke, *Military Obligation*, chapters IX, X and XI.
6   *CCR 1307–13*, 50, 260–5.
7   *Parliamentary Writs*, I, 304, 286, 289, 293, 333, 336–7.

military service against the Scots.[8] In the latter case, the summons was not just to muster troops, as it stated that the Prior was expected to appear in person.[9] Even so, it is doubtful that the Prior actually took part in any battle during the Scottish wars. He is not included in any lists of those serving under the earls, as other lords are, nor mentioned in any secondary works by modern historians.[10] Such service was common, both for spiritual and temporal lords. The Prior was performing the expected feudal service and anything above this was voluntary, as indicated by letters patent for January 1338, when the king granted that the decision of Prior Thame to send ten men-at-arms to Scotland and to maintain them for nine months of his own free will would not become a precedent.[11] Four examples illustrate the development of the Prior's military role in service to the crown beyond performance of the standard feudal service to his appointment to defensive military positions both on land and on sea, and then finally to active participation in offensive campaigns.

Case 1: Prior Thame, Keeper of Southampton, 1339

From the later 1330s, examples materialise that indicate the Prior's changing military role, from service owed to official appointments. This change coincides with the beginning of the Hundred Years War. The first was Prior Thame's commission as keeper of Southampton in 1339, accounts of which are extant.[12] The Prior was commissioned to send 300 men-at-arms to Southampton on 12 April, although the close rolls suggest that he was already there by mid-January.[13] One account roll, which includes the terms of Thame's indenture, notes his formal appointment as keeper of Southampton on 29 August, with a commitment to provide 20 men-at-arms, 10 armed men and 40 archers, initially for 32 days (until Michaelmas).[14] Given the figure of 300 men-at-arms mentioned in the commission, the Prior needed to muster more men than could be provided by the English Hospitaller knights alone. Nevertheless, there are indications from the names of those serving that Prior Thame did indeed call on those with links to Hospitaller families, especially the Archer family: Richard Archer, Adam Archer and William Archer esquires, all served in the first session of service. In the second period of service, from Michaelmas until 8 November, a

[8] *Ibid.*, 463, 468, 488, 491, 495, 502, 505; *CCR 1313–18*, 292, 473, 484, 562, 622–3.
[9] *Parliamentary Writs*, I, 588.
[10] See *The Roll of Arms of the Princes, Barons, and Knights who Attended King Edward I to the Siege of Caerlaverock in 1300*, ed. T. Wright, London, 1864; N. M. Fryde, *The Tyranny and Fall of Edward II, 1321–1326*, Cambridge, 1979; C. McNamee, *The Wars of the Bruces: Scotland, England and Ireland 1306–1328*, East Linton, 1997; J. R. S. Phillips, *Aymer de Valence Earl of Pembroke 1307–1324*, Oxford, 1972; M. C. Prestwich, *The Three Edwards: War and State in England 1272–1377*, London, 1980; M. C. Prestwich, *War, Politics and Finance under Edward I*, London, 1972. None of the above refers to the Prior performing military service in Scotland.
[11] *Rot. Parl.*, II, 100; *CPR 1338–40*, 11.
[12] TNA E 101/22/6–7, TNA E 101/22/10, TNA E 101/22/17.
[13] *Foedera*, London, II, 1079; *CCR 1337–9*, 635.
[14] TNA E 101/22/10.

James Thame and Hugo Archer esquires were amongst those recruited.[15] At least one other Hospitaller, Brother William Multon, commander of Godsfield, was involved in the Prior's duties. It was by his hand that the weapons used by the Prior were delivered back to the custodians of armaments in Southampton on 4 January 1340.[16] Although the Prior was ordered to return the weapons on 6 November and an inventory of weapons was duly drawn up, it appears that he continued in his post as keeper of Southampton until 27 November. It was from 29 August until the latter date that the exchequer was later ordered to pay him.[17]

The fact that the Prior was paid only from the starting date of the formal indenture indicates that during 1339 his military service graduated from feudal or voluntary before 29 August, to paid employment from that date. In the earlier part of the year, he was commissioned to array men for the defence of Southampton and several other maritime counties, from which he was later excused because of his duties in Southampton. There is no mention of payments for these or for his duties as keeper during these months. Only from 29 August do we find accounts and payments that indicate a more integrated role, which is supported by an entry four days earlier in the close rolls showing him in a supervisory role concerning Southampton's defences.[18] While the accounts note the daily rate of payment for knights (2s.), men-at-arms (1s.) and archers (3d.) under the Prior's control, they do not mention the Prior's wages.[19] He was later to negotiate this with the exchequer, but given that the knights were paid 2s., it seems almost certain that Thame was paid more than this, probably at the standard daily rate for a banneret (4s.). That the Prior and his men were paid strongly suggests that there was a limit to the voluntary service, such as that offered in 1337 in Scotland, that the Prior was prepared to provide in order to keep in favour with the king. To Lewis' comment that the Hospitallers were a rare example of voluntary and gratuitous service we need to add that it was also rare for the Hospitallers to offer such service.[20]

Case 2: Priors as Admirals of the Fleet

Prior John Pavely, 1360

The second example of the Prior of St John in military service to the crown was again in a time of crisis, the French raid on Winchelsea, when Edward III was abroad. On 2 March 1360, Prior Pavely was ordered to be on the alert to resist an expected French invasion and to 'abide in the seaward ports' with men-at-arms, armed men and archers.[21] This 'invasion' came on 15 March, when the French

---

[15] *Ibid.*

[16] TNA E 101/22/6.

[17] *Ibid.*; TNA E 101/22/17; *CCR 1339–41*, 305.

[18] This also orders the king's receiver in Southampton to arm the Hospitallers, indicating other brethren were being used, *ibid.*, 185.

[19] TNA E 101/22/10.

[20] *Rot. Parl.*, II, 100; *CCR 1339–41*, 305; Lewis, 'Recruitment and Organisation', 13–14.

[21] *CCR 1360–1364*, 99.

landed at Winchelsea. This was more of a raid than an invasion, as they only stayed in England for one night.[22] Nevertheless, orders were sent to the arrayers to raise men and assemble fleets to repel a further attack. As the regular admirals of the fleet were out of the country with the king, Prior Pavely was appointed by the council as admiral of the fleet on 26 March.[23] Why Pavely was appointed, and not someone else, is perhaps answered by the later service of Prior Radington who, as admiral of the southern fleet in 1385, had responsibility for protecting the ports of Sandwich and Rye, near places where the Hospitallers held lands and could array men quickly. Rye is close to Winchelsea, and it is possible that Prior Pavely had duties for the safe custody of the same area.[24] As with Prior Thame in 1339, it appears that Pavely's general feudal service led to a more official level of service. Of the events of 1339 and 1360, Hewitt has commented: 'The men left at home to guard the coasts had been organised and kept in readiness to repel invasion. They gained no ransoms, no spoils, no fame. The chroniclers do not even mention them, nor do the military historians.'[25] Their role in the defence of the country, however, was vital, and Pavely's successful mobilisation against a further invasion appears to have set a precedent for his immediate successors to hold the post of admiral of the southern fleet on a more permanent basis.

Prior Hales, 1376–77

Prior Robert Hales was to serve the crown in more official positions than any previous Prior: on one of the minority councils, on a diplomatic mission and as treasurer. His first form of service, however, was military. At the beginning of his term as Prior, he was commissioned to muster his men in defence of the country. This applied to other Hospitallers, as is evident from a similar request to the turco-polier Richard Overton.[26] Hales was first appointed admiral of the southern fleet on 24 November 1376 and reappointed on 14 August 1377.[27] Apart from ensuring the safety of the seas and maritime lands, he also adjudicated over breaches of trading agreements, as was the case with the attack on a Genoese ship near Southampton in March 1377, which the Prior dealt with in May.[28] This, 'attack' was, perhaps, a result of the order in February for the admirals to arrest ships and assemble a fleet in the Thames by 16 March, to resist an expected invasion.[29] Such events are of interest, as they may explain how the Prior's role developed from a military to a diplomatic one; dealing with infractions of trading agreements when they (Hales and Radington) were admirals was a first step in the interplay of military and diplomatic roles that the Priors developed in the later fourteenth century.

---

[22] H. J. Hewitt, *The Organisation of War under Edward III, 1338–62*, Manchester, 1966, 19; W. L. Clowes, *The Royal Navy: A History from the Earliest Times to the Present*, I, London, 1897, 277.

[23] TNA C 76/40, m. 13.

[24] Prior Radington is noted as having safe custody of Sandwich, Rye and other vills, TNA E 364/19, m. 5d.

[25] Hewitt, *The Organisation of War*, 21.

[26] *CCR 1369–1374*, 568, 18 June 1373.

[27] *Foedera*, Hague, III, 52, 68.

[28] *CCR 1374–7*, 495, 506.

[29] G. A. Holmes, *The Good Parliament*, Oxford, 1975, 164.

A foreign account survives for Hales' second term as admiral, which includes a copy of his indenture of service.[30] This shows that he was contracted to serve for a three-month period with 134 men-at-arms, consisting of the Prior himself, nine knights, 124 'scutifiers' (squires), and 130 archers.[31] The treaty rolls suggest that this three-month period started from 18 September 1377 and continued until mid-December, which corresponds with the foreign account rolls that cite accounts for service in October.[32] The date of 18 September does not match the formal date of appointment, which perhaps suggests that, as with Prior Thame in 1339, for the first 35 days he was doing obligatory service followed by paid service.[33] It is also from 18 September that Hales had Walter Haule and John Legg (the king's sergeants-at-arms) appointed as his deputy admirals, which again indicates the official nature of the appointment; these appointments appear on the patent rolls on 8 October.[34]

The foreign account rolls also indicate that Prior Hales was able to provide the number of men stated in the indenture, although there were six rather than nine knights. The account dated Trinity term 1378 but referring to service in 1377, states the Prior, six knights and 127 squires made up the 134 men-at-arms, plus 130 archers, who in total were paid for 99 days' service in Southampton and London from 19 October 1377 until 26 January 1378.[35] Various other payments are noted on 5, 8, 12 and 21 October and 18 January. Hales was paid 4s. a day, the standard rate for a banneret.[36] There is no specific mention of brethren other than the Prior serving militarily, but the precedent of Prior Thame in 1339 using Brother William Multon, shows it was possible. The number of knights contracted could have been easily drawn from Hospitaller brethren and it may be that Hales called on his own tenants, as these would be the easiest to mobilise quickly. In addition, we do know that William Melchbourne, the Prior's clerk and attorney, was involved in the payment of the soldiers.[37] Thus we have an example of the English exchequer issuing payment and members of the Order administering those payments.

Prior Radington, 1385

Prior John Radington served as admiral of the southern fleet from 29 January 1385 to 21 February 1386 but, as with Prior Hales, his indenture of service was dated slightly later, from 3 March 1385, because it was from that date that action was required.[38] None of the accounts by Radington refer to service earlier than this date.[39] By looking at the treaty rolls (C 76), in combination with the accounts various (E 101) and foreign account rolls (E 364), we can reconstruct Radington's duties as

30 TNA E 364/13.
31 *Ibid.*, m. 2d.
32 TNA C 76/61, mm. 14, 16, 19, 27; TNA E 364/13, m. 2d.
33 The *HBC* states Hales' appointment lasted until 4 December 1377, but he appears to have still been acting in that capacity until at least 12 December, TNA C 76/61, m. 16.
34 TNA C 76/61, m. 27; *CPR 1377–1381*, 26.
35 TNA E 364/13, m. 2d.
36 *Ibid.*
37 *Ibid.*
38 TNA E 101/68/10/241.
39 TNA E 364/19, m. 5; TNA E 364/20, m. 5.

admiral in 1385. They show a preliminary period of mustering forces, followed by active service at sea. Radington's indenture of 3 March, for three months, contracted him to find 300 men-at-arms (knights and esquires) and 400 archers for the 'war on the water'.[40] Radington's duties (and those of his counterpart Percy, the northern admiral) started immediately, by providing safe conduct for the French ambassadors on 4 March.[41] As admiral it was his task to organise safe conducts and this seems to have preoccupied him up until the end of April. Throughout March, April and May the Prior had letters of protection for knights, squires and merchants that were in or going to be in the king's service abroad, such as that to Hugh Despenser, knight, on 23 March, or Stephen Beyford, the king's hostler, on 13 April, and 14 others. This was a major task, as illustrated by the further 21 protections that were issued between 15 April and 1 May.[42] Radington himself had letters of protection from 3 April, which indicates that he was expecting to leave the country in the near future.[43]

Two foreign accounts, which relate to service from April to August inclusive, give further details of the service at sea and suggest that Radington, like Hales, was able to deliver the full complement of troops stated in the indenture. The first account is in three parts that directly follow each other. Part one begins by repeating the information contained in the indenture of 3 March, but specifies the composition of the force in more detail as 300 men-at-arms and 'balistars' (i.e. arbalesters or cross-bowmen), and 400 archers, and the daily payments to be made: 8d. to the two former categories and 6d. to the archers from 18 April.[44] Part two details payments made at the exchequer to two of Radington's clerks for the soldiers' wages on 3 March, 11 April, 13 May and 23 December totalling £3,521 9s. 4d.[45] The final part gives us a complete breakdown of Radington's force, including payments to the Prior himself, for 91 days' active service at sea from 29 April to 29 July. Radington was paid 4s. a day. The men-at-arms were made up of 17 knights paid 2s. and 282 squires at 12d. per day. The Prior plus men-at-arms, then, made up the full company of troops specified in the indenture. However, in addition, there were 292 'armed men' (as opposed to men-at-arms) paid at 8d. per day, the 'balistars' referred to earlier. Finally, the accounts show payments for 400 archers at 6d. per day.[46]

The accounts for Priors Thame, Hales and Radington are very revealing of the duties and even position of the Prior in English society. Firstly, it is significant that the Prior was paid for his services. This contracting of large forces of troops was becoming usual during the fourteenth century, and the timing of Radington's indenture, almost simultaneous with the last feudal summons in June 1385 (which did not include the Prior), verifies the declining importance of feudal obligation.[47]

[40] TNA E 101/68/10/241.
[41] TNA C 76/69, m. 6.
[42] TNA C 76/69, mm. 4, 5.
[43] TNA C 76/69, m. 2.
[44] TNA E 364/20, m. 5.
[45] The two clerks were William Melchbourne, who had performed the same task for Prior Hales in 1377, and Thomas Whiston, *ibid.*
[46] *Ibid.*
[47] See N. B. Lewis, 'The Last Medieval Summons of the English Feudal Levy, 13 June 1385',

The evidence of the indenture for Prior Thame suggests that this had been so at least since the beginning of Edward III's reign.[48] Second, that the Priors were chosen as admirals is perhaps explained because they could actually provide the number of men stated in the contract. One of the reasons for Thame being called to serve as keeper of Southampton was due to the previous keeper's failure to muster enough troops. The accounts of both Hales and Radington show that they made up the required numbers without struggle. The progression from keeper of a maritime county to admiral is explicable in that, by the latter fourteenth century, an admiral's duties incorporated responsibilities previously undertaken by keepers, such as the protection of strategic ports. Third, the rate of pay that both Hales and Radington received (and probably Thame too), 4s. per day, puts them firmly in the ranks of the bannerets, as opposed to knights, at least with regard to military matters. The Prior's military status as a banneret was forming in the early fourteenth century, as indicated by Prior Archer's summons in 1322 for military service against the Scots, when he was described as 'banneret or knight'.[49] Hales, however, was also paid at the rate of a banneret for his attendance on the second protectorate council of Richard II, and was assessed for the 1379 poll tax to pay at the rate of a baron (40s.), so it appears that there was some crossover between military duty and political status.[50]

Finally, the accounts suggest that Hales and Radington both did active service at sea, which very few admirals did, as the post of admiral in England was 'more administrative than operational'.[51] Admirals often went to sea with their fleets, but were not often expected to fight battles. Perhaps English Priors were exceptions because of their naval experience in the Mediterranean, such as Hales' participation in the 1365 siege of Alexandria. Prior Hales was in service at sea from 19 October 1377, which is why Walter Haule and John Legg (the king's sergeants-at-arms) were made his deputies in his office as admiral on 18 September.[52] He was granted protection until Easter on 3 December and was noted to be in the king's service at sea on 12 December.[53] In the case of Radington, we know that the service referred to in the accounts concerned the blockade of Sluys in May 1385 by himself and the admiral of the north.[54] Presumably, his participation in such a campaign was seen as essentially defensive, as a large French fleet was harboured at Sluys in

EHR, LXXIII, 1958, 1–26, and the rejoinder by J. J. N. Palmer, 'The Last Summons of the Feudal Army in England (1385)', EHR, LXXXIII, 1968, 771–5. According to Palmer, 772, the greater part of the army that served in Scotland was *not* summoned by feudal levy.

[48] TNA E 101/22/10.

[49] Parliamentary Writs, I, 588.

[50] J. F. Baldwin, The King's Council in England during the Middle Ages, Oxford, 1913, 123; Rot. Parl., III, 58; On the difference between bannerets and barons, see C. Given-Wilson, The English Nobility in the Late Middle Ages: The Fourteenth-Century Political Community, 2nd edn, London, 1996, 60–4.

[51] N. A. M. Rodger, The Safeguard of the Sea: A Naval History of Great Britain, I, London, 1997, 131–2.

[52] TNA E 364/13, m. 2d; C 76/61, m. 27; CPR 1377–1381, 26, records the substitutions on 8 October.

[53] TNA C 76/61, mm. 16, 19.

[54] C. de la Roncière, Histoire de la Marine Française, II, Paris, 1900, 80; Die Recesse und Andere Akten der Hansetage von 1256–1430, III, ed. K. Koppmann, Leipzig, 1875, 197.

preparation for invasion. A similar argument had been used to justify the raids on the French coast in 1337.[55]

Case 3: Priors in the Late Fifteenth Century

Prior Langstrother and the battle of Tewkesbury

Compared with the accounts for Hales and Radington, the surviving records for our final examples are not so plentiful, but they do illustrate that, if required, the Prior of St John could be called on to perform military functions in the fifteenth and early sixteenth centuries. While this chapter has dealt with the Prior's military service to the crown against foreign attack, something needs to be said about Prior Langstrother's role leading up to and during the battle of Tewkesbury. Above all else Langstrother was a soldier, from a family not unfamiliar with acts of violence, the ravishment of Joan Boys being one example.[56] Born c. 1416–17, Langstrother was a member of the Order, and thus had started his military training, by the age of 17 or 18, had become a preceptor by 26, was lieutenant turcopolier by 28, castellan of Rhodes at 29, and possibly captain of St Peter's Castle by the time he was 47.[57] When Prior Botyll died, Langstrother (about 51 or 52 years old) was bailiff of Eagle, grand commander of Cyprus, and seneschal of the Grand Master on Rhodes.[58] Apart from his military obligations to the Order, he also served, amongst other duties, as Hospitaller ambassador to Venice and the papal court in Rome, and as the Grand Master's proctor general in England, and he was entrusted as a collector of indulgence money for the defence of Rhodes.[59] He was, in other words, a very experienced soldier and an important figure within and without the Order, possibly a future Grand Master, whose international standing and income outside the realm of England, as grand commander of Cyprus, gave him a certain amount of independence from the crown that other English Priors did not enjoy.[60]

This independence might explain why Langstrother felt confident enough to side with Henry VI against Edward IV, even after the death of his 'master', Warwick, at the battle of Barnet (1471), though in the context of the Wars of the Roses, he may well have considered Edward IV to have been a usurper.[61] In any case, his actions over the previous year against Edward IV probably extinguished any chance of reconciliation. Langstrother had secretly met with Warwick and others at Clerken-

---

[55] G. L. Harriss, 'War and the Emergence of the English Parliament, 1297–1360', *JMH*, II, 1976, 35–56 at 39.

[56] *Paston Letters*, ed. Davis, I, 69–71.

[57] NLM 351, 135; NLM 352, 128v–131; NLM 355, 170; NLM 356, 141–2; NLM 357, 153v–154; O'Malley, *English Knights Hospitaller*, 316.

[58] NLM 375, 101r; NLM 378, 148.

[59] NLM 364, 119; NLM 364, 118–118r; *CPL 1447–1455*, 261–2.

[60] Furthermore, it has been suggested that Langstrother had business interests in the Aegean, which would have generated income, O'Malley, *English Knights Hospitaller*, 288.

[61] M. A. Hicks, 'Bastard Feudalism, Overmighty Subjects and Idols of the Multitude during the Wars of the Roses' in *History*, 85, 2000, 386–403 at 388.

well in March 1470, thus implicating him in the Lincolnshire rebellion.[62] He was considered enough of a danger that Edward IV had him arrested the following month (around Easter), and although he was for some time at liberty under surety of the archbishop of Canterbury, he was eventually confined to the Tower of London (as was Henry VI). While, on 28 July, another Hospitaller, future Prior William Tornay, was pardoned for his part in disturbances before 11 July, Langstrother was not.[63] Following his release from the Tower in early October, he continued to have a military presence to ensure stability in the London area, being appointed a commissioner of the peace for Middlesex in October 1470 and January 1471.[64]

Langstrother certainly would have taken part in the battle of Barnet, if he had not been sent on diplomatic business to France, and to escort Queen Margaret and Prince Edward back to England (see Chapter 4). After their arrival at Weymouth, Langstrother was one of those who rallied support on the way to Tewkesbury. It was these actions, perhaps more than his part in the battle of Tewkesbury, which determined his execution on 6 May 1471. As for his role in the battle, Langstrother and Lord Wenlock held the middle ground, acting as Prince Edward's advisors, but when the battle was lost Langstrother fled for the sanctuary of Tewkesbury Abbey.[65] Neither this sanctuary nor his position as Prior prevented him from gaining the undesirable distinction of being the first and only Hospitaller Prior to be executed by an English monarch.

Prior Multon, warden of the marches, 1474–80

Robert Multon was employed in service to the crown from the beginning of his administration. Only a few months after his appointment as Prior, he was commissioned (24 June 1474) as warden of the east and middle marches towards Scotland for seven years, second in command to the earl of Northumberland.[66] He was to be paid well for holding this position, as both the patent and close rolls testify in July and August 1475: 2,000 marks per annum (£1,333), with provision for payment of 6,000 marks per annum (£3,999) in times of war.[67] However, no references to active service during his appointment as warden survive. This is not surprising because by this time, as Storey has pointed out, the office of warden was 'regarded largely as a source of revenue', granted by the king to reward his supporters, with many wardens absent from the marches and their duties delegated to deputies.[68] This appears to be so in Multon's case, as contemporary with his post as warden was his

[62] 'Chronicle of the Rebellion in Lincolnshire' ed. J. G. Nichols, *Camden Miscellany*, I, Camden Society, First Series, XXXIX, London, 1847, 8.

[63] *The Great Chronicle of London*, ed. A. H. Thomas and I. D. Thornley, London, 1938, 210–11; *CPR 1467–1477*, 17.

[64] *CPR 1467–1477*, 248, 622.

[65] *Hall's Chronicle*, ed. H. Ellis, London, 1809, 300; *Historie of the Arrivall of Edward IV in England and the Finall Recouerye of his Kingdomes from Henry VI AD MCCCCLXXI*, ed. J. Bruce, Camden Society, First Series, I, 1838, 22, 28, 31.

[66] *Rot. Scot.*, II, London, 1819, 442.

[67] *CPR 1467–77*, 545, 22 July 1475; *CCR 1468–76*, 386, 2 August 1475.

[68] R. L. Storey, 'The Wardens of the Marches of England towards Scotland, 1377–1489', *EHR*, LXXII, 1957, 593–615 at 606.

commission, with Henry, earl of Essex and others, to take a muster of soldiers to be sent to France at St Katherine's Mede, London, on 23 May 1475. This indicates that his initial appointment as a keeper of the marches related to the intended French campaign, in which Northumberland served in 1475.[69]

Multon is rather a special case. His appointment as warden seems to have been less to do with his position as Prior and more to do with royal favour and his local connections in the north-east, being the commander of Mount St John (near Thirsk, Yorkshire), a post he held both before his appointment as Prior and after his resignation in 1476. Long after this resignation, he formed part of Northumberland's retinue which attended Henry VII during his tour of the north in 1486, after the suppression of Lovell's rebellion.[70] He is later noted in the Scotch rolls (December 1490) as deputy lieutenant of the east and middle marches, and a reference in the patent rolls to the appointment in February 1494 of a new constable for Newcastle castle 'in the king's gift by the death of Robert Multon' suggests that he had also held that position.[71] Clearly Multon had the favour of both Edward IV and Henry VII, and illustrates that it was not only Priors of St John who were coming into royal service, but other senior members of the Order in England.[72]

Case 4: Prior Docwra in the 1513 French campaign

The final example of the Prior's military service to the king, involved in the invasion of France, shows him in an offensive rather than a defensive capacity, as in the previous cases. It could be argued that direct military action against other Christians was symbolic of the laicisation of the Prior's office and not appropriate for a Prior of St John. Certainly, Patrick Paniter, secretary to James IV of Scotland, implied this in June 1513 when he complained to the Grand Master that the Prior's participation in the vanguard of the English army was unchristian.[73] Paniter, however, had his own agenda – to gain control of Torphichen commandery – which Docwra was accused (falsely) of allocating to George Dundas.[74] Docwra's participation in an offensive role is explained by the papal mandate that was given to Henry VIII for the attack on France. On 22 February 1513, the Prior and fellow Hospitallers Thomas Newport, Thomas Sheffield, Lancelot Docwra and William Weston were appointed to attend the king with 300 men and be ready for safe conduct across the Channel

---

[69] *CPR 1467–1477*, 526.

[70] *Joannis Lelandi antiquari de rebus Britannicis Collectanea*, ed. T. Hearne, 6 vols, London, 1774, IV, 186.

[71] *Rot. Scot.*, II, 494; *CPR 1485–94*, 456.

[72] Senior members, here, means commanders/preceptors. Multon's favour is indicated by the payment on 29 September 1480, of £40 paid to him 'by way of gift', TNA E 28/92/24. This term, of course, was often a euphemism for payment of some sort of wages. Multon also served as an ambassador to Scotland when commander of Mount St John in 1487, 1488 and 1490, *Rot. Scot.*, II, 482, 487, 493.

[73] *The Letters of James the Fourth, 1505–1513*, ed. R. L. Mackie, Edinburgh, 1953, 309.

[74] *Ibid.*, 219; O'Malley, *English Knights Hospitaller*, 262–4.

to attack France at the Pope's command.[75] Technically, then, the Prior and his men had legitimacy for their part in the English host because of the papal dispensation. Nevertheless, Docwra's participation in the actual invasion of French territory was much more aggressive than Radington's part in the blockade of Sluys.

Docwra received letters of protection on 23 April and it appears from the treaty rolls that he and others were mustering their force in early May to leave from Southampton.[76] The *Chronicle of Calais* tells us that the Prior landed at Calais on 7 June, 'with dyvars gentlemen and men of warre to goo in the forward'.[77] He and his retinue then formed part of the advance force led by the earl of Shrewsbury that invaded France on 13 June, advancing three miles outside the English pale, where they stayed until the forward came to them.[78] They met no resistance, so the Prior did not have to engage in battle, but there can be little doubt that he was required to do so if necessary. It is almost certain that, as Docwra was part of Shrewsbury's host, he was also involved in the siege of Thérouanne that began on 16 June.[79] He appears to have still been overseas involved in 'our war' the following February, preceding his diplomatic role in June 1514.[80]

Conclusion

These examples provide an insight into the Prior's military role for the crown. This went beyond the usual grants of money and victuals, which all spiritual and temporal lords were bound to supply and which the Prior continued to provide throughout the later middle ages, to holding official positions and contracting to provide troops for war.[81] In addition to the examples given, we know that the Priors performed other military duties when required, such as Prior Thame's provision of men-at-arms and archers in May 1347, or Prior John Pavely's service in 1370.[82] These examples suggest that the Prior had a greater military role in the fourteenth than in the fifteenth or sixteenth centuries. His military service appears to antedate both his diplomatic duties and his greater involvement in national politics, beyond attendance at parliament. Indeed, there is a close correspondence between the Prior's military duties and his first diplomatic missions, and the former may well be responsible for the latter.

Just why there was a long gap in military service after 1385 is difficult to explain. It could have been a consequence of the Great Schism, with the Hospi-

75 *L&P HVIII 1513–1514*, I, 838.
76 TNA C 76/194, mm. 5, 17.
77 *The Chronicle of Calais in the Reigns of Henry VII and Henry VIII to the Year 1540*, ed. J. G. Nichols, Camden Society, XXXV, 1846, 10.
78 *Ibid.*, 11.
79 *Ibid.*, 11–12.
80 TNA C 76/194, m. 18.
81 For example, the Priors contributed financial support for military purposes in 1404 and 1416, *CFR 1399–1405*, 252; *CPR 1416–1422*, 279.
82 TNA C 76/24, m. 10; *Issue Rolls of Thomas Brantingham*, ed. F. Devon, London, 1835, 20–1; TNA E 403/440, m. 24. Prior Pavely also 'lent' £133 6s. 8d. to Edward III on 13 July 1370.

tallers supporting the French-influenced Avignon papacy. The activities of Juan Fernandez de Heredia (Grand Master 1377–96), who had fought on the French side at the battle of Poitiers (1356), and as Grand Master was resident in Avignon for many years, could have cast suspicion on the loyalties of the English Hospitallers to the English crown.[83] If so, however, why did it not stop Priors serving in other roles, such as Radington as ambassador in the 1390s or Grendon on the temporary council of 1415? A more plausible explanation is that the renewal of the Hospitallers' military campaigning in the eastern Mediterranean meant that the Prior was absent from England for long periods. Nevertheless, as the examples of Priors Multon, Langstrother and Docwra illustrate, the potential of the Prior's military resources was not lost on the kings of late medieval England. The Priors were frequently used on commissions of the peace from the later fifteenth century onwards, and Henry VIII even considered using the English Hospitallers to safeguard Calais on a permanent basis in the late 1520s.[84] The examples of Multon as warden of the Scottish marches and Docwra in 1513 indicate that both Prior and other Hospitaller brethren were being put to greater secular military use in the late fifteenth and early sixteenth centuries.

The evidence, particularly that of the later fourteenth century, raises questions beyond the Prior's military role to the Prior's political status, at a time when such issues were becoming important in the evolution of parliament.[85] For example, how did the Prior, paid as a banneret (ranked between barons and knights), come to be accepted as the first lay baron in parliament? In comparison with Prior Thame, who was keeper of Southampton, Priors Pavely, Hales and Radington, as admirals of the southern fleet, were holding positions that from the mid-fourteenth century (starting with the earls of Suffolk and Salisbury in 1337) were normally associated with the higher nobility.[86] This could indicate either an increase in importance of the Prior in the later fourteenth century or that the Priors were the last of the knightly holders of the office. Priors were described as knights or bannerets in the early 1320s. Sherborne has noted that bannerets 'were a relatively small and select group who had achieved their rank either as a result of noble birth or by a promotion' and that most were drawn from baronial families.[87] The position of Prior of St John was not hereditary, so the rank of banneret came with the job, at least by the early fourteenth century. If, for example, Hugh Archer and James Thame, armigers, who served as men-at-arms in 1339, were relatives of Priors Archer and Thame (which is highly likely), that might indicate that Priors came from gentry families in the early fourteenth century.[88] Priors from the later fourteenth century may even have come from a knightly background: a John Pavely, knight, was one of the founding members of the Order of the Garter; Sir Stephen Hales was keeper of Norfolk

[83] He was captured by the English at Poitiers, Nicholson, *Knights Hospitaller*, 107; Tipton, 'English Hospitallers', 104.

[84] *CPR 1485–1494*, 482, 484, 486, 489–1, 493, 495–8, 500, 503–4, 506–8; *CPR 1494–1509*, 618, 638–9, 650, 663; *L&P HVIII, 1526–27*, IV, 1302.

[85] Given-Wilson, *English Nobility*, 60–3.

[86] TNA E 101/22/7; Rodger, *Safeguard of the Sea*, 134.

[87] J. W. Sherborne, 'Indentured Retinues and English Expeditions to France, 1369–1380', *EHR*, LXXIX, 1964, 718–46 at 737.

[88] TNA E 101/22/10.

and Suffolk at the same time that Prior Hales was admiral of the southern fleet; a Sir Francis Hales was an envoy in 1375.[89] The difficulty in establishing family links makes this hard to confirm. It is possible, however, that it was the position of Prior that was elevated, regardless of an individual Prior's background. As the contract system came to replace feudal service, a reliable source of fighting men was needed, and the Prior, as a great landowner, could potentially summon many squires, who made up the bulk of men-at-arms in the fourteenth century; the acquisition of the Templar lands had provided not only greater wealth for the Prior, but also more available manpower, both of which the crown used.

Finally, the changes in the Prior's military service reflect the transformation taking place in general with regard to military service in England. The decline of the feudal summons does not reflect a loss of sense of duty on the part of the lords. Indeed, it appears that there was an element of choice, and Hales for one has been criticised by modern historians for having 'long since forsaken the saddle for a more rewarding career in the corrupt court politics that marked the later years of Edward III'.[90] Priors came from families that had strong military traditions and saw it as their duty to serve their kings as well as their Order. It just so happened that the Prior's service developed at a time when Hospitaller military activity in the Mediterranean was in a lull and the Prior was based mainly in England. Noticeably, it is also in this period of prolonged residence that the political role of the Prior started, slowly, to develop. At a national level, this meant a change from a mere summons to parliament to trier of petitions, before even greater integration as a member of the king's council from the 1450s.[91] On an international level, it comprised ambassadorial commissions from 1380.[92] The Prior's military service appears to have led to his political service both at home and abroad.

[89] TNA E 364/13, m. 1; Holmes, *Good Parliament*, 34.
[90] Tipton, 'English Hospitallers', 96; Nicholson, 'Hospitallers in England', 39–40.
[91] *Rot. Parl.*, II, 268.
[92] *Foedera*, Hague, III, 105.

4

International Ambassador

Overview

This chapter examines the Prior of St John's role in crown international relations, as opposed to his role as the main Hospitaller representative in England. In contrast to the presumption of past histories of the Hospitallers, it is argued that the Prior's role was not the same throughout the later medieval period and that four distinct phases are discernible: Firstly, from 1380 until 1395, under Priors Hales and Radington, occasional diplomatic duties were undertaken. Secondly, between 1395 and 1440, there was a lull in diplomatic involvement, with only one mission in 1406. Thirdly, from Prior Robert Botyll (1440–68) until the death of Prior Kendal in 1501, the Priors of England took a regular and active part in ambassadorial duties. Finally, Prior Docwra (1501–27) was much more intensively involved than previous Priors to the extent that he qualifies as one of the principal diplomatic envoys on whom both Henry VII and Henry VIII called. This chapter will concentrate on the three active phases to trace the development of the Prior's role and only briefly mention the intervening period to comment on Grendon's 1406 mission. During the final years of the Order in England (1527–40), the Prior's international role was virtually non-existent, restricted mainly to activities within the realm, such as attending on foreign envoys in London.

Very little has been written on the Prior's role as a diplomat between 1300 and 1540, and what has been written only lists the missions he took part in. The only reference to an English Prior as a crown diplomat in the standard work on the English Hospitallers is to Prior Docwra, who rode with Henry VIII at his meeting with Francis I at the Field of the Cloth of Gold in 1520.[1] More recent research has commented on the Prior's diplomatic role in the Tudor period, noting that the Priors 'could hold significant political or diplomatic positions' and describing Prior Docwra as 'a diplomat of skill', as he was, but does not elucidate.[2] Sire devoted a short chapter to the tongue of England, but there is nothing on the Prior's role as a diplomat for the king. Robert Malory is mentioned as a royal servant, but no

---

[1] King, *Knights of St John*, 89.
[2] Tyerman, *England and Crusades*, 355.

example or reference is given.[3] O'Malley gives a good general commentary on the diplomatic role of the English Hospitallers between 1460 and 1540, but does not focus on the Prior in particular, and so mentions some, but not all, of his missions.[4] Finally, Sarnowsky has a paragraph on the Prior's role in international relations between 1440 and 1501, which lists the embassies in which the Priors took part, but omits the roles that Priors John Langstrother and John Weston played in English diplomacy between 1469 and 1489.[5] As mentioned in Chapter 1, the above works rely mainly on Hospitaller sources. They concentrate on Anglo-Hospitaller relations from a Hospitaller viewpoint, overlooking the fact that the Prior and his brethren were English and were part of English society. In this chapter, English primary sources are focused on to demonstrate the development of the Prior's role in diplomacy and to emphasise that the Hospitallers' relationship with the crown was mainly one of peaceful co-existence rather than of conflict, to the extent that from 1380 the Prior served with increasing regularity in English diplomatic missions.

Diplomatic Background

The Prior occasionally served as a diplomat for the crown before the fourteenth century, but he was not regularly employed in this role. Previous research has stated that in the twelfth and thirteenth centuries Templar and Hospitaller brethren acted as ambassadors for the English crown on a regular basis.[6] This was true more for the Templars than the Hospitallers. The sources indicate that the Prior of St John was rarely used. For example, John of Salisbury's letters mention the Hospitallers on diplomatic service on only one occasion (1166) in 27 years (1153–80) and the Prior is not mentioned by name.[7] This, perhaps, is not surprising, given that the Hospitallers were a new religious order in England in the mid-twelfth century. The Prior appears only twice on the close rolls (1225) in 23 years (1204–27), both entries concerning the same mission.[8] Two missions, at most, in 72 years are hardly regular.[9]

There is some evidence that the Prior was an envoy on three occasions in the thirteenth century, in 1225, 1244 and 1264, but this does not make him a regular diplomat. These are outside the timeframe of this study, but will be touched upon

[3] Sire, *Knights of Malta*, 185. Sire relies on P. J. C. Field's article on Malory. Field's article does not mention the Prior in a diplomatic role, with the references to him as a servant meaning his attendance at parliament and great council. See Field, 'Sir Robert Malory'.
[4] O'Malley, *English Knights Hospitaller*, chapters 5 and 6 *passim*.
[5] Sarnowsky, 'Kings and Priors', 89.
[6] Nicholson, 'The Military Orders', 210.
[7] *The Letters of John of Salisbury*, 2 vols, ed. W. J. Millor, H. E. Butler and C. N. L. Brooke, London and Oxford, 1955–79, II, 160. This mission concerned the wish for reconciliation between the king and Archbishop Becket, who was in exile.
[8] *Rot. Lit. Claus.*, II, 11, 70–1, concerning a mission to the Pope.
[9] Neither do the printed memoranda rolls mention the Prior as a diplomat. See *The Memoranda Roll for the Michaelmas Term of the First Year of the Reign of King John (1199–1200)*, ed. H. G. Richardson, Rolls Series, London, 1943; *The Memoranda Roll of the King's Remembrancer for Michaelmas 1230 – Trinity 1231*, ed. C. Robinson, Rolls Society XI, Princeton, NJ, 1933.

briefly to illustrate that, although not used regularly, there was a precedent for the Prior to serve as an ambassador. The first instance was on 3 January 1225, when Prior Robert Dynham was part of an embassy sent to the duke of Austria to negotiate a marriage between Henry III and the duke's daughter.[10] This was during the minority of Henry III and was one of a number of options for the young king, who finally married Eleanor of Provence. The second occasion was on 15 July 1244, when Prior Thierry de Nussa was in a party appointed and given credence to hear what compensation the king of Scotland was willing to give for acts against England.[11] The final instance was on 15 August 1264, when Prior Robert Maunby was appointed one of the proctors to present the king of France with a proposed peace treaty.[12]

The three examples illustrate three themes, which are valid for English Priors' later service in international affairs. First, whether described as negotiators, proctors or hearers, they were equally involved in diplomatic activity, as the letters of credence in 1244 testify. Second, the Priors were not restricted to one geographical or subject area of foreign policy and were used both with neighbours, as with Scotland and France, and to more distant locations, as with Austria, for peace treaties, marriage negotiations and message bearing. Not all royal envoys were used in such a versatile manner. That the Prior was used in a multipurpose way is perhaps explained by his membership of an international order and the resulting geographical contacts that ensued. Third, in contrast to the two missions up until 1225, which only concerned ecclesiastical matters, the three missions from 1225 to 1264 were all to secular rulers, a strong indication of a trend towards the Prior's involvement in lay matters.

The Prior of St John in International Relations, 1380–95

There are two sides to international relations – war and diplomacy – which were 'born as twins', as Queller aptly puts it.[13] During the first half of the fourteenth century, the crown used the Prior of St John's military resources on a number of occasions. However, it was not until the last quarter of the century, during the administrations of Priors Hales and Radington, that the Prior was part of a diplomatic mission. Even then, the Prior was an infrequent envoy (see Figure 5). For both Hales and Radington, commissions were given in the second part of their terms in office, once they had become familiar to the establishment and after performing other duties. When employed, they were mainly concerned with Scotland or for trading disputes, the latter perhaps overlapping with their previous roles as admirals of the fleet.

The first example of a diplomatic office dates from 6 September 1380, when Prior Robert Hales (1372–81) was appointed to a commission headed by John of

---

[10] *CPR, 1216–1225*, 558; *Diplomatic Documents Preserved in the Public Record Office*, I, ed. P. Chaplais, London, 1964, 109.

[11] *CPR 1232–1247*, 432.

[12] *CPR 1258–1266*, 366.

[13] D. E. Queller, *The Office of Ambassador in the Middle Ages*, Princeton, NJ, 1967, 3.

Gaunt, temporary keeper of the Scottish marches, to look at breaches of the truce with Scotland in the east and west marches.[14] Hales was one of the junior members of this party along with Richard Scrope and John Waltham, attending on the archbishop of York.[15] Negotiations had been in progress since September 1377, when an Anglo-Scottish conference agreed that Gaunt and Robert II's eldest son John, earl of Carrick, should meet to settle border disputes, which they did on 18 January 1378. This was the first of a number of meetings during the following years, for most of which time Gaunt was lieutenant of the Scottish Marches.[16] The negotiations with the Scots (headed by William, earl of Douglas) of September and October 1380 took place at Berwick and were successful in negotiating a truce until June the following year, due to Gaunt's willingness to hear the Scottish position. Noticeably the warlike earl of Northumberland and other members of the Percy family were omitted from the delegation, whereas usually the earls were included as the traditional keepers of the Scottish Marches.

Although other members of his family had been envoys and Prior Hales himself had served in a military office as admiral of the southern fleet between 1376 and 1377, this was Hales' first and only diplomatic role.[17] Hales' role in these discussions is undocumented, but there are indications of his duties. First, he spent about six months at Berwick and on the Scottish border during these negotiations, on occasion sending servants to England on Hospitaller business.[18] This length of service suggests his detailed involvement in the negotiations. Gaunt also stayed in the marches after the indenture of 1 November, and it is likely that Hales was with him, involved in the post-agreement details.[19] As a member of an order, he was aware of canon law and his later appointment as treasurer indicates that he was skilled at poring over the details of negotiations. Other members of the embassy, such as Scrope and Waltham, were also trained in law (in Scrope's case both civil and canon), which raises another possible role. It is feasible that Hales was there as a military escort. His reputation suggests that he was qualified to be such, having taken part in the siege of Alexandria in 1365 and with experience from his previous naval appointments.[20]

Hales' involvement in crown affairs was cut short by his murder in June 1381 during the Peasants' Revolt.[21] The next commission was not until five years later,

---

[14] TNA C 71/60; *Foedera*, Hague, III, III, 105.

[15] TNA C 71/60; *Rot. Scot.*, II, 29.

[16] A. Goodman, *John of Gaunt: The Exercise of Princely Power in Fourteenth Century Europe*, London, 1992, 73–6. Gaunt was appointed lieutenant in February 1379, reappointed in August 1380 and remained so until 1384.

[17] Sir Francis Hales had been part of the party at Bruges for talks with Burgundy and France in 1375, see Holmes, *The Good Parliament*, 34; *Foedera*, Hague, III, III, 52, 68; 'The Anglo-French Negotiations at Bruges, 1374–1377', ed. E. Perroy, *Camden Miscellany XIX*, Camden 3rd Series, LXXX, 1952, 9–12. There is no mention of Prior Hales in any negotiations in TNA C 71/59.

[18] TNA C 71/60, on 21 September 1380 and 18 February 1381. By the latter date Hales was Richard II's treasurer.

[19] Goodman, *John of Gaunt*, 77. Gaunt was still at Durham on 11 November, three days after the opening of the Northampton parliament.

[20] Luttrell, 'English Contributions to the Hospitaller Castle at Bodrum', 164.

[21] Tipton, 'English Hospitallers', 99–101.

in February 1386, when his successor John Radington (Prior 1382–95) was made the king's special ambassador to Cyprus, Rhodes and to other (unnamed) kings and states.[22] He had the power to negotiate peace and concord with various states, but the details were left vague. Given the imprecise nature of the 1386 mission and that the places mentioned were in the eastern Mediterranean, it is likely that the Prior was going to Rhodes and that the king gave him letters of credence to perform duties en route. The presentations to benefices by the Prior's lieutenant in England confirm that Radington was abroad by June 1386 and that he did not return until after April 1388 (see Appendix 2).[23]

A year later, in December 1389, the Prior was appointed as one of eight who were to negotiate a compensation claim by Genoese merchants who had had their vessel seized by the treasurer of Calais after it left Seville and brought to Sandwich.[24] The Prior was a natural choice. He was familiar with the Genoese merchants through his own dealings with them. His appointment can also be explained through previous knowledge of such disputes because, as admiral of the fleet west of the Thames in 1385, Radington had himself seized ships during sea disputes with France.[25]

Radington was abroad from May 1390 to January 1393. The *Westminster Chronicle* cites him as one of the English knights who, in March 1390, asked permission to go to the relief of El Mahadia, Tunisia, which was under siege by the Mamluks.[26] However, it is unlikely that he ever went there, as for most of the time that he was abroad, he was a crown envoy. In January 1391 Radington and Thomas Percy formed part of the embassy headed by John of Gaunt that was appointed to deal with the claims of the Teutonic Knights and the Hanseatic League concerning English attacks on their ships. They were also to ensure the ratification of the 1388 trade treaty that had been negotiated. The Prior's appointment to this mission is understandable, as Konrad von Wallenrode, Grand Master of the Teutonic Knights, was one of those with whom negotiations were held. Radington, as a member of a fellow military order, was a suitable envoy to Wallenrode. Additionally, as admirals of the fleet, Radington and Percy had first-hand knowledge of the sea disputes. Wallenrode was not satisfied with the initial negotiations concerning the claims of Hanse merchants attacked by English ships. This was later resolved, but Radington and Percy were pressed for damages amounting to £1,000 and were still involved in negotiations in February the following year.[27]

Soon after completing this mission, Radington was again involved in diplomatic duty attending John of Gaunt in November 1392.[28] In April a truce had

---

[22] *Foedera*, Hague, III, III, 192.

[23] The Prior presented to all Hospitaller benefices when he was in England. When he was abroad, one senior preceptor was made his lieutenant and presented. This means the presentations give us a fairly accurate guide as to when the Prior was in or out of the country and thus when he was on diplomatic duty or going to the Hospitaller Convent.

[24] *CPR 1388–1392*, 173–4.

[25] W. Laird, *The Royal Navy: A History from the Earliest Times to the Present*, I, London, 1897, 296–7.

[26] *The Westminster Chronicle 1381–1394*, ed. L. C. Hector and B. F. Harvey, Oxford, 1982, 432. The siege actually took place between July and September 1390.

[27] *The Diplomatic Correspondence of Richard II*, ed. E. Perroy, Camden 3rd series, LXVIII, 1933, 226–8; Baldwin, *The King's Council*, 498.

[28] Perroy, *Diplomatic Correspondence*, 114–15.

been signed with France, but both countries were keen for a permanent settlement, which the November negotiations concerned. The death of Richard's first wife, Anne of Bohemia, in June 1394 paved the way for further ties through Richard's marriage to Isabella of France in November 1396. The connection to Gaunt and family continued during 1392–93, with Radington accompanying Henry, earl of Derby (later Henry IV) during his expedition to the Holy Land, which included two diplomatic missions to the king of Cyprus.[29] The account books for the journey indicate that Radington was with Henry from 23 December 1392 until 20 March 1393.[30] He, Otto Grandison and other knights and esquires went to the king of Cyprus at Famagusta and Nicosia during early February 1393 in an attempt to win the king's allegiance to the Roman papacy.[31] That the Prior was part of a delegation on behalf of the English crown to get Cypriot allegiance to Rome, when the Hospitaller headquarters supported the Avignon papacy, and indeed Grand Master Heredia (1377–96) was based at Avignon from 1382 to 1396, is significant. It indicates that when crown and Hospitaller policies differed, the Prior was expected to support his king. As it appears that Radington was not sanctioned by the Order for his actions, one assumes that the Hospitallers recognised the difficult position that some priories were put in during the difficult years of the Schism.

Radington's final mission was in August 1394 as part of a twelve-man delegation, headed by Walter Skirlaw, bishop of Durham, to Scotland. This was empowered to agree a lasting peace and final concord.[32] These negotiations were a development of the truce of Leulingham of 1389. Prior Radington had not been involved in the negotiation of that truce, but many of those with him in 1394 were and continued to be between 1389 and 1394.[33] The regularity of those involved in these negotiations is no surprise. For example, the 1394 delegation had a strong representation from those who had interests in the north of England, with three members of the Percy family and a Neville amongst the party. The earl of Northumberland was traditionally a warden of the Scottish Marches and thus expected to be involved in any arbitration.

Although the Hospitaller Priors of the later fourteenth century started to serve as diplomats, it is clear that that neither Hales nor Radington was a regular envoy and most negotiations did not involve them. Both were military men and were employed in that capacity by the king.[34] Also, the level of involvement differed with each Prior. Hales was involved in the negotiations with Scotland over a number of months, as

[29] *Expedition to Prussia and the Holy Land made by Henry Earl of Derby (afterwards King Henry IV) in the Years 1390–91 and 1392–93*, ed. L. Toulmin Smith, Camden Society LII, London, 1894, 150, 226, 279.

[30] *Ibid.*, 150, 279. Radington supplied Henry with money in Venice and organised shipping from there to Jaffa and back. Given that they were both in Prussia in November, it is highly likely that they travelled from there to Venice together.

[31] *Ibid.*, 226; A. Luttrell, 'The Hospitallers in Cyprus after 1386', in *The Hospitaller State on Rhodes and its Western Provinces, 1306–1462*, ed. A. Luttrell, Aldershot, 1999, 1–20 at 4.

[32] TNA C 71/73.

[33] TNA C 71/72–3. Heron and Mitford are mentioned in connection with Leulingham in an entry for 26 October 1393.

[34] Hales had an international reputation and he had been part of the force that attacked Alexandria in October 1365, see Luttrell, 'Hospitallers at Rhodes', 298–9.

was Radington with the Teutonic Knights. Radington, however, was not always involved in the minutiae of agreements. If he was not on the delegation to Scotland in 1394 in a practical capacity, and as his interest in the Scottish marches was limited, then one assumes that he had a more ceremonial role. He was one of the high-status officials that the Scots expected to be part of such an embassy. Unlike Hales in 1380, Radington in 1394 was one of the senior envoys. Neither was he there in a military capacity, because the knights present adequately performed this task. Hales only took part in one diplomatic mission, so it is not possible to judge if any pattern of service was developing. However, a number of conclusions can be made on Radington's five missions. Little information exists on the first mission to Cyprus with which to judge its importance, but it is likely that Radington was going to Rhodes on Hospitaller business and would continue on to Cyprus. The other four missions took place within the space of five years. The first two were concerned with mercantile agreements and the final two with establishing truces and peace. For Radington we can see a clear development from minor to major envoy, including participation in important missions under the leading English diplomat of the day, John of Gaunt.

Priors Walter Grendon (1396–1417), William Hulles (1417–32) and Robert Malory (1432–40) had little or no involvement in crown diplomatic service. This was largely due to lengthy absences abroad. Grendon's initial activities were in service for the Hospitallers. He was in England at the time of his appointment as Prior in September 1396, but he gained licence to go to Rhodes for three years on 28 December 1397, had attorneys appointed on 1 January 1398 and was granted letters for his safe passage the following day.[35] Over the following six years he was only in England for a few months in 1401. Considering these long periods of absence abroad, it is not surprising that Grendon did not partake in diplomatic (or other) activity for the crown in the first half of his administration.

From May 1405, however, Prior Grendon was in England almost continuously until his death in 1417. His only assignment came soon after his return. On 4 June 1406, he was appointed to a commission headed by Edmund Stafford, bishop of Exeter, to deal with infractions of the truce with the Teutonic Knights and Hanse merchants.[36] This commission was a continuation of negotiations over compensation that had begun the previous year. In August 1405, commissioners had been appointed to the Hanse towns concerning the return of plundered goods.[37] The commission was acted upon and on 28 July the constable of Dover castle and the warden of the Cinque Ports were ordered to arrest all those from the *Falcon* barge of Sandwich, which had captured and spoiled the Prussian ship *Christopher*, and bring them before the commissioners at Michaelmas.[38] It is no coincidence that Grendon was chosen for this mission. Like Radington in 1391 he, as the senior Hospitaller in England, was the natural choice of envoy to the head of another military order.

[35] *Foedera*, Hague, III, IV, 141; *CPR 1396–1399*, 273.
[36] *Rot. Parl.*, III, 574; *CPR 1405–1408*, 153; *CPR 1405–1408*, 234; *CCR 1405–1409*, 62; *Royal and Historical Letters during the Reign of Henry the Fourth*, 2 vols, ed. F. Hingeston and C. Randolph, Rolls Series, London, 1860–5, II, 116.
[37] *Ibid.*, 80–2; BL MS Cotton Nero B II, f. 49.
[38] *CPR 1405–1408*, 237.

Grendon's inclusion in the mission makes evident an emerging pattern of service by the Prior when the Teutonic Knights were involved; Prior Botyll was later also an envoy. However, it is important to stress that although the missions were to the Teutonic Knights, they concerned English trading agreements, not crusading.

With the exception of this one diplomatic role, there is no indication that Grendon further represented the crown in international relations. Although commissioned to go in person to attend the Council of Pisa, which aimed at resolving the schism in the Western Church, he did not leave with the party that departed from Southampton in February 1409, is not mentioned in the proceedings of the Council, and the evidence of presentations to benefices in 1409 suggest that he stayed in England.[39] It is difficult to explain with any certainty why he took part in only one minor commission even though he was based in England from 1405 to his death in 1417. One can rule out lack of diplomatic experience, because he had been one of the Grand Master's envoys to Theodore I in 1400 over negotiations to purchase the Despotate of the Morea (south-east Peloponnese).[40] Although the king chose his envoys, it is possible that Grendon avoided selection for crown business in his first ten years as prior, by spending lengthy periods abroad, with the intention of serving his Order.

The composition of the missions in which the Prior of St John took part between 1380 and 1406 is worthy of analysis, especially given his peculiar position of having both lay and ecclesiastical status. How do we class the Prior in these missions, as a layman or an ecclesiastic? Although he was essentially a temporal lord, the missions that he participated in suggest that the ambiguity was utilised and he was used in both capacities: as a high-status lay envoy to Scotland and France, a member of a fellow military order to the Teutonic Knights, and an ecclesiastic on missions to the papacy.

From 1380 until the middle of the fifteenth century, the ratio of lay to ecclesiastical representatives on missions in which the Prior was involved was fairly even. Where there was a discrepancy, it tended to be lay members that were in the majority, noticeably the missions to Scotland in 1394 and to the Teutonic Knights in 1406. However, the majority of the ecclesiastics involved in these missions were those dealing with the administrative details of negotiations. There was normally one important member of the clergy, for example the archbishop of York and the bishop of Durham in 1380 and 1394 respectively, but the others, such as Richard Scrope, John Waltham, Thomas Stanley and Alan Newark, were included for their legal skills. These were talented men, often at the beginning of their careers and hoping to gain favour, as was the case with Scrope, a member of a powerful northern family, who later became bishop of Lichfield (1386) and archbishop of York (1398–1405).

Another factor is that the Prior was an irregular diplomat before 1440, while the majority of personnel were constant. For example, the Scots Rolls record that Gerard

---

39 *Foedera*, London, VIII, 567; A. Landi, *Il papa deposto, Pisa 1409: l'idea conciliare nel Grande Scisma*, Turin, 1985; J. H. Wylie, *History of England under Henry the Fourth*, 4 vols, London, 1884–98, III, 367–8; see Appendix 2.

40 *Monumenta Peloponnesiaca: Documents for the History of the Peloponnese in the Fourteenth and Fifteenth Centuries*, ed. J. Chrysostomides, Camberley, 1995, 415.

Heron and John Mitford were involved in negotiations with Scotland in October 1393, prior to their commission in August the following year.[41] In February 1394, out of an eight-man embassy headed by the earl of Northumberland, one (Scrope) had been involved in negotiations since 1380 and a further five were included in the August 1394 commission that included Prior Radington. This is a clear example of the consistency of personnel.[42] It also confirms the predominance of lay negotiators over ecclesiastical in embassies to Scotland. The local interests represented by the embassies to Scotland explain this last point. The 1380 embassy included Alexander Neville, archbishop of York, and Richard Scrope, both ecclesiastics but from powerful northern families. John of Gaunt had interests through the duchy of Lancaster, inherited from his first wife. The geographical interest is even more pronounced in the 1394 embassy to Scotland, with the bishop of Durham, three members of the Percy family and a Neville. Other lay members were included who came from families with a record of long service to the crown. William Ufford's father, Robert, for example, had helped Edward III come to power and had been a founder member of the Order of the Garter. Hales and Radington come into this last category, both of whom had relatives (Francis Hales, Baldwin Radington) in royal service.

The Intensification of Diplomatic Service, 1440–1501

Robert Botyll, 1440–68

Before the middle of the fifteenth century, the Prior of St John in England played only an occasional role in international relations. From the election of Robert Botyll (1440) the regularity of service was more frequent (see Figure 6), and this pattern continued until the death of Prior Thomas Docwra in 1527.[43] The beginning of Botyll's office coincided with the Mamluk attack on Rhodes (1440–44) and in this crisis situation Botyll's duties to the Hospitallers took precedence over those to the crown. In spite of deteriorating relations with France, the king and his council reluctantly recognised that the Prior's first duty was to the Order. On 26 February 1441 Botyll had licence to take weapons and money for his journey to Rhodes and was further granted licence to export silver on 10 April.[44] He also had letters of safe conduct for himself and Focald Rochechuart, the preceptor of Flanders, who was accompanying Botyll with 100 men.[45] Recognition of his Hospitaller duties was still subject to Botyll's fulfilling his crown commissions. Henry VI had intended

---

[41] TNA C 71/73.

[42] TNA C 71/72. The envoys were John Gilbert, bishop of St David's, Richard le Scrope, bishop of Coventry and Lichfield, Henry Percy, earl of Northumberland, Ralph, Lord Neville, Thomas Furnival, Adam Newark, Gerard Heron and John Mitford.

[43] TNA E 28/63/37; *Official Correspondence of Thomas Bekynton, Secretary to Henry VI and Bishop of Bath and Wells*, 2 vols, ed. G. Williams, Roll Series, London, 1872, I, 78–9. Prior Malory was dead by 10 May 1440, by which time Botyll had been elected Prior by the English brethren.

[44] TNA C 76/123, mm. 12, 22.

[45] TNA C 76/123, m. 22.

Botyll to be one of his envoys to the diet at Mainz in November 1441, which was to discuss Church unity, fragmented since the appointment in 1439 of the anti-pope Felix V by the Council of Basle. Nevertheless, on 29 April 1441, Botyll and other English Hospitallers were allowed to go to Rhodes to help resist the Mamluks and encourage the Grand Master to revive the English-held office of turcopolier.[46] On 18 May, letters of protection for three years were authorised by privy seal to him and his brethren to go to Rhodes.[47]

Although Botyll was meant to go to Mainz afterwards, he remained on Rhodes and was still there in February the following year, when the king ordered him to be at Frankfurt by 23 April, to which the Mainz diet had been transferred.[48] At Frankfurt he was to meet the other English ambassadors, such as Adam Moleyns, who had left London around 15 March.[49] These diets were part of a series (Nuremberg 1438, Mainz 1441, Frankfurt 1442, Nuremberg 1443 and 1444, and Frankfurt 1445), at which it was proposed, amongst other things, that a new general council (the Council of Lyon) should be held to settle the disputes between the Council of Basle (1431–49) and Pope Eugenius IV. The dispute was in essence a power struggle between the cardinals and the popes, which had begun under the papacy of Eugenius IV's predecessor, Martin V, who had allegedly favoured his family members, mistreated the cardinals and acted against their property and person. As a consequence, the cardinals wanted a general council to draw up reforms governing the conduct of popes when acting against a cardinal, namely that no pope acted without the consent of the majority of cardinals. Eugenius at first agreed to the Council of Basle, but later dissolved it, which in turn provoked the cardinals to repeat the Council of Constance resolution that the Council was superior to the Pope, and therefore asserting the superiority of Council of Basle over Martin V and Eugenius IV.[50]

Prior Botyll's first diplomatic activity coincided with this series of diets, but his participation was delayed until a later stage by his journey to Rhodes. Although he was abroad from the middle of 1441 until 1444, he did not go to Frankfurt with the other English envoys and was replaced by John Lowe, bishop of St Asaph.[51] Botyll was in Rome in February and April 1446 for the Hospitallers' general chapter, where he protested against the obstinacy of the French tongue concerning the alleged illegal use of its privileges and the payment of responsions. This stance reflects the growing tensions between England and France at this time over Normandy and the English decision to surrender Maine, which had apparently been informally agreed

---

[46] *Bekynton Correspondence*, I, 80–4. Williams gives the year as 1440, which matches the AD date of MCCCCXL. However, the year is also given in the text as XIX Henry VI, which was April 1441. Ferguson repeats this error by suggesting that Botyll was commissioned to attend Mainz in April 1439, when Malory was still Prior. See JFerguson, *English Diplomacy*, 116.

[47] TNA C 76/123, m. 3.

[48] *Bekynton Correspondence*, I, 89–90.

[49] TNA C 76/124, m. 22; Ferguson, *English Diplomacy*, 118.

[50] L. Pastor, *The History of the Popes from the Close of the Middle Ages*, 6th edn, 40 vols, tr. F. I. Antrobus, R. F. Kerr, E. Graf, E. F. Peeler, Nendeln, 1968–9, I, 282–94.

[51] M. Harvey, *England, Rome and the Papacy 1417–1464: The Study of a Relationship*, Manchester, 1993, 170–1.

since the Treaty of Tours of May 1444.[52] Although Botyll was in Rome, and thus in a position to take part in any diplomatic mission, there is no evidence of any further missions until 1447.

Botyll was present as a crown representative at a later stage of negotiations, aimed at securing the resignation of the anti-pope, Felix V. Both England and France were keen to participate in the peacemaking process between the Council and the Pope, and therefore gain influence for their advantage. Botyll was an envoy in this context. On 24 July 1447, he was advanced wages of £336 for six months from 23 August as one of the envoys to the two-pronged negotiations, at Lyon for the Council and afterwards to Eugenius IV, and to France concerning Maine.[53] On 16 August the envoys were given power to treat for a lasting peace with France.[54] At Lyon, Botyll and the other ambassadors were instructed to meet the envoys of Germany and France and the duke of Savoy in order to secure the abdication of Felix V. The English envoys arrived late, by which time the talks had adjourned to Geneva. However, the talks ended in stalemate and the English envoys retired to Bourges, where the French persuaded them to delay their journey to Rome to offer submission to Eugenius IV.[55] While in Bourges, the ambassadors negotiated, that is tried to delay, the surrender of Maine, to which Henry VI had agreed in December 1446, and an agreement was reached on 15 October that included a truce from 1 May 1448 until January 1449.[56]

For the other part of the mission, Botyll was to be accompanied to Rome by Vincent Clement, a Catalan employed in English service and a critic of the Council of Basle, and Thomas Candour.[57] However on 10 February 1448, Botyll was still in France due to the longer than expected negotiations with the Basle representatives. An extra £224 was authorised to him for a further four months.[58] Finally, in July 1448 Botyll and Clement set out separately from the French embassy for Rome to present the terms of the agreement to Nicholas V. The English arrived first, but the Pope did not accept the agreement. The French arrived presenting the same terms, which were accepted, as the Pope was keen to have French support. This was of concern to England as Nicholas attempted to vie for French support against Basle by offering indulgences if Charles VII would invade Savoy, Felix V's homeland and main base of support.[59] With strained Anglo-French relations, however, there was no guarantee that the money raised would not be used against England. The English embassy, based in Viterbo, was virtually divorced from the negotiations,

---

[52] R. Valentini, 'Un capitolo generale degli Ospitalieri di S. Giovanni tenuto in Vaticano nel 1446', *Archivio Storico di Malta*, VII, Rome, 1935–36, 155–6; Harvey, *England, Rome and the Papacy*, 54; J. A. Tuck, *Crown and Nobility: England 1272–1461*, 2nd edn, Oxford, 1999, 255–7.

[53] TNA E 101/324/15; TNA E 404/63/135; *Foedera*, Hague, V, I, 183–4; Ferguson, *English Diplomacy*, 139.

[54] 'Calendar of French Rolls: Henry VI', *The Forty-Eighth Annual Report of the Deputy Keeper of the Public Records*, London, 1887, 375.

[55] Ferguson, *English Diplomacy*, 140.

[56] BL Egerton Charter 208; B. P. Wolffe, *Henry VI*, 2nd edn, London, 2001, 194; J. R. Lander, *Government and Community: England, 1450–1509*, Cambridge, MA,, 1980, 182.

[57] TNA E 404/63/162.

[58] TNA E 404/64/122; TNA E 404/65/102; TNA E 101/324/15.

[59] N. Housley, *The Later Crusades: From Lyons to Alcazar, 1274–1580*, Oxford, 1992, 249.

and the French dealt with the details of the agreement.[60] Nevertheless, Botyll and Clement were part of the Anglo-French delegation that returned to Lausanne on 10 August 1448 to present the agreement to Felix V. This was agreed on 1 April 1449, Botyll and Clement signing for England, sending a copy to Nicholas V, and informing him that Charles VII wanted a General Council in France, to which they had not agreed.[61] Three days later Botyll guaranteed Felix V's followers that there would be no recriminations on his abdication.[62]

In total, Botyll was paid for 651 days service (out of 653 days) between 23 August 1447 and 5 June 1449, which means that he was constantly engaged in diplomatic service, as opposed to Dudley who was paid at the same rate of 40s. a day for 371 days.[63] The implication is that Botyll was continually involved in the details of the negotiations. Botyll did not return to England until about 20 June 1449, when he presented to a benefice for the first time since May 1447. During his commission, his Hospitaller duties had taken second place to those due to the king, even if he was employed on essentially ecclesiastical business. This is a stark contrast to the situation in 1441–42 when his Hospitaller duties came first. Further emphasis of this change is illustrated by the papal grant, at Henry VI's request, on 1 June 1448 that, due to 'his divers occupations', Botyll need not go in person to any general chapter on Rhodes or elsewhere, but could send a proctor. If he did go, he had licence to leave immediately the chapter was over without permission from the Grand Master.[64] That the English government were able to get papal assent for this is, as in 1418, an example of the advantages that could be gained by gaining influence over the Pope. Although Nicholas V had courted French support against Basle, he was not anti-English. Indeed, as Tommaso Parentucelli, he had served under Niccolò Albergati who had English sympathies. Soon after Nicholas had been elected, Henry VI's proctor to Rome, William Grey, was promoted to 'cubicularius', an honour indicative of good Anglo-papal relations.[65] Botyll managed also to get papal approval for the reinstatement of the turcopolier, the highest English office in the Convent on Rhodes. These were the expected rewards for England's support for Eugenius IV during the struggle with Basle.

Prior Botyll is next mentioned as an ambassador to France and to the Pope in the council records of 27 May 1450.[66] It is possible that he was going to attend the conference at Bonport in July, a last attempt to save English interests in Normandy, although there is no direct reference to his being there.[67] He was then appointed as an envoy to Utrecht, the Pope, and the king of Aragon on 29 April for three

---

[60] Harvey, *England, Rome and the Papacy*, 185–6.

[61] *Ibid.*, 186.

[62] 'John Benet's Chronicle for the years 1400 to 1462', ed. G. L. Harriss and M. A. Harriss, *Camden Miscellany* XXIV, Camden 4th series, IX, 1972, 158. Benet was a member of Botyll's household; Ferguson, *English Diplomacy*, 140.

[63] TNA E 101/324/15.

[64] *CPL 1447–1455*, 187.

[65] Harvey, *England, Rome and the Papacy*, 185.

[66] TNA E 28/80/56; *CPR 1446–1452*, 376. He was intended to serve until mid-September.

[67] *Narratives of the Expulsion of the English from Normandy 1449–1450*, ed. J. Stevenson, Rolls Series, London, 1863, 387–495.

months.[68] No evidence exists to confirm his participation in the latter two parts of the commission, and his attendance at king's council suggests that he did not take part. However, his participation in the first part of this mission is confirmed by his absence from king's council after 1 May until 27 July, almost exactly three months.[69] Botyll led this party whose brief was to discuss with the Teutonic Knights and the Hanseatic League damages to be paid to merchants who had suffered at the hands of English ships.[70] The Prior used his diplomatic skills to exploit the internal rivalries within the league, with the aim of limiting the damages to be paid. He was successful in dividing the league so that no agreement could be reached with all parties and individual agreements were made with the Teutonic Knights and Cologne for the resumption of trade.[71] As was the case for Radington in 1391 and Grendon in 1406, the Prior was a natural choice of envoy to another military order.

Botyll's next commission, which he again led, was in March 1453 as one of the ambassadors appointed to go to Calais to treat with the ambassadors of the duke of Burgundy.[72] Their brief was to agree reparations for breaches made by the subjects of either party of the commercial treaty of 1439 and perpetual truce of 1443.[73] Botyll had left England by 27 March, when his deputy presented on his behalf, but was back by 9 May when he attended the king's council.[74] The mission required a second journey and he was abroad again between 26 June and 10 July, returning the following day.[75]

It was five years before Botyll next appeared as an envoy. On 14 May 1458 he was part of a 22-man embassy to Burgundy, headed by Richard Neville, earl of Warwick.[76] This large and high-powered embassy had as its stated aim the resolution of acts contrary to the truce with Philip the Good and power, if necessary, to make a truce with his son Charles, count of Charolais.[77] However, the composition of both embassies, as Hicks has commented, seems 'unduly prestigious for dealing with routine border infractions'.[78] Behind the cover of these negotiations, Richard, duke of York, was simultaneously negotiating with Charles VII and with Philip the Good to strengthen his own position, and by the end of the summer, according to Lander, a secret arrangement with Burgundy had been made for marriages involving Edward, prince of Wales, York's son Edward, earl of March, and Henry Beaufort, duke of Somerset, on the English side, although in the end nothing came

---

[68] TNA E 404/67/141.

[69] TNA E 28/81/5; TNA E 28/81/55.

[70] TNA C 76/133, mm. 1, 9.

[71] Ferguson, *English Diplomacy*, 104.

[72] TNA E 28/83/1. On 2 March Botyll had been awarded partial expenses for this expedition and he is again mentioned as ambassador in a council on 3 March, at which he was present. Parliament was in session at this time.

[73] TNA E 404/69/195; TNA E 404/69/104–6; *Rot. Parl.*, V, 237.

[74] TNA E 28/83/7.

[75] TNA E 28/83/19; E 28/83/23–4; E 28/83/34; TNA E 404/69/193–6.

[76] 'John Benet's Chronicle', 221–2.

[77] *Foedera*, Hague, V, II, 80.

[78] Hicks, *Warwick the Kingmaker*, 151. Philip the Good's embassy was headed by the count of Estampes.

of this.[79] In this context, the Prior appears to have been sympathetic to, if not part of, the Yorkist camp. He was at the very least acceptable to them. It brings new light to the letters written, supposedly by Henry VI, to the Grand Master and the castellan John Langstrother in June 1459 that Botyll's presence was considered 'full necessarie for many causes', informing them that the Prior would not be going to the general chapter in October and requesting that Botyll should not be called to general chapters in the future.[80] It also indicates how, between Henry VI's letter of 1448 to the Grand Master and that of 1459, the Prior's service to the crown had changed from preferable to essential.

Returning to Botyll's possible links with the Yorkists, even if we take Henry VI's incapacity into account, which meant that Botyll served on king's council regularly between 1453 and 1456, it is certainly odd that, after the intensity of his diplomatic activity between 1447 and 1453, Botyll was then not commissioned until five years later, in what was a very strongly Yorkist influenced embassy. It may indicate that the attempted reconciliation between Henry VI, the duke of York and the earl of Warwick was the impetus for the Prior's return to diplomatic duty.[81] Botyll was probably included as one of the technical negotiators, but it is likely he was also included, along with others, to enhance the status of the embassy. He is, after all, listed fourth of 22 envoys, with only Warwick, Bishop Beauchamp and Viscount Bourchier above him. Botyll's inclusion in the embassy reflects the diplomatic and political tightrope that the Prior had to walk in times of instability. He was a trusted advisor of Henry VI, but he needed to keep on good terms with the leading magnates of the realm. It was particularly important not to offend Warwick who, as captain of Calais, controlled the seas through which the English Hospitallers travelled, traded and gained news of events on Rhodes.

The change of dynasty that came with the deposition of Henry VI and accession of Edward IV did not affect Botyll's diplomatic duties. On 12 November 1461 Botyll was head commissioner concerning infractions at sea of the truce with Burgundy.[82] In contrast to the last embassy with which he was involved, this commission was much smaller, as it was a subsection of the embassy, merely dealing with the details of the negotiations.[83] The Prior is next mentioned on 8 February 1462 in an embassy headed by Lawrence Booth, bishop of Durham, to James Douglas, earl of Ross. These negotiations, by which the exiled earl of Ross, Donald Balagh and his son John and their subjects were to become liegemen of Edward IV and assist Edward should the Scots invade England, dated back to June 1461. They were confirmed in London on 8 February by the ambassadors of the earl, and were signed by both parties on 13 February 1462. Ratification of the treaty took place on 17 March, with a clause that, if a truce was made with Scotland, the earl of Ross and his compan-

[79] Lander, *Government and Community*, 200; C. L. Scofield, *The Life and Reign of Edward the Fourth*, 2 vols, London, 1923, I, 28.

[80] *POPC*, VI, 299–301.

[81] Lander, *Government and Community*, 200; M. R. Thielmans, *Bourgogne et Angleterre, Rélations Politiques et Economiques Entre Les Pays-Bas Bourguignons et l'Angleterre, 1435–1467*, Brussels, 1966, 331–2; *Paston Letters*, II, 340.

[82] *Foedera*, Hague, V, II, 106.

[83] Scofield, *Edward the Fourth*, I, 213.

ions would be included, to guarantee their immunity from accusations of treason.[84] The negotiations with the earl of Ross were to counter the threat of a feared joint invasion of England by the Scots and Margaret of Anjou. While Mary of Guelders, the Scottish regent, wanted to make peace with Edward IV, James Kennedy, bishop of St Andrews, managed to sway support in favour of Queen Margaret.[85] Botyll was still involved in negotiations with Scotland, for which he had 15 days' safe conduct, on 17 June 1462, but no agreement resulted.[86]

Botyll's penultimate commission was on 9 January 1466, headed by the earl of Warwick, in order to conclude a truce with Burgundy.[87] The meeting took place in March, but was not a productive one, perhaps due to animosity between the earl of Warwick and Charles, count of Charolais, heir of the duke of Burgundy, as Warwick (according to the Crowland Chronicler) favoured an alliance between England and France, rather than with Burgundy. The English embassy then went to meet a French mission at Calais, again without any satisfactory result.[88] Botyll's final mission was on 26 December 1467, when he was empowered to treat for an extension to the truce with Brittany (in force since 1464) until 1 July, when alliances were being considered with Burgundy, France and Brittany.[89] This was a reaction to the setback of a Franco-Burgundian truce. Earlier in the year, England had been negotiating a 30-year commercial treaty with Burgundy and the ambassadors had signed an agreement on 20 November. However, the news of a six-month truce between Burgundy and France meant that Edward IV refused to ratify the treaty and appointed a new embassy. Thus Botyll's mission was one of ensuring the support of Brittany, but also perhaps to make plans for assistance, should France threaten to invade Brittany. When the threat became serious only a couple of months after the extension of the truce had expired, Brittany switched its allegiance to the French in September 1468, and a month later Burgundy, by the Treaty of Peronne, agreed not to side with England, should she invade France. Despite these temporary changes of allegiance, relations with both Brittany and Burgundy were re-established by the end of the year.[90]

The final three years of Botyll's diplomatic service coincided with the English government wavering between a treaty with France or Burgundy, Edward IV favouring Burgundy and Warwick preferring France.[91] Edward IV, on the advice of his council, perhaps hoping to recover lost French lands, and through suspicion of France, decided on a commercial treaty with Burgundy, which was to the advantage of the Calais staple, and would secure an ally in case of war. The evidence

[84] TNA C 71/102, m. 17; BL MS Royal 13 B XI, f. 2; *Foedera*, Hague, V, II, 107–9. N. Macdougall, *James III: A Political Study*, Edinburgh, 1982, 59–60.

[85] Lander, *Government and Community*, 233–4; Macdougall, *James III*, 52–3.

[86] Scofield, *Edward the Fourth*, I, 248; A. I. Dunlop, *The Life and Times of James Kennedy, Bishop of St Andrews*, Edinburgh and London, 1950, 221–2.

[87] BL MS Royal 13 B XI, ff. 83v–89; *Foedera*, Hague, V, II, 143.

[88] *The Crowland Chronicle Continuations: 1459–1486*, ed. N. Pronay and J. Cox, London, 1986, 115; C. Hare (M. Andrews), *The Life of Louis XI the Rebel Dauphin and the Statesman King*, London, 1907, 125; Lander, *Government and Community*, 244.

[89] BL MS Royal 13 B XI, f. 83v; Scofield, *Edward the Fourth*, I, 443.

[90] Lander, *Government and Community*, 246–7.

[91] *Crowland Chronicle*, 115.

suggests that Botyll favoured this policy. It is perhaps significant that four of his nine missions were to Burgundy. One would expect him to favour Burgundy, for the Hospitallers' involvement in the wool trade meant they had a common interest with the Calais merchants, who needed Burgundian favour to trade with Flanders, who in turn needed English wool. This may explain his participation in the 1466 mission to Burgundy at St Omer, but his absence from the following embassy that met the French at Calais.

Like the preceding period, during Prior Botyll's administration the lay–ecclesiastical ratio of embassies was fairly even, but if anything favoured lay members, perhaps indicating a move to using secular lawyers. Apart from the expected superior numbers of clerics on the 1447–9 mission concerning the dispute between Basle and the papacy, only the 1453 mission to Burgundy had a majority of ecclesiastics, whereas the 1458 and 1466 embassies were overwhelmingly lay. As in the preceding period, the majority of ecclesiastics were in administrative roles. However, a development from the period 1380 to 1440 was that the continuity of those on missions with the Prior was much more regular. Thomas Kent was in four embassies, Richard Neville, John Wenlock, Vincent Clement, Robert Stillington and Peter Taster in two. This suggests the gradual development of a professional pool of diplomats. Equally, it illustrates the increased service of the Prior. Whereas in the preceding 60 years the Priors had served in seven missions in total, Botyll took part in nine over 20 years. That may seem far from prolific, but is still a significant increase on previous Priors. The nine missions amount to 27 per cent of the total number of major missions (34) between 1447 and 1467. However, six of the total number of missions were concurrent with those Botyll served in. If one deducts these to leave the total that he could realistically have taken part in, then his participation increases to 32 per cent, which is a substantial proportion and involved a major commitment in time.

How did his contemporary diplomats fare in comparison? To conclude on this we need to take a sample period from a time when the Prior was active and diplomatic activity was intense, such as 1447–49 (14 missions in three years). The crown appointed 38 envoys during these three years. Most of these (25) were only employed on one mission. Prior Botyll and eight others took part in two missions and Robert Roos was employed on three. The most active, however, in five missions each were the ill-fated Adam Moleyns, keeper of the privy seal, the court favourite John Sutton, Lord Dudley, and Thomas Kent. Five missions out of 14 is a substantial number considering that many of the embassies ran simultaneously. Botyll's two missions suggest that between 1447 and 1449 he was not as regular an envoy as those who were members of king's council and court were, but he was nevertheless a constant one. Furthermore, Potter, looking at foreign policy in Henry VIII's reign, has classified those sent on three or more missions for the whole of his reign as part of a 'core' of diplomats.[92] If the same holds true for Henry VI and Edward IV's reigns, then over the whole of his administration Botyll qualifies to be in such a core.

Another development during Botyll's office was the use of foreigners as envoys.

---

[92] D. Potter, 'Foreign Policy', in *The Reign of Henry VIII: Politics, Policy and Piety*, ed. D. MacCulloch, Basingstoke, 1995, 101–33 at 103.

The Catalan Vincent Clement played a prominent part in the 1447–9 mission that secured Felix V's resignation.[93] At that time he was in the service of Lord Dudley, who also went on the mission. Clement is an early example of a member of the humanist school who came to England to seek employment with the crown, hoping to enhance his ecclesiastical career. In his case this succeeded as, by the 1458 mission to Burgundy, he was papal collector to England. Other (English) humanists, such as John Tiptoft, earl of Worcester, who had studied at Padua, served in diplomatic missions.[94] Foreigners from the former Byzantine Empire also came into English service, at least temporarily, such as Demetrios Palaeologos (1455), John Argyropoulos (1456, also in service in Italy) and Franculos Sernopoulos (1456, 1459).[95]

The constant use of the Prior from the mid-fifteenth century can thus be understood in the context of early Renaissance developments and diplomatic changes in the Italian states that had a knock-on effect in England. The complex alliances and rivalries between the Italian states, including the papacy, led to the development of a highly advanced system of diplomacy.[96] Clough has suggested that English monarchs from Henry VI onwards were aware of these changes and adopted the same diplomatic format to ensure the efficient conduct of business.[97] It was essential, therefore, to have skilled diplomats such as Vincent Clement, especially those fluent in Ciceronian Latin, the language of diplomacy.[98] Botyll was thus an ideal candidate. He was aware of the current diplomatic format in Italy through his association with the English hospice in Rome.[99] The Hospitaller general chapters were held in Latin, and we know that Botyll was proficient from his oration at the 1446 general chapter in Rome.[100] As a leading Hospitaller, his papal connections added to his suitability for diplomatic service.

Langstrother, Weston and Kendal, 1469–1501

Botyll's successor, Prior John Langstrother (1469–71), after the Readeption of Henry VI in September 1470, was appointed treasurer by Warwick for the second time and was also involved in diplomatic duties (see Figure 7).[101] On 13 February 1471, Langstrother was named as one of the envoys, headed by George Neville, archbishop of York, to Louis XI to seek a ten-year truce.[102] The previous month French

---

[93] Harvey, *England, Rome and the Papacy*, 185.
[94] Lander, *Government and Community*, 161.
[95] TNA E403/806, m. 6 for Palaeologos; TNA E 403/807, m. 10 for Argyropoulos; TNA E 403/809, m. 2, TNA E 403/817, m. 9, TNA E404/71/52 for Sernopoulos.
[96] M. Mallett, 'Diplomacy and War in Later Fifteenth Century Italy', *Proceedings of the British Academy*, London, LXVII, 1981, 268–88 at 273.
[97] C. Clough, 'Late Fifteenth Century English Monarchs subject to Italian Renaissance Influence' in *England and the Continent in the Middle Ages: Studies in Memory of Andrew Martindale: Proceedings of the 1996 Harlaxton Symposium*, ed. J. Mitchell and M. Moran, Stamford, 2000, 32.
[98] *Ibid.*, 31.
[99] J. Allen, 'Englishmen in Rome and the Hospice 1362–1474', in *The English Hospice in Rome: The Venerabile*, XXI, Exeter, 1962, 43–81 at 53, 56; B. Newns, 'The Hospice of St Thomas and the English Crown 1474–1538', in *ibid.*, 150.
[100] Valentini, 'Un capitolo generale 1446', 155–6.
[101] *Foedera*, Hague, V, II, 178. He was re-appointed treasurer on 20 October 1470.
[102] *Foedera*, Hague, V, II, 184–7.

ambassadors had been in London, discussing trading agreements and a possible joint invasion of Burgundy. Around 17 February Langstrother and the other ambassadors set out for France to confirm the agreement and to escort Queen Margaret and the Prince Edward back to England.[103] The intended return on 27 February was delayed due to bad weather and Langstrother waited on the queen, the prince and his wife at Honfleur.[104] A second attempt was made on 24 March, but was also delayed, and they finally arrived in Weymouth on 14 April.[105] He was attendant upon Margaret until his participation in and death after the battle of Tewkesbury.[106] Edward IV was also wary of Langstrother's successor, William Tornay (1471–74). Like Langstrother, Tornay had acted against Edward IV, probably under Langstrother's orders. He and Langstrother had taken part in the insurrections against Edward, but Tornay was pardoned on 28 July 1470.[107] Although he swore on 3 July 1471 to acknowledge Edward, Yorkist Prince of Wales, as heir to the crown, he did not hold any important royal office and was not an envoy in international relations.[108]

After Tornay's death, there was a power struggle for the English Priory between Robert Multon and John Weston that prevented any participation in crown affairs. Despite the Lancastrian sympathies of his kin, Prior John Weston (1477–89), once elected to Edward's satisfaction, did serve him as an envoy.[109] His first mission took place during the precarious diplomatic period between the death of Charles the Bold, duke of Burgundy in 1477 and the Treaty of Arras in 1482. By the Treaty of Pécquigny (1475), Edward IV and Louis XI had agreed, amongst other things, a seven-year truce, an annual pension to be paid to Edward, and a treaty of amity, which included a commercial agreement and a marriage between the Dauphin Charles and Edward's daughter, Elizabeth.[110] Charles the Bold, the last Valois duke of Burgundy, died at the siege of Nancy in January 1477, and this created an unstable international situation, as Louis saw it as a chance to invade Burgundy. Charles' daughter and heir, Mary, married Archduke Maximilian in August the same year to counter the threat of invasion.[111] Over the next few years, Louis and Maximilian competed for Edward IV's support, support he was not financially capable of giving. Edward IV wished to remain on good terms with both France and Burgundy, in the former case to retain his annual pension and to conclude the marriage, and in the latter case because of English commercial interests in the important cities of the Low Countries, under Burgundian control.

---

103   Lander, *Government and Community*, 279; TNA E 404/71/6/41; *Foedera*, Hague, V, II, 189; *Historie of the Arrivall of Edward IV*, I, 22.

104   Scofield, *Edward the Fourth*, I, 564.

105   *Historie of the Arrivall of Edward IV*, 14–15; Scofield, *Edward the Fourth*, I, 582.

106   *Crowland Chronicle*, 127; Scofield, *Edward the Fourth*, I, 583; *Death and Dissent*, 113.

107   *Foedera*, Hague, V, II, 175. Prior Langstrother remained imprisoned in the Tower until the Readeption.

108   *Rot. Parl.*, VI, 234.

109   *The Lisle Letters*, 6 vols, ed. M. St Clare Byrne, Chicago, 1981, I, 329. According to Byrne, the Lancastrian sympathies of Edmund Weston, brother of Prior John Weston, brought royal favour to the family on the accession of Henry VII.

110   Scofield, *Edward the Fourth*, II, 140–3.

111   Lander, *Government and Community*, 292–303.

Prior Weston was involved in relations with both sides. On 6 July 1480 he went to Gravesend to meet Margaret of York, duchess of Burgundy, and escorted her to Greenwich in the royal barge.[112] Margaret was in England as an envoy on behalf of Maximilian, her visit culminating in an alliance with Burgundy the following month.[113] Meanwhile, on 24 August 1480, Weston and Thomas Langton were made ambassadors to Louis XI to negotiate a truce and demand the marriage between the Dauphin Charles and Edward IV's daughter Elizabeth, as agreed by the Treaty of Pécquigny, for which Edward had asked Louis for confirmation after Charles the Bold's death.[114] Weston had replaced John, Lord Howard, as help for Rhodes, then under Ottoman siege, was another item on the agenda.[115] The fall of Otranto to the Ottomans earlier that month, for which Sixtus IV had issued a crusade appeal, was another topic to be discussed. Apart from his fellow ambassador, Weston was also accompanied by members of his household, including two members of the Cely family, William and Richard junior, whose letters elaborate on the Prior's itinerary during the negotiations.[116] They tell us that on 1 September the Prior was preparing for his journey across the Channel.[117] The following day Weston, in Dover and expected to arrive at Boulogne on 3 September, asked George Cely to meet him there with foreign currency.[118] The talks were unsuccessful for England, and hence for a crusade. Louis, suspicious of England's alliance with Burgundy and talks with Brittany, told Weston and Langton that they might as well return to England. Louis presented Weston with letters that Edward IV had written to Maximilian and Margaret, which suggested that Louis was in contact or had an understanding with Archduke Maximilian, nominally in competition with Louis for Edward's support. This gives us a hint of the analytical skills needed to be a diplomat.[119] It was information that meant that it cannot have been a surprise when, two years later, Louis renounced the English marriage agreement and arranged with Maximilian for the dauphin to marry Margaret of Austria by the Treaty of Arras.[120]

Another aspect of this mission, again requiring analytical skills and concerning intelligence work, may have been to gauge just how angry Louis was that England was in contact with Burgundy, and thus assess the likelihood of war. This is implied in the Cely letters, where George Cely in Calais, whose merchants also had an interest in knowing, asked his brother Richard to enquire from the Prior if war was likely, and received assurances a few days later that Weston thought that there would not be war.[121] The Prior returned to England via Calais and met the king at Eltham on 11 November to report on the mission, staying there just long enough to

---

112 *Cely Letters*, 85–6; Scofield, *Edward the Fourth*, II, 285. Scofield gives the wrong date of 24 June.

113 Lander, *Government and Community*, 303.

114 *Foedera*, Hague, V, III, 112; Scofield, *Edward the Fourth*, II, 140–3.

115 *Ibid.*, 291.

116 *Cely Letters*, 86.

117 *Ibid.*, 86–7.

118 *Ibid.*, 87.

119 Scofield, *Edward the Fourth*, II, 298.

120 Lander, *Government and Community*, 303.

121 *Cely Letters*, 96–100.

attend Princess Bridget's baptism, and then returning to London the same night.[122] The Prior's mission had lasted over two months. One advantage for the Prior of serving as a crown diplomat was that, as a member of an international religious order, he had the freedom to move outside England, in a period when such access was increasingly restricted.

Due to his absence on Rhodes, for where he left in early August 1481, Prior Weston did not serve again as an envoy until the reign of Henry VII. Weston appears not to have returned to England until the autumn of 1485, after the battle of Bosworth. As one of the eight witnesses called to testify concerning the request for a papal dispensation for Henry VII to marry Elizabeth of York, he stated that he had known Elizabeth for ten years and Henry since 24 August, two days after Bosworth, the possible date of his return.[123] He was certainly back for the November parliament, where he presented a petition requesting the upholding of the Hospitallers' privileges.[124]

Henry VII, as founder of a new dynasty, placed international acceptance for his regime at the forefront of his foreign policy. His main aim was to secure his hold on power and to increase the wealth of the monarchy, and his foreign policy aimed to secure his position at home. Essential for this was the ceasing of hostilities with Scotland and Weston first appears as an envoy for Henry in this arena.[125] On 6 May 1486, Weston was appointed part of a six-man mission to the ambassadors of James III. King James viewed the change of dynasty in England to be to Scotland's advantage and had agreed to negotiations, which took place during June and July. A concord was agreed on 3 July, ratified in London on 26 July for a three-year truce as a precursor of a lasting peace, which was to be accompanied by two proposed marriages between James III's second son, James, and Edward's daughter, Katherine, and between James III himself and Edward IV's widow, Elizabeth Woodville.[126] James III inspected the concord and gave confirmation in Edinburgh on 24 October. Further confirmation of the treaty was given two years later.[127] This was part of a long process of negotiations with Scotland that culminated in the Treaty of Ayton in 1497, which concluded the first lasting peace between the two countries since 1328.[128]

The following year, on 2 June 1487, Weston was once again an envoy, this time as the king's 'orator' to Innocent VIII.[129] He arrived in Rome on 15 October, where he joined the turcopolier and future Prior of England, John Kendal, who had been in Rome since March as the Grand Master's ambassador to the Pope.[130] This mission

---

[122] *Ibid.*, 89–92, 95–6. Reporting on the Prior's meeting with Edward IV on 11 November at Eltham, Richard Cely wrote on 15 November that the king had made Weston 'ryught whelcum', *ibid.*, 95; Scofield, *Edward the Fourth*, II, 299–300.

[123] S. B. Chrimes, *Henry VII*, 2nd edn, New Haven, CT, and London, 1999, 331.

[124] *Rot. Parl.*, VI, 313. However, he was not appointed on the opening day (7 November) as a trier of petitions in this parliament, perhaps because he had not yet returned.

[125] *Foedera*, Hague, V, II, 169–72.

[126] TNA C 71/106, ff. 1–4; N. Macdougall, *James IV*, 2nd edn, East Linton, 1997, 13.

[127] *Foedera*, Hague, V, III, 181, 192–3.

[128] Chrimes, *Henry VII*, 278.

[129] *CPL 1484–1492*, 195.

[130] *Cely Letters*, 116; *CVSP*, 164.

concerned the negotiations on who should have custody of the fugitive Djem, son of Mehmed II and younger brother of Bayezid, in Hospitaller custody since July 1482. Whilst Kendal, as Hospitaller custodian of Djem during the discussions, continued to take part in negotiations with the papacy, Weston, who had been there to ensure France did not get custody of Djem, and therefore payment of the pension from the Ottoman sultan, headed back to England and was at Calais on 22 January 1488 awaiting a safe crossing.[131]

Weston's final diplomatic appointment was to Ferdinand and Isabella of Spain in March 1488. Weston headed this delegation, which had authority to conclude a truce or lasting peace.[132] The negotiations, initially aimed at seeking aid to preserve Breton independence, ended with the Treaty of Medina del Campo in March the following year, which included an extremely beneficial trade agreement for England, an important mutual commitment not to aid each other's rebels, and a marriage between Prince Arthur and Princess Catherine, which finally took place in November 1501.[133]

Weston continued the tendency of more regular involvement in foreign affairs by the Priors of St John that began with Botyll. His relative lack of service under Edward IV was due first to internal Hospitaller struggles for control of the English Priory and secondly to his absence from England, rather than to any animosity between the crown and Hospitallers. Edward viewed Prior Tornay with suspicion, but his failure to serve as an envoy was also due to the brevity of his term of office. Prior Multon did not serve as envoy, partly due to a short tenure and partly because of the disputed election with John Weston. His other duties in Edward IV's reign, when he was preceptor of Mount St John, and later under Henry VII as ambassador to Scotland, show that both kings considered him suitable to hold important office, including envoy.

John Kendal (1489–1501) succeeded Weston and served as a crown envoy throughout his office as Prior. The first of these missions was a direct result of the Perkin Warbeck affair, in which Kendal was later implicated.[134] In November 1491, Perkin Warbeck, son of the controller of Tournai, appeared in Ireland claiming to be Richard, duke of York. He managed to gain the recognition of a number of foreign powers, including Scotland. To counteract this, on 12 June 1492 Henry sent an embassy that included Kendal, headed by Richard Fox, keeper of the privy seal and recently appointed bishop of Bath and Wells, to France to negotiate a truce or peace and a trade agreement. Charles VIII, however, angry at English interference in Brittany, to which France had laid claim since the death of Duke Francis II in September 1488, invited Warbeck to France and treated him as if he was a prince, a factor that prompted Henry to invade and besiege Boulogne in October. However, neither power wanted war, and soon negotiations started, which led to the

---

[131] *Cely Letters*, 241–3; S. dei Conti, *Le Storie de' Suri Tempi dal 1475 al 1510*, 2 vols, tr. F. Calabrò and D. Zanelli, Rome, 1883, 325. Djem was in Hospitaller custody first on Rhodes and then in France between 1482 and 1489, when he was transferred to the papacy. The French did not gain custody of him until a month before his death in 1495.

[132] *Foedera*, Hague, V, III, 189.

[133] Lander, *Government and Community*, 341.

[134] *Ibid.*, 342–3; I. Arthurson, *The Perkin Warbeck Conspiracy 1491–1499*, Stroud, 1994, 98.

Treaty of Étaples on 3 November.[135] By the treaty, Charles VIII, keen to press his claim to the crown of Naples, agreed to pay the cost of the war, the money owed by Anne of Brittany, and the arrears of Edward IV's pension granted by the Treaty of Pécquigny. A commercial agreement also opened French markets to English merchants and revived the wine trade with Gascony. Most importantly, Charles VIII agreed not to assist English rebels. Charles, playing on Henry's dynastic insecurity, used Warbeck to end English involvement in Brittany, which they had agreed to defend by the Treaty of Redon (February 1489), and in return expelled Perkin Warbeck from his court.

The second embassy of which Kendal was a part was on 14 December 1495. Richard Fox, now bishop of Durham, headed the embassy to Archduke Philip the Fair to conclude a pact of peace and trade, the Magnus Intercursus.[136] Negotiations were conducted throughout the early part of 1496 and an agreement was reached on 20 February and finally sealed by Philip in December.[137] This was accompanied by confirmation of the marriage of Prince Arthur to Catherine of Aragon, daughter of Ferdinand and Isabella and sister of Juana, wife of Philip the Fair, which was agreed on 1 October 1496, and had already been negotiated in the Treaty of Medina del Campo.[138]

As well as diplomatic duties abroad, Kendal also took part in the diplomatic entourage on special occasions when visiting foreign dignitaries were present. He was, for example, at the feast of the tournament held at Westminster between 9 and 13 November 1494.[139] He was also in the king's presence in 1500, when Henry VII met Archduke Philip.[140] On that occasion, the king and queen arrived at Calais on 8 May, and Kendal followed two days later. On 29 May, Kendal was sent as ambassador to meet Philip at St Omer, where he was received with great honour, and rode side by side with the archduke.[141] The details of the talks are not known, but almost certainly concerned the forthcoming meeting between the king and the archduke. On 9 June, the king and queen met Philip at St Peter's church outside Calais for a banquet and an evening of dancing. Kendal returned to England with the royal party on 16 June.[142] The following year (1501) Kendal was commissioned to participate in the preparations for Catherine of Aragon's arrival in England, due in August or September, for her marriage to Prince Arthur. Lord Willoughby de Broke was given the task of receiving the princess on her arrival, and Kendal and eight others were to attend on Willoughby, when required. Their role was to include receiving

[135] *Foedera*, Hague, V, IV, 45; Lander, *Government and Community*, 343–4.

[136] TNA E 30/624/1, 3.

[137] *Foedera*, Hague, V, IV, 82–7.

[138] Chrimes, *Henry VII*, 278.

[139] *Letters and Papers Illustrative of the Reigns of Richard III and Henry VII*, 2 vols, ed. J Gairdner, London, 1861–3, I, 402; S. Anglo, *Spectacle, Pageantry and Early Tudor Policy*, 2nd edn, Oxford, 1997, 53. Anglo does not mention Priors John Weston, Kendal or Docwra.

[140] *Letters Richard III and Henry VII*, II, 87.

[141] *Great Chronicle of London*, 292–3.

[142] *Chronicle of Calais*, 3–4. The footnotes give Docwra as Prior in 1500, but in fact Kendal was still Prior.

Catherine on her arrival in London and escorting her to and from her lodgings.[143] The marriage took place on 14 November, but Kendal died before April 1501 so took no part in the preparations to receive the princess. In summary, Kendal was involved in the main ambassadorial missions during his Priorship, which indicates that he formed part of the core of Henry VII's diplomatic corps. His previous experience whilst turcopolier, as the Grand Master's resident ambassador in Rome provided excellent credentials for service to Henry VII.

The composition of embassies from 1470 up until about 1507 reversed the previous lay to clerical ratio, in that ecclesiastics were more numerous. This was so whether the embassy was to France (1471), Scotland (1486), Castile (1488) or the emperor (1495). Only the 1492 mission to France had a narrow (three to two, plus the Prior) lay majority. Moreover, this change was due to an increase in the number of high-status clergy in these embassies. The 1471 mission to France included three bishops, George Neville, John Hales and Robert Tully. John Alcock and John Russell were in the 1486 mission to Scotland. A number of reasons possibly explain this trend. Firstly, the humanist influences in Henry VII's court that began in Henry VI's reign escalated in the latter half of the fifteenth century. Some Englishmen, both lay such as John Tiptoft, and ecclesiastics such as Robert Flemming, John Shirwood and John Gunthorpe, seeking advancement through royal service, went abroad to gain a humanist education.[144] Gunthorpe, who had William Grey, bishop of Ely, as an influential patron, served on many diplomatic missions like those to Castile in August 1466 and in March 1470. He continued to serve under Henry VII, and accompanied Prior John Weston during the negotiations for the Treaty of Medina del Campo with Castile during 1488–9.[145] Weston headed the 1488 mission, accompanied by other skilled envoys such as Christopher Urswick, which gives us a good indication of his experience and reputation as a diplomat. Weston's description the previous year as the king's 'orator' to the Pope raises the possibility that he served as a proctor for the king to the Roman Curia, at the same time that turcopolier John Kendal was procurator for the Grand Master of the Order. Weston, like Botyll, was a natural choice as envoy, with both diplomatic skills and papal connections. Secondly, in an effort to secure his dynasty, Henry VII had a deliberate policy of constantly engaging both laymen and ecclesiastics on commissions. This was especially necessary (in Henry VII's view) to remind the clergy, always conscious of their independence, of their duty to the crown.

Continuing the trend of the previous period, there was a consistency of service by the Prior and his fellow envoys. Priors Langstrother, Weston and Kendal in total served in nine missions between 1470 and 1495, as well as attending on the king for meetings with other monarchs. This sounds like occasional service but, if one takes into account when they were available for service, a different picture emerges. Langstrother is difficult to assess because his Priorship commenced during a time of struggle for power between Henry VI and Edward IV, in which Langstrother was imprisoned in the Tower for some time. Nevertheless, between October 1470 and

---

[143] *Letters Richard III and Henry VII*, II, 103–5. The others were Lords Risley, Tyrrell, Hungerford, Owen, Poyntes, Wingfield, Sandys and Darrell.

[144] Clough, 'Late Fifteenth Century English Monarchs', 307–10.

[145] *Ibid.*, 312.

May 1471, apart from being treasurer, he served on one mission. Weston served on two missions for Edward IV in 1480, was then absent from England until 1485, but in his last three years as Prior served on three missions. Finally, Kendal served on four missions between 1492 and 1496. This may not be numerous, but it is regular for the periods when the Priors were in England.

The regular personnel were mainly ecclesiastics with a legal background such as John Russell, Henry Sharp, Christopher Urswick, Henry Ainsworth and Richard Fox. The lay membership also tended to have a greater status. Those that were included usually held positions in the king's household, such as Thomas Lovell in 1486 or had a practical reason for being included, like Warwick as captain of Calais in 1471 or Sir James Tyrell, lieutenant of Guînes, in 1492. The Prior was included as an information gatherer as well as a high-status official. It was no coincidence, for example, that Weston was patron of the Celys, a wealthy merchant family, who were merchants of the staple of Calais. They, as their obligation as client entailed and as their letters testify, provided the Prior with valuable and up-to-date information from the continent, as well as supplying him with foreign currency and fabrics from Flanders. Weston had, for example, requested news from Calais in June 1480. Unfortunately the type of news is not stated, but it is likely to have been general, such as the goods that he had ordered through the Celys, or news of Rhodes from returning merchants.[146]

Docwra, the Professional Diplomat, 1501–27

Kendal was replaced by Thomas Docwra (1502–27). Docwra spent his first years as Prior on Rhodes and between 1501 and 1504 Brother Thomas Newport, turcopolier, was his lieutenant in England.[147] Once he returned, Docwra served regularly as an envoy, as his predecessors since Prior Botyll had done (see Figure 8). In April 1506 Docwra was one of the ambassadors who made a truce and trade agreement with Philip the Fair. On 12 January Philip and his wife Juana, queen of Castile, had been sailing from Zealand to Spain, when a storm had forced them to take refuge in England, where they stayed a little over three months. Henry VII took the opportunity to conclude a favourable commercial agreement and gained a promise of the surrender of Edmund de la Pole, in exile in Flanders. The ambassadors were also to negotiate a marriage between the widowed Henry and Margaret of Savoy, which did not materialise.[148] The treaty was agreed on 4 April, approved by Henry at Westminster on 20 April, further discussed by both sets of ambassadors in London on 30 April, and ratified on 15 May.[149] This was part of other

[146] Mallett, 'Diplomacy and War', 274; see *Cely Letters*, 79–80.
[147] Newport was at first president during the vacancy, and still in that position in March 1502. By August Docwra had been officially recognised by the Pope and Grand Master as the new Prior of England and Newport was presenting as his lieutenant. Docwra did not present until January 1506. See also BL MS Lansdowne 200 for chapters of the English Priory.
[148] Lander, *Government and Community*, 348.
[149] *Foedera*, Hague, V, IV, 223–7.

negotiations that followed on from the Treaty of Windsor that had been agreed in February, by which Henry VII had recognised Philip as king of Castile, and committed himself to help him against his father-in-law, Ferdinand of Aragon.[150] Before Philip departed on 23 April, Ferdinand had married Germaine de Foix, thereby strengthening relations with France, which made an Anglo-Castilian alliance even more crucial. To this end, another commission was appointed in July to discuss a marriage between Philip's son, Charles (the future Charles I of Castile in 1516 and Emperor Charles V in 1519) and Mary, Henry VII's daughter, and to confirm the treaty of friendship. Docwra was not included in the initial party, which was headed by Nicholas West, bishop of Ely.[151] The death of Philip in September 1506 delayed the marriage negotiations while other options were considered, but the pact against Ferdinand continued, due to Ferdinand's alliance with France. By 12 October the following year, Docwra had been included in the embassy headed by Richard Fox to the representatives of the young Archduke Charles.[152] Docwra and the other ambassadors left England for Calais on 27 October where they met their counterparts to arrange the terms of the marriage.[153] They reached an agreement on 2 November and Henry gave his consent at Westminster on 8 December. Both sets of ambassadors, including Docwra, signed the agreement at a special ceremony at Calais on 21 December.[154] The simultaneous second negotiation on the confirmation of the 'amicable truce', which Docwra was also involved in, followed exactly the same timetable as the marriage negotiations, with the addition that the Emperor Maximilian agreed to it on 22 February 1508 and gave confirmation on his grandson's behalf on 26 March.[155] The hoped-for agreement of Ferdinand of Aragon for the marriage was not forthcoming and eventually Henry VII decided to do without his permission and the betrothal was publicly announced on 17 December at Westminster in the presence of the ambassadors of Castile and England, including Docwra.[156] The marriage never materialised, however, and Mary was later to become queen of France.[157]

Prior Docwra's next appointment, his first for Henry VIII, was in March 1510, when he and Nicholas West negotiated a peace treaty with France, the details of which were agreed on 23 March. The same ambassadors were also appointed on 20 June to negotiate a marriage.[158] On 11 May it was noted that Docwra had intended to go to France to ratify the peace treaty, but his visit was delayed until the king was of full age (28 June).[159] Docwra was in Paris by 15 July and was still

[150] Lander, *Government and Community*, 349–50.
[151] *Foedera*, Hague, V, IV, 233. The other commissioners were William Bennington, Robert Robins and Giles Lord Daubeney, captain of Calais.
[152] *Foedera*, Hague, V, IV, 239–46.
[153] *Chronicle of Calais*, 6. The notes to the Calais chronicle gives the year as 1508, but this is incorrect, as 27 October, 23 Henry VII, was in 1507.
[154] *Foedera*, Hague, V, IV, 239–46; *Chronicle of Calais*, 6.
[155] *Foedera*, Hague, V, IV, 246–50, 250–5.
[156] *Foedera*, Hague, V, IV, 265–6. Catherine of Aragon also attended.
[157] Chrimes, *Henry VII*, 277.
[158] *Foedera*, Hague, VI, I, 12–13.
[159] *L&P HVIII 1509–1513*, I, 282, 299, 302.

there on 23 July when the bishop of Paris acknowledged the 745,000 gold crowns due from Louis XII to Henry VIII outstanding from the 1492 treaty.[160]

A year and a half later, on 4 February 1512, Docwra was appointed ambassador to the Fifth Lateran Council, due to open on 7 April, but his commission was cancelled and instead he was deployed concerning preparations for the invasion of France. Following the invasion in 1513, in which Docwra took part, and the capture of Tournai, he next served as an ambassador in 1514, when he was one of the king's council negotiating the peace at Baynard's Castle, London, on 16 June.[161] A resulting peace settlement was outlined on 7 August by Charles Somerset, recently created earl of Worcester, Docwra and Nicholas West and was agreed on 18 August.[162] This included the arrangement of a marriage between Henry's sister Mary and Louis XII.[163] The English ambassadors left London after 29 August and they arrived at Boulogne on 3 September. The following day peace was made between England and France through the marriage treaty of Princess Mary to Louis XII.[164] On 8 September 1514 Worcester, Docwra and West wrote to Henry VIII from Abbeville informing him of the arrangements prior to the wedding.[165] Henry replied with instructions for the escort of Princess Mary to France and for the ambassadors to convey that the marriage was meant to strengthen the alliance. After the solemnisation of the marriage, they were to return to England, and not go to the coronation in Paris.[166] However, these instructions were changed and they were still in France on 7 November 1514, when Docwra and the others wrote to the king from Paris informing him that the queen had been crowned two days earlier. They also noted that negotiation for the place and time of fixing the alliance was scheduled after 20 April 1515, but that Louis wanted an earlier date, as he intended to recover Asti and Milan. Louis died in December 1514 before he could realise his plans.[167]

After the marriage, Docwra returned to England. On 3 May 1515, he was at an evening dinner at Greenwich, sitting at the Venetian ambassador's table. He was there to impress, which he did wearing 'very superb chains'.[168] He intended, however, to go to Rome and Venice, as noted by the Venetian ambassador in Paris the previous year.[169] It seems he planned to go further, as on 12 November 1515 Grand Master Carretto wrote to Henry VIII of his intent to detain Docwra on Rhodes.[170] This journey did not take place and in May 1516 Docwra was first in London for the queen of Scotland's visit, and later at Newcastle-on-Tyne accom-

[160]   *Ibid.*, 313–14; *Foedera*, Hague, VI, I, 15–16.
[161]   *Chronicle of Calais*, 10–14; *L&P HVIII 1513–1514*, I, 1301.
[162]   *Foedera*, Hague, VI, I, 73–4.
[163]   *CMSP 1385–1618*, 438–440; *L&P HVIII 1513–1514*, I, 1376, 1380–1.
[164]   *The Ancient Kalendars and Inventories of the Treasury of His Majesty's Exchequer*, ed. F. Palgrave, 3 vols, Record Commission, London, 1836, III, 402; *L&P HVIII 1513–1514*, I, 1370, 1388–9.
[165]   *Ibid.*, 1374–5.
[166]   *Ibid.*, 1387–8.
[167]   *Ibid.*, 1440–2.
[168]   S. Giustinian, *Four Years at the Court of Henry VIII 1515–1519*, tr. R. Brown, 2 vols, London, 1854, I, 91; *L&P HVIII 1515–1516*, II, 120.
[169]   *L&P HVIII 1513–1514*, I, 1388–9.
[170]   BL MS Cotton MS Otho C IX, f. 24.

panying the ambassadors of Scotland.[171] At this point he was acting as interpreter between Charles Brandon, duke of Suffolk, and Sebastiano Giustinian, the Venetian ambassador, but he is later noted in negotiations with France and Scotland as one of the potential hostages demanded by John Stewart, duke of Albany, to guarantee his safe conduct.[172] The following year Docwra was in Castile to settle merchant disputes. Later in 1517, he and Tommaso Spinelli, the resident ambassador of England, were with King Charles of Castile on 20 September on diplomatic business, perhaps as part of the background negotiations to the Treaty of London of the following year.[173] On 4 May 1518 Spinelli informed Henry VIII that Prior Docwra was at Almadén (Castile) on 23 April.[174] He was still there in early September, clearly on a diplomatic mission to Charles of Castile before he returned to England to take part in negotiations with France later that month.

On 2 October 1518 the details of the peace treaty made at London were agreed. Docwra was one of the signatories, along with Charles Somerset, Nicholas West and Nicholas Vaux.[175] Two days later the details of the marriage treaty, also formulated by Docwra and the others, were agreed.[176] Final ratification was needed and on 25 October the Prior was preparing to go to France as an ambassador.[177] On 9 November Docwra was commissioned to take the oath of Francis I regarding the marriage of Henry's two-year-old daughter Mary to the king's son Francis, the dauphin, as agreed on 4 October. He was also to take the oath for the peace treaty made on 2 October, to arrange a meeting between the two kings, and to surrender Tournai on payment of 50,000 francs in gold crowns.[178] Docwra, West and the earl of Worcester, 'thes iii being chefe ambassadors into Fraunce to finishe the marriage', arrived in Calais on 14 November 1518.[179] On 14 December, in Notre Dame Cathedral, Francis I swore to abide by the treaty negotiated on 2 October (Treaty of London) in the presence of the English ambassadors.[180] The following day Docwra and the others wrote to Wolsey from Paris describing the oath taken and other details concerning the surrender of Tournai.[181] On 16 December the marriage treaty was ratified and authorisation for implementation was given on 18 December 1518.[182] The ramifications of the treaties continued into the following year and Docwra remained involved. On 4 February 1519, Docwra and the other ambassadors wrote to Wolsey on events concerning the surrender of Tournai. They had left Péronne on 27 January and arrived in Tournai on 30 January.[183] On

[171] *L&P HVIII 1515–1516*, II, 532, 536.

[172] Giustinian, *Court of Henry VIII*, I, 223; *L&P HVIII 1515–1516*, II, 535, 712–13.

[173] *L&P HVIII 1517–18*, II, 1168–70.

[174] *Ibid.*, 1283–4. Charles often resided at Almadén.

[175] *Foedera*, Hague, VI, I, 163–4; *L&P HVIII 1517–1518*, II, 1372–73.

[176] *L&P HVIII 1517–1518*, II, 1374.

[177] Giustinian, *Court of Henry VIII*, II, 235–8.

[178] *Foedera*, Hague, VI, I, 163–4, 167; *L&P HVIII 1517–1518*, II, 1396–98.

[179] *Chronicle of Calais*, 17–18; *L&P HVIII 1517–1518*, II, 1387–8; *L&P HVIII 1519–1521*, III, 30.

[180] *L&P HVIII 1517–1518*, II, 1420; *Foedera*, Hague, VI, I, 163–4, gives the date as 10 December.

[181] *L&P HVIII 1517–1518*, II, 1421.

[182] *Foedera*, Hague, VI, I, 164, 167.

[183] *L&P HVIII 1519–1521*, III, 16–17.

8 February they acknowledged receipt of 50,000 francs from Francis I at Tournai for the surrender of the town, its recently reinforced castle and the abbey of St Amand, and the surrender took place two days later.[184]

Docwra continued to serve Henry VIII in an international capacity at home as well as abroad in the later years of his administration. Indeed, after the election of Philippe de Villiers de L'Isle Adam as Grand Master on 22 January 1521 in preference to Docwra, it was natural for him to engage himself more in English affairs.[185] One such occasion was the planned meeting of Francis I and Henry VIII, as envisaged in the previously agreed treaties. On 26 March 1520 the Prior, as first lay baron, was summoned to attend Henry at the meeting with Francis at Calais (the Field of the Cloth of Gold), planned for 7 to 23 June.[186] In April, tournaments were arranged to take place prior to the meeting, and Docwra set out in the advance embassy headed by Wolsey on 1 June.[187] At the meeting, Docwra was one of the English judges of the jousting contests with the soon-to-be-executed duke of Buckingham, the earl of Northumberland, the earl of Worcester and Edward Poynings.[188] Docwra's status as provincial head of a military order and a veteran of the 1480 siege of Rhodes made him a worthy and high-status judge of the contest.

The following year, on 10 July, Docwra was appointed as one of the 35 temporal lords to attend the king at a meeting with Charles V at Gravelines and Calais. He was the first baron mentioned, directly below dukes, marquises and earls. Also included in the entourage, further down the list, was the Hospitaller Brother Thomas Newport, bailiff of Eagle, as a knight of Lincolnshire.[189] In one account of the Calais conference (which ran from 7 August to November) Cardinal Duprat's secretary notes that Docwra was attending on Wolsey in August, and that he was still there in October.[190] On 20 October, Docwra was appointed messenger between Wolsey and Charles V.[191] He set out immediately and was involved in negotiations on 26 October, when he and the other envoys wrote to Wolsey to update him on negotiations with the emperor, and further briefs were sent between 28 and 30 October.[192] Simultaneously he was involved in talks with the French. These talks, however, did not go well and on 3 November Charles' chancellor, Mercurino Gattinara (in Calais), informed Charles that Francis would not accept Docwra's brief, probably because he had heard of Henry's agreement with Charles that neither would make new alliances with France for the following two years.[193] Docwra shuffled between negotiations with the French and the emperor throughout the congress.

---

[184] *Chronicle of Calais*, 18; *Foedera*, Hague, VI, I, 175; *L&P HVIII 1519–1521*, III, 18, 20.

[185] K. M. Setton, *The Papacy and the Levant (1204–1571)*, 4 vols, Philadelphia, 1976–84, III, 203.

[186] *L&P HVIII 1519–1521*, III, 235; J. G. Russell, *The Field of Cloth of Gold. Men and Manners in 1520*, London, 1969, 56, 193.

[187] *Chronicle of Calais*, 20; Russell, *Field of Cloth of Gold*, 86.

[188] *Ibid.*, 116.

[189] *Chronicle of Calais*, 20–1; *L&P HVIII 1519–1521*, III, 325–6; Giustinian, *Court of Henry VIII*, II, 238. Charles V (Charles I of Castile).

[190] *L&P HVIII 1521–1523*, III, 696, 777.

[191] *Ibid.*, 706.

[192] *Ibid.*, 713; 717–19.

[193] *Ibid.*, 732–3.

On 10 November Docwra was with the emperor at Oudenarde, but Wolsey recalled him, and he returned on 17 November 1521.[194]

In 1522 Docwra was again on diplomatic duty when he was appointed to attend the king at Canterbury on 26 May, prior to the meeting with Charles V, and to ride with the king to the meeting at Dover castle.[195] Negotiations with the emperor's ambassadors for a marriage between Charles and the six-year-old princess Mary had been in progress since the beginning of the year and were agreed in March. Charles arrived in England on 26 May and met Henry the same day. After making their way to London and meeting his supposed bride-to-be, Charles and Henry concluded the treaty at Windsor on 10 June and the formal betrothal was announced nine days later.[196] Docwra was abroad on diplomatic duty again from April 1523 for most of the year. On 12 November 1523 Richard Sampson, the resident ambassador to Castile, wrote to Wolsey from Pamplona that the Prior was entering Languedoc and had been involved with negotiations with the emperor.[197] However, he does not seem to have been involved in any preparations for a reconquest of Rhodes, but was abroad on the king's business. It is indicative of the increasingly lay nature of the role of the English Prior that despite repeated calls for Docwra to appear on Rhodes in the years before its fall in December 1522, he did not go. Instead, he was employed by Wolsey in his attempt to create a new order in Europe encapsulated in the Treaty of London and in the attempts to maintain this policy in the following years. Docwra's diplomatic duties continued unaffected by the loss of Rhodes. On 24 May 1524 he was commissioned to treat with the emperor's ambassadors for a joint invasion of France.[198] A treaty with Charles was concluded by Docwra on 25 June with his counterpart Cardinal Louis Duprat to assist the duke of Bourbon to invade France.[199] The following year, on 6 April 1525, Docwra was in Rome and on 8 September he was commissioned to accompany the Venetian ambassadors at the ratification treaty between Henry VIII and Francis I.[200] At the time of his appointment he was in Toledo, where in October he delivered Henry's letters to the resident ambassador, Richard Sampson.[201]

Prior Docwra was involved in diplomacy for the crown more than any other English Hospitaller Prior. Over a period of 20 years, he was a regular participant in missions, 15 in all. Only his absence from England at the beginning of his Priorship and his failing health in his later years prevented further involvement. He participated in embassies to Scotland, Castile and the emperor, but most frequently to France. He was, in other words, a central figure in the major diplomatic missions between 1506 and 1525.

The composition of Docwra's earlier missions, under Henry VII, continued to have a strong and high-status ecclesiastical presence, with both Archbishop

[194] Ibid., 739, 751; BL MS Cotton Galba B VII, ff. 130–56.
[195] L&P HVIII 1521–1523, III, 966–7.
[196] A. Weir, Henry VIII: King and Court, London, 2001, 239–43.
[197] L&P HVIII 1521–1523, III, 1469.
[198] L&P HVIII 1524–6, IV, 148.
[199] Ibid., 148.
[200] Ibid., 546, 732.
[201] Ibid., 750.

Wareham and Bishop Fox in the 1506 embassy to Philip the Fair, and Fox in the embassy to Archduke Charles the following year. From the accession of Henry VIII, the pre-1470 equilibrium between lay and ecclesiastic was restored. From 1518 the missions that Docwra took part in had predominantly lay members. The exception was Richard Sampson, the musically gifted dean of Windsor and future bishop of Chichester, who was resident ambassador to Charles V from 1522 to 1525. As with the previous two periods, regardless of the lay–clerical ratio, there was a uniformity of personnel involved in Docwra's missions. Nicholas West took part in six missions, Charles Somerset, newly created earl of Worcester, in three embassies, Nicholas Vaux, Tommaso Spinelli, and Richard Sampson in two missions. The use of Spinelli, relative of Leonardo Spinelli, the papal ambassador to London in 1514, and Sampson shows a continuity of humanist influence in Henry VIII's reign, as one expects considering the education of the king and the courtiers, like William Blount and Lord Mountjoy, who surrounded him. Spinelli and Sampson also illustrate the tendency from 1517 for Docwra to work with resident ambassadors to lay powers, a trend emerging in Henry VII's reign.[202]

Docwra died in the spring of 1527 and was succeeded by the turcopolier William Weston. Unlike Docwra, Weston was not active as an envoy, and only rarely attended on foreign envoys to London. On 17 December 1528, Weston, accompanied by a sizeable retinue, was one of those who welcomed Venetian ambassador Luca Falier on his arrival in London and escorted him to his lodgings.[203] A second instance was in July 1535 when Weston attended on Charles Morette, the French ambassador in London, with similar duties.[204] It appears, then, that the Hospitaller Prior had been 'downgraded' to attend on envoys, rather than actively to negotiate with them.

Conclusion

Although Priors had partaken very occasionally in international relations in the thirteenth century, after 1264 the Prior was not included in a diplomatic mission until 1380. This was not because the Priors in between were untalented men, but that the king chose to employ their talents elsewhere, or not at all. Prior Joseph de Chauncy, for example, was never an envoy of Edward I, but served him well as treasurer of England between 1273 and 1280. Others served in administrative and military capacities, such as Philip de Thame, as keeper of Southampton in 1338–39. Between 1380 and 1440 the Priors' involvement in international relations was irregular and restricted to individual Priors. Hales and Radington were envoys, but Grendon, Hulles and Malory took virtually no part, although in the case of the latter two this may have been partly due to the long minority (1422–37) of Henry VI, when the king's council were reluctant to engage in important diplomacy. In contrast, from 1440 until 1527, diplomatic service for the king was common. Finally

[202] Clough, 'Late Fifteenth Century English Monarchs', 300.
[203] *CVSP, 1527–33*, 179–80, 185–6.
[204] *L&P HVIII 1535*, VIII, 402.

the last Prior before the Dissolution, William Weston (1527–40), was not part of a diplomatic mission, but did attend on foreign envoys visiting England.

One explanation for their participation in missions is geographical pragmatism. The Prior, based at Clerkenwell just north of London, was more convenient to call on than lords who had their seats in more remote areas of the country. This element of geographical convenience helps to explain the composition of the other members of missions. For example Warwick, as captain of Calais, headed the 1458 and 1466 negotiations with Burgundy partly because they were held in Calais. The Prior's position as Hospitaller Prior is another reason for inclusion in missions. From 1312, as head of the only military order in England (except for the much smaller Order of St Thomas), he was an appropriate envoy, most notably, to the Teutonic Knights and Hanseatic League. It is no coincidence that one of the first missions (in 1451) headed by the Prior of St John was to the Teutonic Knights.

A third reason, perhaps, is the particular skills in information gathering specific to training in a military order. The Hospitallers often used espionage to keep themselves informed of the Ottomans, Mamluks and their other rivals in the eastern Mediterranean, the Venetians. Many English Hospitallers, including Thomas Docwra, served at St Peter's Castle on the Anatolian coast, from where they could report on Ottoman military manoeuvres.[205] In Europe, the Prior, in common with ecclesiastical diplomats, enjoyed a greater geographical freedom and diplomatic immunity than was the case for most lay envoys. His pan-European connections as a member of an international military order with preceptories all over Europe allowed him access to a potential network of information that was able to report on military as well as diplomatic developments. Familiarity with intelligence work and training in a military order qualified those Priors skilled in these spheres as suitable envoys who could, apart from fulfilling their diplomatic duties, gather and, crucially, comprehend other useful information, such as the movement of enemy troops. Contemporary correspondence shows that the Grand Master regularly gave the king, and later Wolsey, updates on Turkish manoeuvres. These dispatches also confirm that the reason for the initial five-year service on Rhodes was military training. In a letter of July 1515 Henry VIII, after his requests to the Grand Master had not been successful, wrote to Pope Leo X that Richard Neville, the brother of both George Lord Abergavenny and court favourite Sir Edward Neville, had recently completed his military education at Rhodes, and requested a preceptory for him.[206]

If proximity to London, the Prior's status as Prior, or special training alone explained his inclusion in diplomatic missions, then why were not all Hospitaller Priors envoys? Regular service as an envoy only started with Prior Botyll who served

---

[205] Docwra, then turcopolier, was elected captain of St Peter's Castle on 23 March 1499, J. Mizzi, *Catalogue of the Records of the Order of St John in the Royal Malta Library*, ed. A. Gabaretta and J. Mizzi, Valletta, 1970, II, I, 85 (NLM 78, f. 83); Luttrell, 'English Contributions to the Hospitaller Castle at Bodrum', 166, 168; O'Malley, *English Knights Hospitaller*, 316–317.

[206] *L&P HVIII 1515–1516*, II, 64, 190. The later report on Ottoman movements mentions an English Hospitaller, Thomas Sheffield, as captain of St Peter's Castle, *ibid.*, 195. He was writing to request the next vacant preceptory for Neville, as the Grand Master had not answered his request, but Neville had to wait a further four years before his appointment to Willoughton.

in various ambassadorial roles over a period of over 20 years. He was an envoy every year between 1447 and 1451 and then for regular periods up until his death in 1468. This is a significant contrast to previous Priors, who had served only occasionally as envoys. It is important to note this because it has not been observed previously. An abrupt change took place from the appointment of Robert Botyll. Just why this was is difficult to say, but possible explanations will be explored below. Firstly, it is possible that all Priors had the potential to be utilised as envoys, but that for various reasons this was not exploited, for example, because the Prior was occupied with assimilating Templar possessions in the first half of the fourteenth century or absent from England on Hospitaller duties up until the late 1440s. That three thirteenth-century Priors, and Priors Hales and Radington in the fourteenth century were used indicates this potential. Absence is a partial explanation, but it is not wholly satisfactory. Why, for example, did Prior Grendon only take part in one minor mission between 1406 and 1417, when we know that he was in England? Another issue raised is whether the Priors' increased service was due to the skill of individual Priors or part of a general trend of greater service. It seems unlikely that most Priors before 1440 were considered unsuitable to be envoys and that most after were. All Priors needed to have a common level of skills to attain their position, indicated in Henry VI's letter of support for Botyll to be confirmed as English Prior, in which he states the qualities needed.[207] Before 1440, Hales and Radington had proved their suitability in royal service. Furthermore, Grendon clearly had the potential to be a crown envoy, which is shown by his service as the Grand Master's ambassador to Theodore I, Byzantine despot of the Morea, in 1400. A key factor in the Priors' increased involvement in diplomacy from the mid-fifteenth century is their greater involvement in English politics more generally. As access to the king, controlled by household members like the chamberlain, became more difficult, a willingness to be involved in politics and diplomacy was one way to gain admission to the king's presence. It was desirable for any lord who wanted to preserve his interests to have such access, and the Prior, wishing the king to confirm Hospitaller privileges such as tax exemptions and allowing responsions, was no exception. Kings, of course, needed to require the Prior's service, but in making themselves available for service, Priors helped to bring this requirement to fruition.

The other envoys on the diplomatic missions in which the Prior was a part were fairly constant from the mid-fifteenth century. For example, Botyll was on several diplomatic missions with Vincent Clement, Thomas Kent and John Wenlock. Both Langstrother's missions were with Henry Sharp. John Weston was accompanied on missions by Thomas Langton and Henry Ainsworth, Kendal with Christopher Urswick and Docwra with Nicholas West. All states used specialists in the field of negotiations, especially lawyers, and this was a trend that increased from 1440. The implication is that the Prior was, from about 1450, part of a developing nucleus of 'professional' diplomats used by the crown, and as before mentioned, research indicates that this had materialised by the reign of Henry VIII.[208]

This general increase in service applied to ecclesiastics as well as lay members

---

[207] *Bekyngton Correspondence*, I, 79.
[208] Potter, 'Foreign Policy', 103.

of society. The composition of the embassies in which the Priors were involved suggests that there was an increase in service by ecclesiastics after the 1440s (see Figure 9). While lay members were in the majority in the later fourteenth and early fifteenth centuries, this began to change from about 1450 up until the advent of the Reformation. Those involved in these embassies were also government ministers. Judging from the composition of the embassies, it was mainly those from an ecclesiastical background who had the skills needed. The Prior of St John was especially useful because he had the required language skills and papal connections, and he was also skilled in the art of information gathering, as the (sadly rare) example of Weston in 1480 illustrates.[209] The skills needed to be an ambassador were partly to do with individual ability, but also a certain amount of training. Allen, looking at the Hospitallers in the Counter-Reformation, has suggested that the Order of St John was viewed by European monarchs and popes as a 'school for ambassadors' and that this role was of more use than their military function.[210] On the evidence presented in this chapter, this theory can also be applied to the Hospitallers in England from the latter half of the fifteenth century. It appears that similar patterns of service and co-operation with local rulers were occurring in other parts of Europe, such as Navarre and Aragon.[211]

There may have been a trend for greater involvement by lords generally, but why in particular did the Prior become involved? Firstly, the Prior's increased participation in English diplomacy coincides with the failure of the Christian powers in general and the military orders in particular to prevent the Turkish advance, poignantly demonstrated by the fall of Constantinople in 1453. The loss of Constantinople made the Hospitallers, the only military order in the eastern Mediterranean, more vulnerable to Ottoman attack and more reliant on the support of European monarchs. These monarchs in turn started to employ the talents of Priors and other Hospitaller brethren for their own use, taking advantage of their weakened position and, perhaps, greater availability. Although the ideal of crusading was still alive and attracted recruits, the immediate relevance of crusading had in effect gone for the leaders of Western Europe. They allowed the occasional indulgence to fund a crusade and muttered sympathetic noises, but took little other practical action. For example, Henry V, Edward IV and Richard III paid lip-service to the crusade ideal, but Henry IV was the last English king designated *crucesignatus*. Regional struggles and an emerging sense of 'nation' seemed to have triumphed over the idea of a united Christendom. The shift of emphasis towards serving the crown was a symptom of this general change in attitudes and allegiance. By the mid-fifteenth century, English Hospitallers, or at least English Priors, may have considered that their loyalty was due to their king first and their Order second. Previous Priors had served the crown, but in return had been allowed to go to Rhodes. Although serving the crown was a good policy for ensuring favour for the Order, that very few Priors

---

[209] The nature of espionage or information gathering means that it is hard to find firm evidence and such a role has to be inferred.

[210] D. Allen, 'The Order of St John as a "School for Ambassadors" in Counter-Reformation Europe', in *The Military Orders: Welfare and Warfare*, ed. H. Nicholson, Aldershot, 1998, 363–379.

[211] Barquero Goñi, 'The Hospitallers and the Kings of Navarre', 349–54.

(once they were Priors) from the mid-fifteenth century went to Rhodes, suggests an element of choice in serving the crown. It may be indicative of the sense of nation-hood that had developed during the Hundred Years War. These changes ushered in a new age of diplomacy, the era of the increasingly professional diplomat, and contributed to the Prior's increased participation both in diplomacy and in national politics.

The diplomatic role of the Prior in service to the crown increased during a time that saw the fall of Constantinople in 1453, three main sieges on Rhodes and the loss of that island in 1522. That is, it increased at exactly the time that one would expect the Prior to intensify his participation in Hospitaller activities. That the opposite happened from the 1440s reflects the changing priorities in this period and points to the secularisation of his office. For example, Docwra's attendance at the May 1522 meeting with Charles V was at a time when one might expect him to be engaged in Hospitaller duties. A month after the May meeting, the Ottoman Turks started their siege of Rhodes, which led to its capitulation in December 1522.[212] Yet Docwra's crown diplomatic duties continued unaffected in 1522 and 1523. Although he later commissioned an English translation of the account of the siege, he seems to have taken no part in plans for the recovery of Rhodes.[213]

The greater involvement of the Priors from the mid-fifteenth century is also indic-ative of a general secularisation of the Order. Many years ago, Jacob commented that it was 'an essential feature of the life of the upper ranks of lay society in later medieval England that the road to success lay in the service of the crown'.[214] This trend was mirrored by the Prior, the English Hospitallers and their relations. John Kendal, for example, acted as an ambassador for Henry VII while still turcopolier. As the Grand Master's proctor in Rome, he was usefully placed for diplomatic missions for the king and was in contact with the other resident English proc-tors in Rome.[215] William Weston, also as turcopolier, performed minor diplomatic duties before becoming Prior, his non-Hospitaller brother Richard made his career in royal service and his nephew Francis was a court favourite. The trend is also apparent from the development of the preceptor of Torphichen's diplomatic role for the Scottish crown, especially in the person of Sir William Knollis, in the later fifteenth century, who served as treasurer under both James III and IV.[216] Leading Hospitallers like the Prior, with a knowledge of military law gained through their membership of the Order, were valuable members of embassies, especially those that dealt with infractions of truces.

Although there was a trend towards secularisation of the Hospitallers, it was never total. The drop in the Prior's diplomatic contribution coincided with the Reformation Parliament of 1529–36. Although Weston demonstrated his loyalty to

212 *L&P HVIII 1521–1523*, III, 1196.

213 *Ibid.*, 1191–3.

214 E. F. Jacob, *The Fifteenth Century 1399–1485*, Oxford, 1961, 326.

215 We know that the English Hospitallers had links with St Thomas's Hospice in Rome from at least 1445, when it received gifts from Prior Botyll and the turcopolier, Hugh Middleton, see Harvey, *England, Rome and the Papacy*, 54.

216 *Rot. Scot.*, II, 495–6, 514; R. Nicholson, *Scotland, The Later Middle Ages*, Edinburgh, 1974, 532; *HBC*, 187–8; Macdougall, *James IV*, 50, 80, 95; see also Macquarrie, *Scotland and the Crusades*, for general comment on Knollis.

Henry by signing the letter in support of his divorce and not challenging the with-drawal of obedience from Rome, the legislation of the following years such as the Acts of Supremacy, Dispensations and Appeals all brought the Order further under crown control.[217] In the November 1534 parliament, it was proposed that Weston was to have 1,000 marks a year and the rest of his possessions were to go to the king. At his death, all was to go to the king, as were the possessions of the precep-tors on their deaths.[218] This did not happen until the suppression of the Order in 1540, but such discussion was bound to affect the status of the Prior both at home and abroad.

While the diplomatic missions that the English Prior took part in are well known to historians of late medieval England, the role of the Prior in these missions is not the focal point of their research. Historians of the crusades know the outline of some of the Priors' duties for the crown, but tend to concentrate on Anglo-Hospi-taller relations and conflict with the lay authorities. They also implicitly assume that the main tasks of the Prior were the good management of the English Priory and the collection of responsions for the struggle in the east and to minimise his duties to the crown. The research presented in this chapter indicates that the function of the Prior in the realm of English diplomacy was greater than has previously been assumed and brings into question the general orthodoxy on his main duties and loyalties.

---

[217] *SR*, III, 454–5, 460–1, 498.
[218] *L&P HVIII 1534*, VII, 515; See BL MS Cotton Cleopatra E. IV, f. 174.

Figure 5: Number of diplomatic duties for the crown, 1380–95[219]

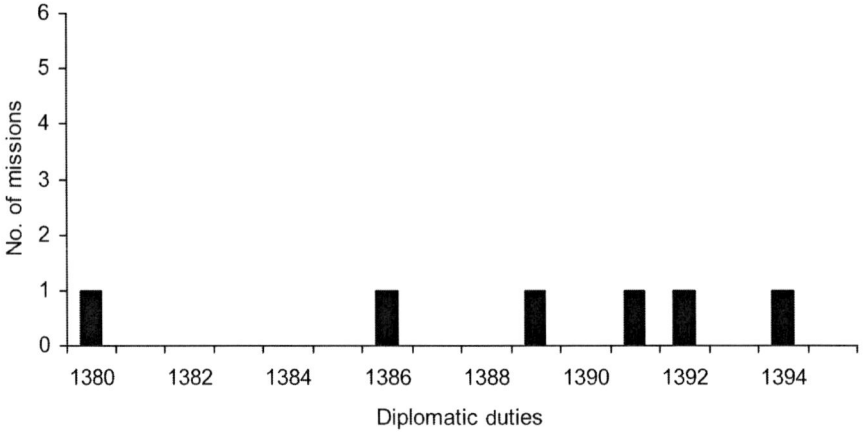

Figure 6: Number of diplomatic duties for the crown, 1440–67

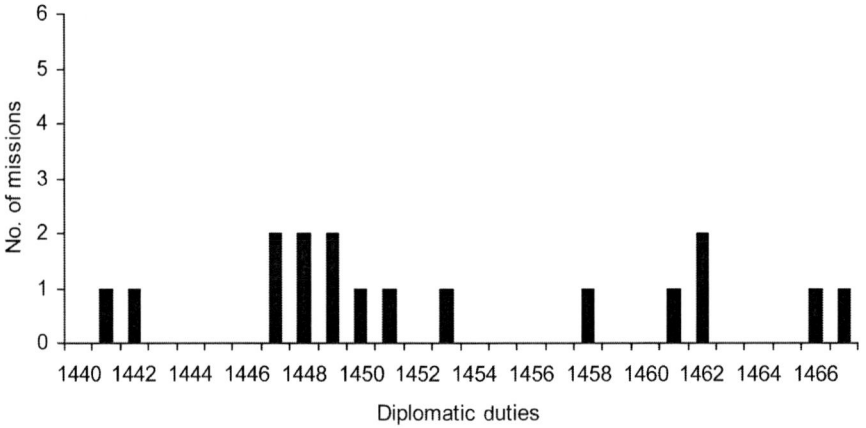

[219] Figures 5 to 9 are based on the various sources fully referenced in the footnotes, including TNA C 71, C 76, E 30; BL MS Cotton Galba B VII; BL MS MS Royal 13 B XI; BL Egerton Charter 208; *Foedera*, Hague; *Rot. Parl.*; *CCR*; *CPR*; *CFR*; *L&P HVIII*.

Figure 7: Number of diplomatic duties for the crown, 1470–1501

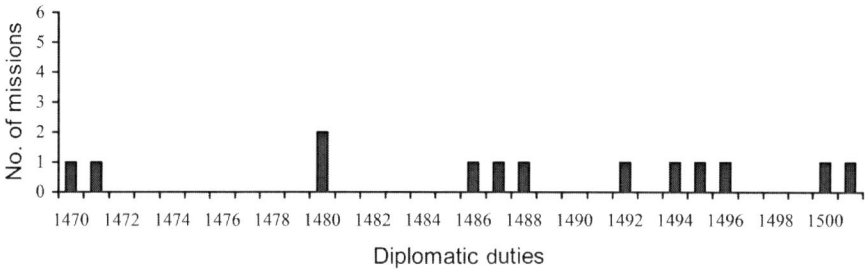

Figure 8: Number of diplomatic duties for the crown, 1506–35

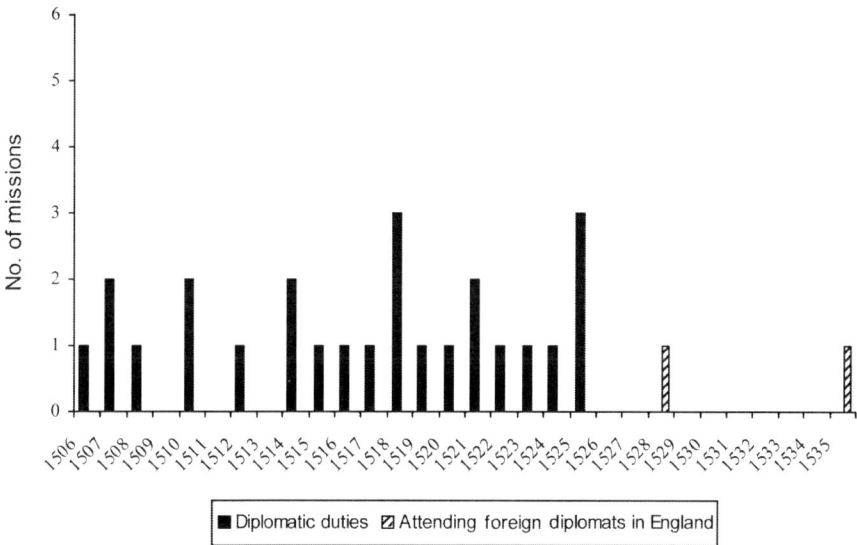

■ Diplomatic duties ☑ Attending foreign diplomats in England

Figure 9: Percentage of ecclesiastic to lay members in embassies containing the Prior, 1380–1525

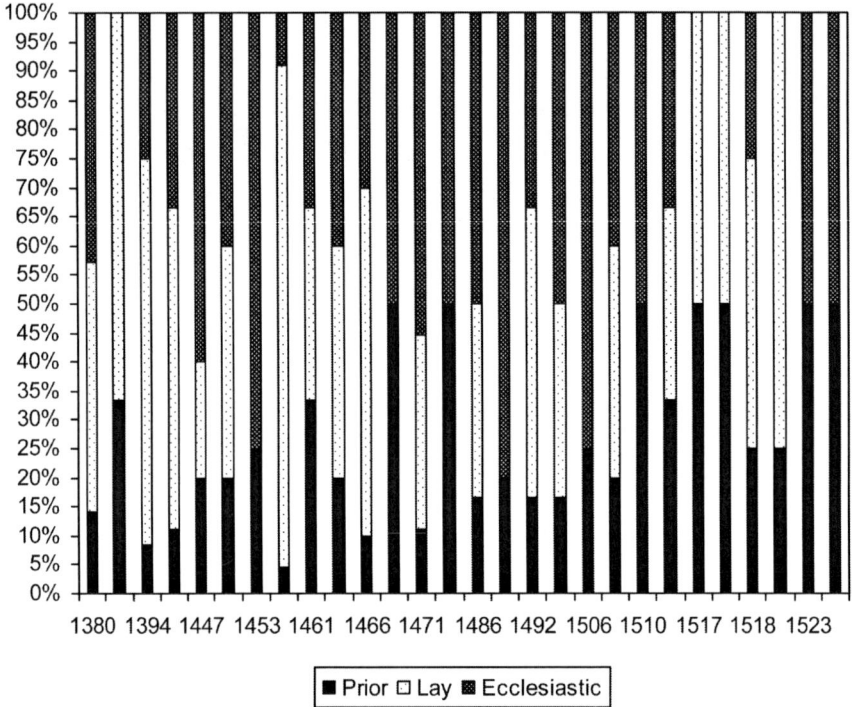

5

National Statesman

'… and so by the counsel of Merlin, the
king let call his barons to council.'[1]

The aim of this chapter is to establish what part the Prior of St John played in
internal politics in England. It will concentrate on his service to the crown as a lay
lord, instead of his role as mediator between the Grand Master in the East and the
local ruler. Rather than deal with the development of parliament and council generally, which has been fully dealt with elsewhere, it will focus on the Prior's activities in
parliament, great council, and king's council.[2] In the process, it will comment on the
misconceptions about the Prior's role in English politics that appear in crusading
histories.

The king took advice, both informally from those he sought counsel, and formally
in parliament, great council, and in king's council. It is the formal gatherings that
are treated here. It is not always easy to define which gathering is which and the
terminology used often confuses matters further. For example, those summoned to
meet in London in September 1297 were to meet with 'others of king's council'
to advise Prince Edward, yet the summons went out to 50 people, which indicates
it was a great council, rather than a meeting of the king's council, and the *Handbook of British Chronology* designates it as a parliament.[3] Furthermore, the research
presented in this chapter suggests that Nicolas' collection of 'privy' council proceedings, extracted from manuscripts in the British Library, contains many meetings
that were really great councils. This adds weight to Dunham's suspicions that many

---

[1] *Le Morte Darthur: Sir Thomas Malory's Book of King Arthur and his Noble Knights of the Round Table*, 2
vols, ed. A. W. Pollard, London, 1900, I, 15.

[2] Apart from the other works mentioned in the text, for the development of council and parliament, see Baldwin, *The King's Council*; N. B. Lewis, 'The "Continual Council" in the Early Years
of Richard II, 1377–80', *EHR*, XLI, 1926, 246–51; E. B. Fryde and E. Miller, eds, *Historical
Studies of the English Parliament*, 2 vols, Cambridge, 1970; G. R. Elton, 'The Early Journals of
the House of Lords', *EHR*, LXXXIX, 1974, 481–512; G. O. Sayles, *The King's Parliament of
England*, London, 1975, 131; J. R. Lander, *Crown and Nobility 1450–1509*, London, 1976; R. G.
Davies and J. H. Denton, eds, *The English Parliament in the Middle Ages*, Manchester, 1981; Brown,
Late Medieval England; A. Goodman, 'Richard II's Councils', in *Richard II: The Art of Kingship*, ed.
A. Goodman and J. Gillespie, Oxford, 1999, 59–82.

[3] *CCR 1296–1302*, 128; *HBC*, 550.

of the records in the *Proceedings and Ordinances of the Privy Council of England* were not king's council, but records of parliament.[4] These difficulties of definition are symptomatic of the close relationship between king's council, great council and parliament. Nevertheless, they can be given separate definitions. The king's council was a regular, usually small, gathering (continual during law terms) of those appointed by the king. Some of its members were constantly in the presence of the king, but increasingly during the late middle ages it made its home at Westminster, and when the king was not there, messengers of the council were sent to him (e.g. to Windsor) for his assent to decisions. The king was not required to inform parliament or great council of the membership of king's council, even on the occasions that it was requested, although this was required in certain circumstances, such as for Henry VI's minority. Indeed, during times of royal minority or madness, those who served on the king's council wanted parliamentary assent in order to avoid accusations of seizing power or misgovernance. The great council was an occasional, summoned, gathering of all the lords and select others. It was often called when urgent business needed to be discussed that could not wait for parliamentary elections. A parliament was a summoned meeting of the lords (i.e. great council), plus elected knights of the counties and others, when considered necessary, such as burgesses. Both parliaments and great councils discussed the same business, with great council often meeting a few days before, and continuing after, parliament, and for this reason they will be considered together in the sections below, so as not to distort the interlinking nature and development of these summoned assemblies.

Parliament and Great Council

This section will examine the development of the Prior's summons to parliament and great council, his place in parliamentary precedence, his pattern of attendance where it can be ascertained, and what he did when he was there. It is likely that the Prior was summoned to parliaments and great councils before 1295, but it is only from this date that records of those summoned became usual practice. Before 1295, summonses only exist for the January 1265 parliament, to which the Prior was summoned, and for 1283, to which he was not summoned.[5] In contrast, lists of summonses exist for all but four parliaments between 1295 and 1540, so it is only from 1295 that the pattern of summonses for the Prior can be discussed.[6]

---

4   See the numerous entries in vols I–VI of *POPC*; W. H. Dunham, ' "The Books of Parliament" and "The Old Record", 1396–1504', *Speculum*, LI, 1976, 694–712 at 706–7.

5   *RDP*, III, 34 (for 1265).

6   J. E. Powell and K. Wallis, *The House of Lords in the Middle Ages*, London, 1968, 219. Lists do not exist for the parliaments of July 1297 and Easter 1298, great council of May 1324 and the 1478 parliament, so they are not included in figures 11 and 12 under the number of parliaments and great councils summoned.

Summonses to great council and parliament

As far as can be known, the Prior was summoned both to great council and to parliament from the time that records begin, regardless of where they were held. In the writs of summonses he is listed with the abbots, master of the Order of Sempringham and the master of the Templars, but his position in the list of summonses varies and cannot be used as an indication of precedence. Between 1295 and 1330 the Prior received summons to parliament with increasing regularity (see Figure 10). From 1330 onwards, he was summoned to almost all parliaments. The same pattern occurs for summonses to great council, irregular at first, but more common after 1330. The change to a more regular summons is explained by the more frequent presence of the Prior in England. Normally writs were issued to those within the realm at the time of summons, or those expected to be at the time of parliament. This is clear when one considers, for example, that the Prior was summoned to Edward II's coronation (25 February) on 18 January 1308, but the very next day (19 January) he was excluded from the lists of summons to the parliament due on 3 March.[7] He was expected to leave the realm shortly after the coronation, as the licences and letters of protection testify.

If one looks at the parliaments and great councils to which the Prior was not summoned, they tend to coincide with his absence from the realm. Prior Tothale was not summoned to the three parliaments of 1308 or the great council of February 1309. This matches with letters of protection granted to him on 30 October 1307 to go abroad on Hospitaller business and a renewal of these on 15 November 1308.[8] His absence is further indicated by the lack of his presentations to ecclesiastical benefices during this period (see Appendix 2), the last being on 22 December 1307 and the next one not until 4 March 1309, the same day he received a summons to the April 1309 parliament.[9] Although Prior Richard Pavely was not summoned to the two great councils of 1317, his letters of protection were granted on the same day that the April parliament was summoned (14 March).[10] Finally, Prior Archer was not summoned to the five parliaments between January 1327 and July 1328. This is explained by a combination of absence abroad, as letters of protection indicate, and failing health, possibly aggravated by the Hospitallers' serious financial problems at that time.[11] The Prior's regular summonses continued in the fifteenth and sixteenth centuries, with the only noticeable absences in the 1420s and for the 1504 parliament again explained by absence abroad (see Figure 11).

---

[7] *RDP*, III, 176.

[8] *CPR 1307–1313*, 10, 143. The letters of protection follow soon after the dissolution of the October 1307 parliament, and it is possible that he petitioned for them in that parliament.

[9] *RDP*, III, 188.

[10] *CPR 1313–1317*, 624. Again, he made no presentations during this time.

[11] *CPR 1324–1327*, 295; *CPR 1327–1330*, 1, 42, 192; *CCR 1327–1330*, 211, 235–6, 359, 365, 379; The decision to replace Prior Archer with Prior Tibertis of Venice had been taken by 1 May 1328 (*CPL 1305–1342*, 488) and Tibertis was voted Prior elect at the Melchbourne provincial chapter of late June and early July that year, subject to confirmation by the Grand Master, 1338 Survey, 215. However, this confirmation did not come until the chapter general at Montpellier in late October 1330 to take effect from 24 June 1331, NLM, 280, f. 2v. Accordingly, until his death in late August 1330, Prior Archer continued to sign recognisances jointly with the Prior elect, and was still summoned to parliaments and great councils in 1328, 1329 and 1330.

What determined the Prior's summons, then, was whether he was expected to be in England when parliament was held. Given that there is evidence, even if limited, of summonses both to parliament and great council in the thirteenth century and that the lack of summonses from the fourteenth century until the dissolution of the Order can be explained either by absence from the realm, illness, an interregnum between Priors, or other services to the king, it seems likely that the Prior from at least the mid-thirteenth century was always summoned to both great council and parliament.

Precedence

This long tradition of summons had implications for the Prior's precedence in parliament, which dispels some longstanding misconceptions on the Prior's place in parliament. It has been stated by a number of historians that the Prior was 'the premier baron of England, ranking above all other lay barons'.[12] This was perhaps true from the mid-fifteenth century and definitely for the early Tudor period, but it was not always so. It is likely that from its inception seating in parliament mirrored the general stratification of late medieval English society, but this cannot be confirmed due to the lack of records: the imaginary plan of a parliament of Edward I is from the Wriothesley manuscript and is thus sixteenth-century in origin.[13]

Although the Prior was summoned to parliament with the spiritual lords, this was not necessarily an indication that he was considered a spiritual lord, or that his place in parliament matched his place on the summons lists, especially as the latter varied. However, the evidence in the parliamentary rolls suggests both that there was some association with the spiritual lords and that his status was changing from the mid-fourteenth century. In 1322, the parliamentary writs refer to Prior Archer as a knight or banneret, the rank below baron.[14] One would think that this firmly placed the Prior as a temporal lord, yet in both 1339 and 1346 Prior Thame was not even listed with the temporal lords in parliament for the granting of aids for war, but amongst the spiritual lords.[15] From 1362 to 1369 Prior Pavely was placed in the lists of triers of petitions in parliament after the spiritual lords and before the earls, a sign that the Prior's status was changing (see Figure 16).[16] This was also the situation for Prior Hales' first years of office, as indicated in 1376, when he was below the bishops and above the earls in a list of 34 names in parliament concerning mainpernors for Lord Latimer, and in 1378, when he was listed below the abbots and above the earls as a trier of petitions.[17] The Prior's position appears to have changed in

---

[12] Tyerman, *England and Crusades*, 355; Sarnowsky, 'Kings and Priors', 85; O'Malley, *English Knights Hospitaller*, 61.

[13] Powell and Wallis, *House of Lords*, Plate XXI, between 492 and 493.

[14] *Parliamentary Writs*, I, 588.

[15] *Rot. Parl.*, II, 103–4, 158. In 1339 he was placed between the dean of York and the abbot of Westminster. In 1446 he was between the abbot of Westminster and the Prior of Canterbury.

[16] *Rot. Parl.*, II, 268, 275, 283, 289, 294, 300. The Prior's role as a trier of petitions is discussed later in the chapter.

[17] *Rot. Parl.*, II, 326–7; *ibid.*, III, 34. See Holmes, *The Good Parliament*, 101–7 for more on the accusations against Latimer.

1379. Firstly, the 1379 parliament decided that Prior Hales would be assessed for the poll tax as a baron, affirming his status as a temporal lord, although he was paid for his service on the 1378–9 minority council according to the wages of a banneret.[18] Moreover, as Powell and Wallis note, by 1381 a distinction had emerged between barons and bannerets and the Prior came between the two.[19] As a trier of petitions in 1379 and (January) 1380, Hales was placed amongst the earls, perhaps due to his increased importance on the minority council.[20] Finally, as a trier of petitions between 1383 and 1385, Prior Radington was once placed between abbots and earls, and three times listed with the barons, but not as the head baron, being below Lord Fitzwalter.[21] All of this evidence suggests that, in the later fourteenth century, the Prior's position in parliamentary precedence was still fluid, although there was a clear move away from the spiritual lords towards association as a temporal lord from the mid-fourteenth century. This was a reflection of the variability of status amongst the temporal lords at this time. Brown has commented that the lords were becoming status conscious by the mid-fourteenth century, indicated by the creation of new titles, the first duke being created in 1337 and first marquis in 1385. Baronial status was also changing from being held by tenure to being hereditary, and there was a sub-division between barons and bannerets.[22] During this period, disputes over rank arose frequently, the first noted case being in 1405 and others continuing into Henry VI's reign.[23]

From 1415 until the Dissolution the Prior was (with two exceptions) placed below earls or viscounts and above the barons as a trier of petitions, an indication that an order of precedence was solidifying during the first half of the fifteenth century.[24] Other evidence verifies this. The presence lists for the Winchester session of the 1449 parliament list the Prior separately, below the duke of Suffolk and above Lord Roos.[25] The Prior is listed above the barons on 30 November 1453 and on 15 March 1454.[26] He was also listed ahead of the barons in the 1455 commission in parliament to strengthen Calais and Berwick.[27] Finally, the daily attendance lists for the 1461 parliament and those from 1509 onwards confirm that the Prior maintained

[18] *Rot. Parl.* III, 58; TNA E 403/475, m. 19.

[19] Powell and Wallis, *House of Lords*, 390.

[20] *Rot. Parl.*, III, 34, 56–7.

[21] *Ibid.*, 151, 167, 185, 204. He was below Lord Fitzwalter in 1383, November 1384 and 1385, and in between the abbot of Hyde and the earl of Oxford in April 1384.

[22] A. L. Brown, 'Parliament, c. 1377–1422', in *The English Parliament in the Middle Ages*, Manchester, ed. R. G. Davies and J. H. Denton, 1981, 109–40 at 114–15.

[23] *Ibid.*, 115.

[24] *Rot. Parl.*, IV, 63, 368; V, 4, 66–7, 129, 278–9, 345, 373, 461–2, 496, 571; VI, 3, 167, 410, 458, 509–10; *Lords Journals*, I, 18–19, lxxvi. The exceptions were 1445 when, although below the earls, the abbots are placed between the Prior and the barons, and 1497 when Lord Dynham was above the Prior.

[25] A. R. Myers, 'A Parliamentary Debate of the Mid-Fifteenth Century', *Bulletin of the John Rylands Library*, XXII, 1938, 388–404 at 402.

[26] R. A. Griffiths, 'The King's Council and the First Protectorate of the Duke of York, 1453–54', *EHR*, XCIX, 1984, 67–82 at 78; *Rot. Parl.*, V, 249.

[27] *Ibid.*, 279–80.

his status ahead of the barons until the dissolution of the Order.[28] The conclusion must be that during the first half of the fifteenth century, the Prior established his right to be placed above the barons. Why this became important is indicated by a later statute of 1539 for the placing of lords in parliament, which stated that all nobility (from dukes down to barons) not holding specific office 'shall sytt and be placed after ther Auncientes as it hathe ben accustomed'.[29] This meant that precedence was decided by the hereditary right, the older the first sitting, the more senior the placing. Such issues were still active in the mid-fifteenth century, as shown by the debate on 20 March 1449 on whether the earl of Arundel in the parliamentary session of October to December 1433 should have been there by new creation or re-admission to his old inheritance.[30] As the Prior's inheritance was not dependent on the production of an heir of the body, it was quite natural that over time he came to be the most senior baron. It is possible that, informally, he was accepted as such at an earlier stage, but it was not until the gradual development of a more formal structure in parliament in the late fourteenth century that precedence of all lords in parliament became an issue.[31] This was linked to the simultaneous development of hereditary right to attend parliament, and led to an increase in attendance at parliament and great council during the fifteenth century.

Attendance at great council and parliament

Figures 10 and 11 indicate that the Prior attended parliament and great council for at least some days during a session, but that is as accurate as one can be before the mid-fifteenth century. Presumably Priors who were triers of petitions were present more often, but they may have been tied up in these meetings rather than in the parliamentary chamber.[32] Evidence of attendance is not as common as summonses. It can be discovered by references in chronicles, petitions in parliament (usually the petitioner was there), the corresponding letters patent, if granted, the rare noted attendances in the rolls of parliament, triers of petitions records, and from the fragments of attendance in the fifteenth century. The lords' journals, from the reign of

---

[28] *The Fane Fragment of the 1461 Lords' Journal*, ed. W. H. Dunham, New Haven, CT, 1935, 3–25; R. L. Virgoe, 'A New Fragment of the Lords' Journal of 1461', *BIHR*, XXXII, 1959, 83–7 at 86–7; BL MS Harley 158, ff. 113–43; K. G. Madison, 'The Seating of the Barons in Parliament, December 1461', *Mediaeval Studies*, XXXVII, 1975, 494–503.

[29] *SR*, III, 1817, 729–30.

[30] *EHD 1327–1485*, IV, 469.

[31] Brown, 'Parliament, c. 1377–1422', 115–16.

[32] Triers of English petitions met in the painted chamber. Triers of overseas petitions met in the Marcolf chamber (named after the mural in that chamber of the dialogues between Solomon and the demon-like being Marcolf). The exact location of the Marcolf chamber is not known, but it was a separate chamber from the white or lesser hall, where the lords met during parliament, *Close Rolls of the Reign of Henry III*, 14 vols, London, 1902–38, VII (1251–3), 290; E. W. Tristram, *English Medieval Wall Painting. The Thirteenth Century*, 2 vols, Oxford, 1950, I, 89, 104; E. W. Tristram, *English Wall Painting of the Fourteenth Century*, London, 1955, 206; P. Binski, *The Painted Chamber at Westminster*, London, 1986, 22, 43, 165; S. Thurley, *The Royal Palaces of Tudor England: Architecture and Court Life 1460–1547*, New Haven, CT, and London, 1993, 5, 6, 7, 209, 259.

Henry VIII, give us a more accurate idea of the Prior's attendance during parliament up until the dissolution of the Order.

The extant evidence suggests that the Prior attended the parliaments and great councils to which he was summoned when in England. Indeed it was in his interest to do so, to uphold the interests of his order. There are very few direct references to the Prior attending parliament in the first half of the fourteenth century, but two exist, for October 1339 and September 1346.[33] However, there are other ways to discover his attendance. It is known, for example, that he attended the February 1305 parliament, because he presented a petition.[34] The presentation of a petition indicates attendance because, as Brand has noted, responses to petitions were given orally as well as in writing, which implies that the petitioner was there.[35] According to Brand, many petitions do not appear on the parliamentary rolls.[36] If so, this disguises the presence of many who attended parliament, including the Prior, but his presence can be reconstructed from related contemporary material. One example surrounds the petition for the Templar lands in 1313. On 25 November 1313, at a king's council meeting at Westminster, the Grand Master's representatives (Brothers Alberto de Nigro Castro and Leonard de Tibertis) requested transfer of the Templars' possessions, and this was granted by letters patent three days later.[37] That the request took place just ten days after parliament was dissolved indicates that it was a referral of a petition originally made at parliament, in which case the Prior was probably at parliament as the petitioner. The link between letters patent and petition in parliament is further indicated in the fifteenth century by Prior Botyll's letters patent of 30 May 1450, granting him wages for diplomatic service from the customs and subsidies. These were issued at Leicester during the parliament there.[38] There is also evidence of attendance at great councils from the 1330s, such as the great council of February 1346, but it is likely that the Prior attended such assemblies much earlier.[39] The attendance of the Prior at parliament is more certain from 1362, when he first became a regular trier of petitions.

Up to this point we have been able to identify that the Prior was both summoned to and attended parliament from the thirteenth century. However, it is not until the mid-fifteenth century that one can ascertain the regularity of his attendance during parliament, and what he did when there. The published extracts of the parliaments and great councils of 1449, 1454 and 1461 give a better indication on these issues, while also illustrating the close relationship of business between parliament, great council and king's council.[40] In 1938, Myers published a transcript of Harley MS

[33] *Rot. Parl.*, II, 103, 158.

[34] *Memoranda de Parliamento: Records of the Parliament Holden at Westminster 1305*, ed. F. W. Maitland, Rolls Series, London, 1893, 201.

[35] P. Brand, 'Petitions and Parliament in the Reign of Edward I', in *Parchment and People*, 14–38 at 37.

[36] *Ibid.*, 23.

[37] TNA E 30/1368, 25 November 1313; *CPR 1313–1317*, 52, 28 November 1313; TNA E 135/1/25, 5 December 1313 for formal receipt of the Templars' possessions.

[38] *CPR 1446–1452*, 376.

[39] *Rot. Parl.*, II, 453.

[40] For 1449, Myers, 'Parliamentary Debate of the Mid-Fifteenth Century'; W. H. Dunham, 'Notes from the Parliament at Winchester, 1449', *Speculum*, XVII, 1942, 402–15; A. R. Myers,

6849, which had two main parts to it; a list of 33 lords who attended the Winchester session (16 June–16 July) of the 1449 parliament, and a debate of 14 lords on an unspecified day (which he later identified as 19 June) of that session on the best way to obtain supplies to send troops to Normandy and Guienne.[41] Myers noted that Prior Botyll appears in the list of those attending the Winchester session, but did not secure a writ of summons to the parliament, the first session of which opened at Westminster on 12 February 1449.[42] Dunham then suggested that Botyll was probably out of the country on diplomatic duty when the summons was issued in January.[43] He was right, as Botyll was on a mission to France and then to the Pope from 23 August 1447 until 6 June 1449.[44] Botyll was not noted at any of the four days for which records exist for the Westminster session and was not appointed as a trier of petitions at this parliament.[45] It is likely that he did not take part in the debate of 19 June, because he had not returned from abroad although, as Dunham has noted, he had returned by 26 June, when his petition concerning fairs and markets was granted by charter at Winchester.[46]

The next indication of attendance on specific days comes from 1453–54, in between the third and fourth sessions of parliament, and during the fourth session.[47] On 30 November 1453, 16 days after parliament had been prorogued, the Prior was one of 52 lords to swear allegiance to Henry VI.[48] Although this meeting was held in the star chamber, it was clearly a great council, as was the next meeting on 5 December. At the latter, 21 lords including the Prior 'assembled in gret counsel as peres of the land' (as opposed to when they met as king's council) and stated that they acted only for the good of the realm during the king's infirmity and until they received greater authority (from parliament).[49] Of the 21 present, only 14 signed, perhaps an indication of who was serving on king's council that month (seven of the 14 served at king's council the next day), but also perhaps showing a reluctance of the others (including Botyll) to serve without parliamentary approval.[50] It is known from the extant records that Botyll attended at least six days of the fourth

'A Parliamentary Debate of 1449', *BIHR*, LI, 1978, 78–83; R. A. Griffiths, 'The Winchester Session of the 1449 Parliament: A Further Comment', *The Huntington Library Quarterly*, XLII, 1979, 181–91; For 1454, BL Harley MS 158, f. 113–113v; Griffiths, 'King's Council and the First Protectorate', 67–82; Dunham, 'Books of Parliament', 694–712; For 1461, see *Fane Fragment*; Virgoe, 'New Fragment', 83–7; Madison, 'Seating of the Barons', 494–503.

[41] Myers, 'Parliamentary Debate of the Mid-Fifteenth Century', 402–4; Myers, 'Parliamentary Debate of 1449', 82.
[42] Myers, 'Parliamentary Debate of the Mid-Fifteenth Century', 394.
[43] Dunham, 'Parliament at Winchester', 406.
[44] TNA E 101/324/15.
[45] *EHD 1327–1485*, IV, 469, 20–1 March, 24 March; Myers, 'Parliamentary Debate of 1449', 81–2, 4 April; *Rot. Parl.*, V, 141.
[46] Dunham, 'Parliament at Winchester', 406.
[47] Griffiths, 'King's Council and First Protectorate', 67–82. Although *HBC* suggests that parliament may still have been in session on 16 April, the entry for 4 April refers to those there as the 'remnant of the Lords', suggesting the other lords had left, *ibid.*, 79.
[48] Griffiths, 'King's Council and First Protectorate', 77–8. Twenty-one of the 22 future protectorate councillors were there. Thirty-one swore the oath that did not serve on the first protectorate and it is clear that all spiritual and temporal lords were expected to take the oath.
[49] *Ibid.*, 78–9.
[50] *POPC*, VI, 164–5.

session of parliament (February–April 1454), when a formal council was established. On 15 March, he was listed as one of 22 in parliament commissioned to create Edward, heir of Henry VI, Prince of Wales and earl of Chester.[51] He was present on 23 March, as one of 12 chosen to go to the king at Windsor and get permission for business such as the appointment of a new chancellor and archbishop of Canterbury, and appointment of a formal king's council.[52] He was also present on 25 March, when the result of the visit was reported to parliament.[53] He attended on 30 March and 2 April, when the letter to the Pope recommending the bishop of Ely as the new archbishop of Canterbury was drawn up and a new chancellor was appointed.[54] Finally, he was in parliament on 4 April, when a new council was named, with the duke of York as protector.[55] On this day, there appears to have been a special meeting after parliament (hence the reference to the 'remnant of the lords') of those who were to serve on the council, in order to get their agreement to serve. Botyll's reply states that he asked to be excused because of his Hospitaller commitments, but assented on condition that the commons be informed of the financial state of the land and the duties the council was to perform.[56] All of the lords expressed their reluctance to serve with one excuse or another to counter accusations of seeking power, but given Botyll's regular attendance from May through to July inclusive, it is likely that he was quite happy to serve on the king's council, subject to not being held responsible for financial mismanagement.[57] His statement, with the request for the commons to be informed, shows he had a good knowledge of parliamentary procedure and the astuteness to ensure that his appointment had the widest backing. From the extant records of this fourth session, then, it is tentatively suggested that Botyll was attending parliament regularly and was deeply involved with its business. This was matched, as shall be shown, by a deep engagement in king's council during these years.

The next insight into attendance is provided from the extracts of the 1461 lords' journal.[58] The parliament was held from 4 November until 21 December, a period of 41 parliamentary days of which the fragment covers only ten days of the latter part of the session. As with 1449 and 1454, it is a glimpse and no more into the attendance habits of those summoned. Information on 8 December is incomplete, so there are only seven days for which full information on attendance is known. Virgoe has also found copies of attendance lists for 5 and 12 December, but as there are no dots or a 'p' to indicate presence, it is not known if those listed actu-

---

[51] *Rot. Parl.*, V, 249. The full list was the archbishop of Canterbury, the archbishop of York, the bishops of London, Durham, Salisbury, Ely, Norwich, Lincoln, Carlisle, the dukes of York and Buckingham, the earls of Pembroke, Warwick, Oxford, Salisbury and Wiltshire, Viscounts Beaumont and Bourgchier, the Prior of St John, lords Fauconburgh, Willoughby and Stourton. This commission appeared on the patent rolls on 13 April, *CPR 1452–1461*, 171–2.

[52] *Rot. Parl.*, V, 240.

[53] *Ibid.*, 241.

[54] *Ibid.*, 450.

[55] Griffiths, 'King's Council and First Protectorate', 79–81. Twenty-two lords are named, including the duke of York.

[56] *Ibid.*, 81.

[57] TNA E 28/84–5.

[58] See *Fane Fragment*; Virgoe, 'New Fragment', *passim.*

ally attended.[59] Given the numbers listed, 75 and 72 respectively, they are likely to be lists of those expected to attend, rather than actual attendance. In addition, as Roskell has pointed out, the unusually large attendance was due to its being Edward IV's first parliament. It is probably unrepresentative of other parliaments in this period.[60] Despite these provisos, actual day-to-day attendance varies enough to give some idea of the attendance habits. First of all, of the 93 lords summoned, 80 are listed as attending. The Prior attended on all seven days for which records exist and was also present on the first day of parliament on 4 November when he was appointed a trier of English petitions.[61] Botyll may have also attended on two other days, on 7 November when licence was given for Brothers John Langstrother (Castellan of Rhodes) and Cencio de Orsini (preceptor of Rome) to carry out a visitation,[62] and on 12 November when Botyll was commissioned, with two others, to determine infractions of the truce with the duke of Burgundy.[63] His attendance appears very good compared to the other barons, of whom only six out of 34 matched the Prior's attendance.[64] Of the abbots, only six of 21 equalled the Prior's attendance, and only one of the six earls.[65] With the exception of the king and the archbishops of Canterbury and York, who attended on all eight days for which information exists, only the bishops made a decent showing in comparison with the Prior and even then less than half (seven out of 16) equalled his attendance.[66] On this evidence, scanty though it may be, the Prior's record of attendance seems to be regular and complements the evidence for 1454.

However, it is not until the regular records of the lords' journals from 1509 that one gets a better idea of actual daily attendance. The Prior was in attendance on 21 January 1510, the first day of Henry VIII's first parliament.[67] He was also present in the first session of the 1512 parliament, as on 4 February Docwra was commissioned to be present at the Lateran council of Monday 19 April 1512.[68] He is noted in parliament on 6 February and 9 March, and on the latter date, as the highest-ranking lord in attendance, adjourned parliament until the following day, due to the absence of the spiritual lords in convocation.[69] More detailed records exist for the sessions in 1515, 1534 and 1536 (see Figures 12–15).

The first session of the 1515 parliament consisted of 45 days. On four days

[59] Virgoe, 'New Fragment', 86–7.
[60] J. S. Roskell, 'The Problem of the Attendance of the Lords in Medieval Parliaments', *BIHR*, XXIX, 1956, 153–204 at 196.
[61] *Fane Fragment*, 5, 7, 11, 14, 17, 21, 24; *Rot. Parl.*, V, 461.
[62] *Foedera*, London, XI, 477; *CPR 1461–1467*, 52. Langstrother was also preceptor of Balsall.
[63] *Ibid.*, 478; *CPR 1461–1467*, 102.
[64] *Fane Fragment*, 94–5. These were Scrope of Bolton, Scrope of Upsal, Grey of Wilton, Stourton, Wenlock and Ferrers. Of course, the Prior had an advantage in that he was based in London.
[65] *Ibid.*, 93–4.
[66] *Ibid.*, 93. That Edward IV attended all eight days further emphasises the unusual nature of this parliament. Most kings only attended on the first and last days of parliament and Edward IV's extended attendance indicates his insecure hold on power. He may, indeed, have demanded high attendance as an indication of support.
[67] *L&P HVIII 1509–1513*, I, 157–8.
[68] *Ibid.*, 511.
[69] *Lords Journals*, I, 14.

parliament was adjourned due to convocation.[70] On another two days (8 February and 2 March) no one was marked as present although business was conducted, and on the former day the speaker of the commons was presented to the king in full parliament.[71] On 19 March, no one is marked as present and there is no record of business, and on 27 March only the archbishops of Canterbury and York are noted as present.[72] Therefore presence lists exist for 37 days, of which the Prior attended on 19 days (51 per cent). This is comparable with William Wareham, Archbishop of Canterbury and chancellor, who attended on 21 of the days.[73] Nevertheless, for someone who was based in the London area, one might have expected him to attend more often, and one possible explanation is that he was involved in other duties, such as his appointment as a trier of overseas petitions on 4 February.[74]

In the second and final session of the 1515 parliament, there were 29 days' business, of which attendance records exist for 27 days (see Figure 13). The Prior attended on 24 days (88.9 per cent), a considerably greater proportion than in the first session.[75] This may have been because fewer petitions were presented during this session, but perhaps also because his Hospitaller duties had eased or been minimised until after parliament, a short assembly at Clerkenwell having concluded the day before parliament opened.[76] This was not the only time that provincial chapters and parliaments followed in quick succession; it was also the case in 1536, when the Clerkenwell chapter ended on 30 May and the Westminster parliament opened on 8 June. It may suggest that Priors Docwra and Weston were arranging provincial chapters near to times when they (and others) were in London for parliament.[77]

The parliament of 1534, session five of eight of the Reformation Parliament, consisted of 44 days, with the Prior attending on 39 days (88.6 per cent), comparable with his attendance at the November 1515 parliament (see Figure 14).[78] This session showed not only a general increase in daily attendance of all lords compared to 1515, but a predominance of temporal over spiritual lords, mainly due to the absence of most bishops after the first few days of parliament. This confirms Chapuys' assertion that certain prelates and other peers were ordered to absent themselves in 1534.[79]

Finally, records exist for all 26 days of the parliament starting on 8 June 1536, the last parliament the Prior attended, with the Prior present on 23 days (see Figure

---

[70] *Ibid.*, 20–1, 23–4, 28–9, 32 for 9 and 16 February, 6 and 13 March.

[71] *Ibid.*, 19–20, 27. Given that the attendance for the rest of parliament ranged between 20 and 40 per day, it is unlikely that full parliament actually meant that all 92 listed (but not marked present) attended on 8 February.

[72] *Ibid.*, 34–5, 38.

[73] *Ibid.*, 19, 21–4, 26, 29, 32–3, 35, 37–42.

[74] *Ibid.*, 18–19. Wareham, who was a trier of English petitions, might also have been expected to attend more regularly. Also Botyll missed sessions of the king's council in 1461 during parliament, when he was trier of petitions.

[75] *Ibid.*, 43–57.

[76] BL MS Cotton Claudius E VI, ff. 156v–157. The next provincial chapter was in April 1516.

[77] TNA LR 2/62; *Lords Journal*, I, 84–5. It was also true for the 1539 parliament, which the Prior did not attend, with the provincial chapter ending on 24 April and parliament starting on 28 April.

[78] *Ibid.*, 58–83.

[79] Fryde and Miller, *Historical Studies*, II, 16.

15).[80] Again the Prior attended the same proportion of days (88.5 per cent) as for November 1515 and 1534. As suggested before, this could be because his Hospitaller business had been dealt with, his provincial chapter having finished on 30 May, but also because he was not a trier of petitions. Unlike Docwra, Weston was never a trier of petitions, and was therefore free to attend parliamentary sessions more frequently.[81] Weston did not attend the parliament of 1539–40, appointing Lords Latimer and Windsor as his proxies for the first session (28 April–23 May 1539).[82] Officially this was due to continuing illness, but perhaps the real reason was the subject matter of the Dissolution of the larger monasteries and the ensuing danger to the Hospitallers, which Weston did not wish to take part in or approve. He had, after all, been well enough to preside over the provincial chapter that ended on 24 April, just four days before parliament opened.[83] Presumably his proxies were still valid during the second session (30 May–28 June 1539).[84] For the third session (12 April–24 July 1540) Weston had no proxy and was not listed. This is unsurprising, considering that from 22 April to 1 May the act to transfer Hospitaller possessions to the king was discussed and concluded.[85] Such a short period of debate suggests that the details were probably worked out in advance of the third session, so there was no point in Weston attending.[86]

Based on the evidence available, it appears that the Prior attended parliament regularly when he was in England. Attendance at parliament, however, was increasingly becoming both a right and duty of all spiritual and temporal lords. Apart from participation in the general business of parliament common to all lords, what did the Prior do when there? One clear indication that the Prior was becoming more actively involved in the government of the realm was his appointment as a trier of private petitions from 1362.

Triers of petitions

The rolls of parliament show that receivers of petitions, who were meant to sort and 'answer' them, were appointed from the 1305 parliament at least, and perhaps from the 1280s.[87] Separate groups of receivers and triers of petitions are listed for most parliaments from 1341 onwards, when the rolls become more consistent in what they record, those triers for England, Wales, Ireland and Scotland (hereafter referred to as triers of English petitions) meeting in the painted chamber and those for Gascony, the Channel Islands and other overseas possessions (hereafter triers of overseas petitions) meeting in the Marcolf chamber at Westminster. What triers did

---

80 *Lords Journals*, I, 83–102.
81 *Ibid.*, 18–19, lxxvi, Docwra was a trier of overseas petitions in 1515 and 1523; *ibid.*, clii, 84–5. Weston was not appointed for the 1529–36 parliament or the June 1536 parliament.
82 *Ibid.*, 103.
83 TNA LR 2/62, ff. 179–200.
84 *Lords Journals*, I, 113–37. The last day the abbots attended was 24 June.
85 *Ibid.*, 132–134. Provision for the English and Irish Hospitallers was discussed between 8 and 10 May, *ibid.*, 136.
86 Hicks has observed that such advance preparation of bills had been common since 1461, M. A. Hicks, *English Political Culture in the Fifteenth Century*, London, 2002, 97.
87 Brand, 'Petitions and Parliament', 34.

exactly is not certain, but it has been suggested that they did have a practical role from at least the early fourteenth century and well into the fifteenth century.[88]

The Prior is first recorded as a trier of overseas petitions in 1362.[89] Although records for triers at all parliaments between 1341 and 1362 are not extant, they are for eight, and the Prior was not appointed at any of these.[90] The Prior was summoned to all eight of these parliaments, which indicates that he was in England, as summonses to the Prior were not issued when he was abroad.[91] Records of presentations in bishops' registers also indicate that the Prior was in England at or near the time of each of these parliaments.[92] Absence, then, is not the explanation for the Prior's lack of appointment before 1362. Remote location can also be ruled out, as all parliaments between 1341 and 1362 were held at Westminster, within easy reach of the Prior's base at Clerkenwell. Either Prior Thame was not considered suitable to be a trier (unlikely considering his military service to the crown), or he did not wish to serve as trier, perhaps viewing it as an administrative burden and distraction from his Hospitaller duties. He was, for example, present at the 1348 parliament, but was active exclusively in assuring Hospitaller privileges.[93] What can be said with some confidence is that Prior Thame (d. December 1353) did not serve as a trier, as seven of the eight extant records for triers up until 1362 fell within his term of office (1335–53) and records for only three parliaments are lost for the period 1341–54. He attended the parliaments of 1346 and 1347, but is not listed as a trier at either.[94] There is even a record of his presentation (on 27 March) to a benefice during the 1351 Westminster parliament, which confirms he was in England.[95] Prior John Pavely, then, was the first known Prior to be a trier of petitions and served as trier in all six parliaments between 1362 and 1369 (see Figure 16).[96] That he was not a trier in 1371, even though summoned to parliament, may be due to failing health, as it appears that he died in that year. This is indicated as in November the

---

[88] Brand suggests that the receivers of petitions at the Easter parliament of 1280 were also to answer them, *ibid.*, 34; W. M. Ormrod, 'On and Off the Record: The Rolls of Parliament, 1337–1377', in *Parchment and People*, 40–1; C. Given-Wilson, 'The Rolls of Parliament 1399–1421', in *Parchment and People*, 60–1; A. Curry, '"A Game of Two Halves:" Parliament 1422–1454', in *Parchment and People*, 83–5.

[89] *Rot. Parl.*, II, 268.

[90] *Ibid*, 126 (1341), 135 (1343), 147 (1344), 157 (1346), 164 (1347), 226 (1351), 236 (1352), 254 (1354). No list of triers exists for the two parliaments of 1348 or for 1355, 1357, 1358, 1360 and 1361.

[91] *CCR 1341–1343*, 113–14; *CCR 1343–1346*, 94, 368; *CCR 1346–1349*, 146, 240; *CCR 1349–1354*, 287–9, 401; *CCR 1354–1360*, 64.

[92] See Appendix 2 for a list of presentations compiled from the bishops' registers in print. In these, the Prior is only mentioned as presenting if he is in England. Otherwise his lieutenant is noted. Thus the records of presentations can be used as a guide to when the Prior was in England or overseas.

[93] *Rot. Parl.*, II, 158, 215, 217, 221.

[94] *Ibid.*, 157, 164.

[95] See Appendix 2.

[96] *Rot. Parl.*, II, 268, 275, 283, 289, 294, 300. As the records of triers between 1355 and 1361 are lost, it is not known if Pavely was appointed at an earlier date. All that can be said is that he was not appointed at the 1354 parliament, perhaps because he had only been Prior a few months and was not well known in government circles.

turcopolier, Richard Overton, requested exemplification of letters patent upholding Hospitaller privileges, a task that the Prior would normally perform.[97]

Prior Pavely was appointed exclusively to try overseas petitions. We can also detect a consistency of personnel appointed as triers during these six parliaments, with Prior Pavely and Sir John Mowbray serving at all six parliaments, the bishops of Durham, Hereford and St David's, the earl of Anjou, Sir Walter Manny and Sir Roger Beauchamp serving at five, and the abbot of St Edmund's, the earls of Stafford, Salisbury and Devon serving at four (see Figure 16). Only two of the 16 triers appointed in 1369 had not served in the previous five parliaments, the rest having served at least three times. This does not count any service they had done in parliaments before 1362 or appointments as triers of English petitions, and quite a few of the triers served on both panels.

Pavely's appointment as a trier marks an important change in the parliamentary role of the Prior. Rather than attending parliament mainly to promote the interests of the Hospitallers, he was taking on a significant government duty. The position of trier was not just an honorary one without duty. Private petitions continued to occupy a great deal of parliamentary time long after chancery ceased to enrol them in about 1332.[98] They had an important role because they decided which petitions were discussed in parliament and which were referred to lower courts, such as king's or common bench.[99] Priors, like other triers, were in a position of relative political power, able to promote their own interests and subdue their opponents. The role of trier was also, in some ways, akin to later Priors' role on the king's council: it dealt with petitions, which occupied king's council also; it meant access to the innermost parts of Westminster Palace where the committees met, as did service on king's council meeting in the star chamber, and it meant frequent meetings with those most influential in the government machinery.

Pavely's immediate successors, Priors Hales and Radington, also served as triers, again for overseas petitions. In contrast to Pavely's first years as Prior, records exist of triers at all four parliaments between 1372 and 1377, to which Hales was summoned, but he was only appointed as trier at the 1378 parliament (see Figure 17).[100] Lists of presentations to benefices suggest he was in England throughout this period, with the possible exception of the November 1373 parliament.[101] He was definitely at the 1376 parliament, where he was busy upholding Hospitaller privileges on lands inherited from the Templars, and he acted as one of the 34 mainpernors for Lord Latimer, who had been accused of abandoning the Calais staple and of bad counsel to Edward III.[102] Hales' appearance as a trier in 1378 and in the following two parliaments (1379, January 1380) is evidence of his increasing involvement in English government, perhaps spurred by the beginning of Richard II's minority, as it coincides with his appointment to the third continual council,

97   *CPR 1370–1374*, 158.
98   Ormrod, 'Rolls of Parliament, 1337–1377', 40–41.
99   Given-Wilson, 'Rolls of Parliament 1399–1421', 60.
100 *Rot. Parl.*, II, 309, 317, 321, 363; *Rot. Parl.*, III, 34.
101 Brother John Noble presented as Hales' lieutenant two days before the opening of parliament (see Appendix 2).
102 *Rot. Parl.*, II, 326, 348; *CPR 1374–1377*, 302, 306.

and was followed both by diplomatic duty (which is why he was not a trier at the November 1380 parliament) and his term of office as treasurer of England.

Prior Radington was a trier of overseas petitions at the four parliaments between 1383 and 1385 (see Figure 18), but then did not serve as a trier again, perhaps due to constant absence abroad for the Order or on diplomatic missions for the crown.[103] This marked the start of a period of 50 years (1386 to 1438), during which time the Prior of St John only served as a trier of petitions twice, once in 1415, when Prior Grendon was a trier of English petitions, and again in 1431, when Prior Hulles was a trier of overseas petitions.[104] The Prior's regular appointment as a trier only recommenced in 1439, when Prior Malory was a trier of English petitions.[105]

Whereas Priors in the fourteenth century had been exclusively triers of overseas petitions, Priors Grendon, Malory and Botyll dealt with English petitions. Botyll was a trier of English petitions in seven out of eight parliaments.[106] The exception, trier of overseas petitions in 1455, is possibly explained by his involvement on two other commissions during that parliament, perhaps to lighten his load because there were fewer overseas petitions to deal with, but more likely as they involved overseas issues: one commission involved Calais and the other stopped the flow of gold and silver out of the realm to Bordeaux and other places.[107] Miller has noted that, in the Tudor period, appointment as a trier was a mark of distinction and that the more senior nobles were appointed as triers for England.[108] If this was also so for the fourteenth and earlier fifteenth century, then the Prior's appointment as a trier of English petitions from 1415 to 1467 is an indication of a gradual increase in status during the fifteenth century.[109] If one follows this logic, then there is a corresponding decrease in status of the later Priors, as they returned to being triers of overseas petitions. Was Prior Docwra, one of the judges at the duke of Buckingham's trial in 1521 and a renowned international statesman, really of lower status than Priors Grendon, Malory or Botyll?[110] Prior Botyll's role as a trier of English petitions could equally suggest a shift in emphasis towards greater involvement in English affairs out of his own preference, and his other duties to the king during his term of office indicate this was so.[111] For example, he regularly attended king's council in the 1450s. He was also on a committee for the defence of Calais and Berwick in 1455 and on another committee in the same year to restrain the export of gold and silver, something unthinkable a century earlier when the Priors themselves, especially Philip Thame, were constantly called to account for illegally sending money abroad.[112] It is possible that Priors had an element of choice to which petitions they

---

[103] *Ibid.*, III, 151, 167, 185, 204.

[104] *Ibid.*, IV, 63, 368.

[105] *Ibid.*, V, 4.

[106] *Ibid.*, 66–7, 129, 278–9, 345, 373, 461–2, 496, 571.

[107] *Ibid.*, 279–80.

[108] H. Miller, *Henry VIII and the English Nobility*, Oxford, 1986, 121–2.

[109] It appears that this was so, as nobles such as John of Gaunt were triers of English petitions.

[110] *Year Books of Henry VIII, 12–14 Henry VIII, 1520–23*, ed. J. H. Baker, Selden Society CXIX, London, 2002, 57, 62.

[111] The change to Botyll being a trier of English petitions was not due to lack of experience abroad, as he was a regular crown diplomat.

[112] *Rot. Parl.*, V, 279–80.

tried according to their individual interests and investments. It is notable that the Prior took a special interest in Calais, important to the English Hospitallers both economically and as a source of information coming from the Convent, just as the English Hospitallers were particularly concerned with St Peter's castle in the East, which the English invested in heavily from its inception.[113] The political situation within England at any particular time also determined the Prior's interests. Just as Botyll was seconded onto the protectorate councils, he served as a trier of English petitions during a period of great instability in English politics.

A final comment, of relevance to the next section, is that many of those who served as triers also served on the king's council. For example, eight of the 11 known councillors (including Prior Hales) appointed at the 1378 Gloucester parliament during Richard II's minority were also regular triers of petitions between 1378–80.[114] This appears to have been a regular occurrence and in 1455, 17 of 33 known councillors (including Prior Botyll) in that year were also triers of petitions and all 11 of those most regular councillors were triers.[115] It appears that selection as a trier of petitions was indicative of further integration into English politics and perhaps a precursor to appointment on the king's council.

King's Council

As opposed to great councils and parliaments, which were temporary summoned assemblies, the king's council was a more permanent body, appointed by the king, unless he was in his minority or not of sound mind, in which case the lords in parliament appointed a council, with the assent of the commons. Before the middle of the fifteenth century, the Prior was not a regular member of the king's council. Joseph Chauncy and Robert Hales attended in their capacity as treasurer of England, but with these exceptions, there are only two instances of the Prior's appointment to council, and both were in special circumstances. Firstly, Prior Hales served on the second minority council of Richard II (1378–79). The issue rolls show that Hales was paid for attendance on 238 days (out of 373) between 26 November 1378 and 3 December 1379, but unfortunately records of exactly which days and the business covered at king's council do not exist.[116] Secondly, Prior Grendon was appointed in 1415 to the temporary council under the duke of Bedford while Henry V was in France, although there is no evidence that Grendon attended, from either attendance lists or payment records.[117] The references in POPC to Prior Radington's presence in council concern great councils, such as those at Clarendon and Reading in

113 Luttrell, 'English Contributions to the Hospitaller Castle at Bodrum', 106.
114 Rot. Parl., III, 34, 56–7, 72; Baldwin, King's Council, 123.
115 Rot. Parl., V, 278–9.
116 TNA E 403/475, m. 19, paid £285 13s. 8d. at the rate of a banneret; TNA E 403/476, m. 12 adds that he was on the council at the assent of the king and with the advice of other magnates at the parliament of Gloucester.
117 TNA E 403/621–4; BL MS Cotton Cleopatra F III, ff. 177v–179; POPC, II, 157.

1389, and not to the continual council, as has been suggested in previous research.[118] The Prior is not named in any of the formal councils of Henry IV or as one of those appointed to the minority council of Henry VI.[119] Furthermore, from the start of Henry VI's minority in 1422, it became more common for council documents to be signed or for those attending to be noted by the clerk of the council, and before 1450 there is no record of the Prior as a councillor.[120] Even on the two recorded occasions that king's council was held at the Hospitallers' Priory at Clerkenwell in November 1437 and May 1439, the Prior was not noted as attending.[121]

The following section will discuss the Prior's attendance at king's council, how his attendance compared to other lords of the council, and what he did when he was there. It will focus on the period when the council and privy seal records were relatively rich, between 1451 and 1463 (see Figures 19–23). The first certain example of the Prior attending king's council as a councillor is on 1 May 1451, at which were discussed the customs and subsidies to the value of £20,000 in the ports of London and Southampton that were granted at the previous parliament (9 February to 1 March 1451).[122] Also attending were the chancellor, treasurer, John Lord Stourton, and the keeper of the privy seal, plus a clerk of the council, Langport.[123] The Prior next attended on 27 July, as did the chancellor, treasurer, the keeper of the privy seal, Andrew Holes and Thomas Tyrell, a member of the king's household.[124] This meeting, like that on 1 May, concerned the tax on customs, specifically noting sums of money paid to the queen rather than to the treasury and that the king had replaced this money. Two other documents dated the same day, but with no attendance noted, concerned the repayment from the tax on London of sums lent by the chancellor for the maintenance of Calais and repairs at Roxburgh Castle on the border with Scotland.[125] At this stage, the Prior did not attend regularly. Between 1 May and 17 August 1451 attendance at king's council was noted on nine days, of which the Prior attended on the two days mentioned above. The Prior was not the only irregular attendee. Of the 15 councillors noted during 1451, only four attended on five days or more. The two most regular of these were the chancellor, Cardinal John Kemp (all nine days), and the treasurer Sir John Beauchamp (six days).[126] Attendance varied considerably, even on a single day. On 18 May, 10 councillors are noted on one document, but only five on the next to be signed. On

---

[118] *POPC*, I, 11–12, 17–18; O'Malley, *English Knights Hospitaller*, 122.

[119] *Rot. Parl.*, III, 486, 530; IV, 175, 201; A. L. Brown, 'The Commons and the Council in the reign of Henry IV', in *Historical Studies of the English Parliament*, ed. E. B. Fryde and E. Miller, Cambridge, 1970, II, 31–60; R. A. Griffiths, *The Reign of King Henry VI: The Exercise of Royal Authority, 1422–1461*, Stroud, 1998, 32–8.

[120] There is no mention of the Prior as a councillor in TNA E 28/1–80, BL MS Cotton Cleopatra F III or BL MS Cotton Cleopatra F IV.

[121] *Ibid.*, f. 136; TNA E 28/60/4.

[122] TNA E 28/81/5.

[123] Clerks of the council should be considered as councillors. In the meeting of 1 May another clerk of the council, Thomas Kent is even referred to as 'our councillor'. Presumably, then, the clerk not only recorded decisions of the council, but contributed to the debate.

[124] TNA E 28/81/55.

[125] TNA E 28/81/53–4.

[126] TNA E 28/81. The other two were John Stafford, archbishop of Canterbury and Ralph Lord Cromwell, chamberlain of the household, who each attended on five days.

21 May only the chancellor was present, apart from the clerk of the council.[127] In 1452, eight days in May, June and July record attendance at council.[128] Fifteen councillors served during these months, but never more than eight at a time and generally there were five or six attending. Ten of the councillors served for three or fewer days, with only the chancellor present on every day, the treasurer on seven, and Reynold Boulers, bishop of Hereford, on six days. The Prior attended on three of the seven days, one in May and the other two in July. On 15 May, the Prior is noted on one of two documents calling various persons to appear before the council.[129] He does not appear to have attended during June, but appears again on 3 and 12 of July, when business dealt with the duties and rent due from the tenants of the bishop of Hereford (himself a councillor), and the summoning of those to appear before council.[130] An even mix of clerics and lay councillors attended, although the lay members tended to hold official positions, such as the treasurer, John Tiptoft, and Robert Whittingham, a member of the king's household.[131]

Up until this point, the Prior was not a core member of the king's council. This changed during 1453. Attendance is recorded on 23 days in the council and privy seal files, and a further six in *POPC* (see Figure 20). Until the onset of the king's madness in August, the Prior's daily attendance in 1453 was about 66 per cent (10 out of 15 days), compared to 22 per cent in 1451 and 37 per cent in 1452.[132] Only the chancellor (12 days) and treasurer (11 days) attended more often and 18 of the 27 councillors mentioned attended on no more than four days. The reason for the Prior's marked rise in king's council attendance appears to be his increased diplomatic duties in 1453, as in both March and July he is noted as an ambassador going to, or in, Calais.[133] Business at the meeting of 3 March, which the Prior attended, dealt with orders to officials at Dover and Sandwich to find and pay for shipping of the Prior and two other ambassadors to Calais.[134] On 10 July, he is noted as in the king's service in 'parts beyond the sea', though he had returned by the following day, when he was present at king's council.[135] Finally, on 20 July he is noted as being sent to Calais on a six-week mission to meet the duke of Burgundy's ambassadors.[136]

---

[127] TNA E 28/81/12, 14, 16.

[128] TNA E 28/82.

[129] TNA E 28/82/33–4.

[130] TNA E 28/82/50, 53. What they were to appear for is unclear due to the deliberately evasive language, which just states 'for certain great and chargeable causes and matters such as move us and our council'.

[131] My research shows that Whittingham first attended on 15 May (TNA E 28/82/33–4), rather than in July as Virgoe claimed, R. L. Virgoe, 'The Composition of the King's Council, 1437–61', *BIHR*, XLIII, 1970, 134–60 at 158–60.

[132] TNA E 28/83. Although the Prior's total attendance for the whole year was 45 per cent of all meetings where those present were noted, this is artificially low due to his diplomatic service in August.

[133] TNA E 28/83/1, 23, 34. One might ask why he was not a councillor during his diplomatic duty of 1447–49. The difference was that in 1453 he was in short embassies across to Calais, rather than the longer and more distant mission of 1447–49. Also, by 1451 he had been Prior for ten years and had proved his worth through previous service to the crown.

[134] TNA E 28/83/1.

[135] TNA E 28/83/23–4.

[136] TNA E 28/83/34.

It appears that the Prior's duties as a councillor, as for the other councillors, were concerned with domestic issues and English diplomacy, but it was in the interest of his order to secure stable government in England after the Cade rebellion of 1450 and in the final stages of the Hundred Years War. Peace in Europe was essential for the Hospitallers. Rhodes was attacked by Mamluks a number of times in the 1440s and the fall of the Byzantine Empire in May 1453 meant that the Hospitallers looked to western governments for support when the Turks inevitably turned their forces towards Rhodes.

Although the onset of Henry VI's madness in early August 1453 coincided with a fall in council attendance, it is likely that attendance dropped due to the summer break, the king's move from London to Windsor, and in the Prior's case, diplomatic duty. The Prior last attended on 10 August. The four documents surviving from this date give no indication of the king's madness and concentrate on the suppression of riots in Northumberland, the restitution of merchants' property and licences for merchants to leave for Aquitaine.[137] For the remainder of August, the treasurer, Thomas Thorpe, speaker at the previous parliament but also a baron of the exchequer, and the dean of St Severin attended regularly, the only other person to attend council was the keeper of the privy seal.[138] The Prior is only recorded at one further meeting that year, on 24 October, when the duke of York was requested to attend a great council.[139]

As for 1453, there are a fair number of documents with which to assess the Prior's attendance at council in 1454. The council and privy seal files record attendance on 29 days. A further seven, possibly, are recorded in *POPC* (see Figure 21). However, before looking at the Prior's attendance, a discrepancy between the two sources in the numbers attending king's council must be addressed which, as alluded to earlier, suggest that many of those entries in Nicolas' collection are records of great council, not king's council. In the council and privy seal files, recorded attendance only occasionally reaches double figures, normally ranging between seven and nine.[140] The only exception to this was when 14 attended on 6 February and 20 attended on 14 February, the first day of parliament.[141] This indicates that these two records are of a great council meeting prior to the parliament proper. The meeting of 6 February even notes that it took place in the great council chamber.[142] In contrast, the meetings recorded in *POPC* normally record attendance at 15 or over, and often more than 20. Twenty-eight are recorded as meeting in the 'council chamber in time of parliament' on 15 March, but surely their business, granting power to the king's doctors to administer medicines to the king, was an issue for great council

---

[137] TNA E 28/83/51–4. Henry VI's madness was not widely known at this time, although possibly some of the councillors were aware of it.

[138] TNA E 28/83/55–9, 64. The treasurer and Thorpe attended on all six recorded days, the dean of St Severin on five and the keeper of the privy seal on two.

[139] *POPC*, VI, 163–4.

[140] TNA E 28/84, E 28/85.

[141] TNA E 28/84/1–2.

[142] TNA E 28/84/1. King's council meetings could take place in the great council chamber, especially if just before or after a meeting of the great council. In the case of 6 February, it is the combination of high attendance and place that indicate a great council.

to consent to and one the king's councillors would want a larger backing for.[143] A similar-sized meeting of 28 on 13 November drew up ordinances for regulating the king's household in 'greet counsail'.[144] For this reason attendances of over 20 have been designated to be great councils. While others of 15 or over have been treated as king's council, many of these too were probably also great councils. Three documents from 18 July 1453 suggest this is a sound approach. The first two note the number of councillors as eight and seven respectively (the Prior was not one) and dealt with a minor petition and the subsidy granted to the king by the convocation of Canterbury province.[145] Both the size and subject matter are consistent with a king's council meeting. In contrast, the same day 24 lords (including the Prior) met in great council to discuss whether the duke of Somerset, accused of treason, should be released on bail.[146] This indicates that, when distinguishing between king's council and great council, size does matter, and attendance figures in the council and privy seal files throughout the period 1451 to 1463 confirm this. However, it is important to stress that, despite the division suggested above, the king's council, great council and parliament were part of the same governing organ, the king's council sitting when great council and parliament were not able.

Moving on to the Prior's attendance at king's council in 1454, as with the previous year, it was relatively high. Only the chancellor attended more often. The Prior attended on 23 out of 29 days recorded in the council and privy seal files and a further six out of seven in *POPC*, giving an average attendance of just over 80 per cent of the days when attendance was noted. This is significantly higher than in the previous year. The reason was the king's madness and the consequent appointment of the duke of York as protector to be advised by a formal council, of which the Prior was a member. It is perhaps indicative of the Prior's increasing importance in English political circles that, in contrast to 1422 when there was also a protector and formal council to which the Prior was not appointed, in 1454 the Prior was appointed to the formal council.

Of the 36 councillors who attended council from the start of the protectorate, 11 out of 12 who attended most regularly (from 11 days by Viscount Bourgchier to all 29 days by the chancellor) were of those who had agreed to serve at the great council on 3 April.[147] For the rest, attendance never reached double figures and was mainly in July, when the duke of York attended, though not to support him as to counter his influence, such as Viscount Beaumont.[148] That those sworn of the council should have attended most regularly can be explained both because they had made a commitment to attend and because they were the only ones who had the incentive of promised payment. Even then payment was in arrears. On 9 July 1456, a warrant for issue was raised for eight councillors.[149] The Prior was to be

143 *POPC*, VI, 166–7.
144 *Ibid.*, 220–33.
145 TNA E 28/85/47–8. Five councillors were noted on both documents, a total of ten councillors in all attending that day.
146 TNA E 28/85/49. Eight of the ten who attended king's council this day, also attended this great council.
147 The twelfth was Lord Dudley, who attended on 19 days.
148 Beaumont was the queen's man and she was opposed to a protectorate.
149 TNA E 404/70/3/81; Virgoe, 'Composition of the King's Council', 153. The eight were the

paid at a rate of £100 per annum, in four equal portions, from 15 April 1454 until 28 March 1456, though examination of the issue rolls shows no trace of actual payment.[150] The warrant for issue is valuable in that it confirms what the attendance notes indicate, that the Prior was one of the core councillors from the start of the first protectorate until the end of the second. This is especially useful as the records for 1455 (17 days) and 1456 (seven days) are less detailed than for 1453–54 and otherwise indicate a drop in the Prior's attendance (see Figures 22 and 23). This in turn may indicate the Prior attended more often than the records imply in 1451 and 1452. However, the lack of payment records for the Prior as a councillor (as opposed to the many payments for his diplomatic duties) in those years, which exist for other councillors, may equally suggest not.[151]

Council business when the Prior attended in 1454 covered a variety of topics, but placed particular emphasis on securing the loyalty of the soldiers based at Calais.[152] However there are some indications that the Prior's service on the council could benefit both Hospitaller kin and the Order itself. For example, when the Prior attended on 11 July, amongst other more important business was a petition from Richard Langstrother (kin of John), parson of St Ives church and a servant of Botyll, to have his presentation to High Ongar church in the diocese of London confirmed by privy seal letters. This was granted the same day. It is hard to doubt that Prior Botyll used his influence to ensure this petition was discussed and to secure a positive decision quickly.[153] Similarly, although not present on 14 July, Botyll gained king's council support for a Hospitaller request to the Pope for indulgence money to be collected in aid of Rhodes in England, Wales and Ireland in 1455, and various letters favouring John Langstrother going to the Pope on the Order's behalf regarding this matter.[154] Although the Prior served on council mainly to serve the king, he did not forego the opportunity to help his order or family when the opportunity arose. This was no more than any other lord did for kin and those in their service.

bishop of Lincoln, the earls of Warwick and Salisbury, Viscount Bourgchier, Prior Botyll, Sir Thomas Stanley, the dean of St Severin and John Say. The following February (1457) John, earl of Shrewsbury, then treasurer, complained (see TNA E 404/71/1/52) he had received nothing for his services on council between 15 April 1454 and 28 March 1456, but neither the E28 files or *POPC* indicate he attended!

[150] TNA E 403/785–835 (Easter term 1451 to Easter term 1466) show no payments to the Prior as a councillor, only payments for diplomatic duty and repayments for small sums he had lent the king.

[151] TNA E 404/69/29, 88, for example, show warrants for issue to John Stafford, archbishop of Canterbury, for two £50 payments for attendance on the 'contynuel counsail' from July to December 1452.

[152] For example, see TNA E 28/84/26–7, 30.

[153] TNA E 28/85/23–4. Other petitions that day dealt with Calais, the subsidy raised by the Canterbury convocation, the costs of reparations to the king's palaces, and business of the duke of York. Richard Langstrother was in the Prior's service from at least June 1448, when he was rector of Quenington, *CPL 1447–1455*, 24.

[154] TNA E 28/85/29–32. Letters were sent to the Pope and cardinals giving crown support for the bid and to the doge of Venice for favour. A further letter was sent to the doge of Venice on 24 July, asking him to favour the Hospitallers, TNA E 28/85/68; see *CPL 1447–1455*, 261–6, for details of the papal decision in early December 1454 in favour of the Hospitallers' request.

For 1455 records exist for the king's council on eight days during parliament (12 November–13 December) and nine items of business directly after parliament on 16 December that help explain better the Prior's role both in parliament and on king's council (see Figure 22). During parliament, the Prior only attended king's council on three days (37.5 per cent). This compares with attendance on five of eight days before and after parliament (62.5 per cent). This difference cannot be explained by a drop in attendance by councillors during parliament, as attendance was constant before, during and after parliament, averaging about ten councillors per meeting.[155] It can be explained by the Prior's role as a trier of overseas petitions and his appointment in the July session (9–31 July) of parliament to two of five commissions, the only person commissioned to more than one.[156] Two other normally regular councillors, the bishop of London and the dean of St Severin, were also mostly absent during parliament. The former was a trier of English petitions and the latter on the commission to stop the flow of gold and silver out of the realm. Of the ten items of business covered on 16 December, seven were petitions.[157] This not only explains why the Prior was absent during parliament, but also indicates why he attended council, mainly to deal with petitions.

There are only a few attendance records for the later years of Henry VI and the start of Edward IV's reign (see Figure 23), and some of those from *POPC* are probably great council rather than king's council records. Records between 1457 and 1462 are particularly sparse, with only nine days noting attendance. The records show that the Prior continued to attend king's council during this period, but they are not enough to judge how regularly. However, for 1456 and 1463 there are numbers comparable with 1451 and 1452 that are worthy of comment. The council and privy seal files record attendance on seven days between March and July 1456, during which a total of 18 councillors attended, but never more than eight at a time.[158] Although York's second protectorate had ended in February, the most regular attendees were still those who had been on this body. Some, such as the archbishop of York, the dukes of York and Buckingham and Viscount Beaumont, only attended during or just after parliament, but others such as the chancellor, the treasurer, the earl of Salisbury, Prior Botyll and the dean of St Severin continued to attend in June and July.[159] The business of the council in March 1456 dealt with petitions left over from the recent parliament, such as the petition of the Italian merchant companies to be exempt from the 20s. levy agreed at the Reading parliament in March 1453 and for letters of safe conduct for natives of the duchy of Guienne.[160] The Prior had been a trier of overseas petitions during the parliament and presumably was

---

[155] On the last two days of parliament it rose to 16 and 15 councillors respectively.

[156] *Rot. Parl.*, V, 278–80. The two commissions were (a) to strengthen Calais and Berwick against invasion and establish regular payments to troops there and (b) to stop the flow of gold and silver out of the realm to Bordeaux and other places.

[157] TNA E 28/87/20–9.

[158] TNA E 28/87. *POPC*, VI, 285–6 records a meeting of 22 lords on 24 January 1456, but the size and fact it took place during the parliament indicates it was a great council.

[159] TNA E 28/87/31–44. The chancellor was Thomas Bourgchier, archbishop of Canterbury and the treasurer Henry Viscount Bourgchier, his brother.

[160] TNA E 28/87/32–4. Prior Botyll was not at the meeting of 13 March, but was there on 16 March.

one of those who referred these petitions to the council, or perhaps brought them with him as unfinished business. In June and July, council business concerned Calais, for example payment of wages claimed by various tradesmen (on hearing that the soldiers had been paid) who had strengthened the fortifications when the duke of Somerset had been captain, as well as payment of the earl of Warwick's wages as captain of Calais.[161]

In 1463, Edward IV's council and privy seal files record attendance on seven days (three in March and four in July).[162] Twenty-two councillors are named as attending, and there is a noticeably higher attendance in March (up to 16) than in July (no more than nine), which again may suggest a great council prior to the April parliament.[163] The Prior attended on five days, the same as the bishop of Norwich, with only the chancellor and John Lord Wenlock attending more regularly. The highest attendance (16) was on 7 March. It included Brother John Langstrother, the only Hospitaller who was not a Prior known to attend council.[164] He was probably there as a follower of Warwick, who also attended, and this with other evidence indicates that long before he was Prior, Langstrother was becoming involved in internal politics.[165] The business before council in March 1463 was mainly financial. On the days the Prior attended in March, it concerned the restraint on the sale of wool at Calais, collection of the tax on wool and trading privileges granted to the Hanse merchants.[166] In July the business was still financial, but geared towards diplomacy and defence, such as the wages of ambassadors sent to St Omer to meet their Burgundian counterparts, the duties of the Calais regiment and the sending of auditors to Calais to check payments to them.[167] The surviving records also indicate the council's judicial role, such as the decision on 5 July in favour of two Venetian merchants who had had their goods confiscated, despite the safe conduct granted to them, and the order for their goods to be returned.[168]

After the 1460s, there are very few council and privy seal files, and most are damaged and illegible, but those that do survive hardly ever note attendance.[169] However, using in particular the star chamber and court of requests proceedings in the National Archives, some of which have been printed, the Lansdowne manuscripts in the British Library, plus various printed extracts, one can reconstruct

---

[161] TNA E 28/87/37, 41.

[162] TNA E 28/89. *POPC* stops in 1461 (vol. VI) and then restarts (vol. VII) in 1540.

[163] A reference to the 'lords councillors of our great council' in the chancery warrants for 5 March further supports this view, *Select Cases before the King's Council 1243–1482*, ed. I. S. Leadam and J. F. Baldwin, Selden Society XXXV, Cambridge, 1918, 114; See also TNA E 28/89/21 for 5 March 1463.

[164] TNA E 28/89/23. John Pavely was ordered to appear before the council in the 1330s with Prior Thame to explain sending money abroad, but neither were there as councillors.

[165] On 17 February, he received a £20 payment from treasury due to the high regard the king held him in, TNA E 403/827A, m. 12; On 7 April, he was one of those (others included a Malory and a Middleton) commissioned to arrest Humphrey Neville and bring him before the council, *CPR 1461–1467*, 279; Hicks, *False, Fleeting Perjur'd Clarence*, 36, notes that there had been an association between Langstrother and Warwick since the 1450s.

[166] TNA E 28/89/21, 23–4.

[167] TNA E 28/89/37, 41.

[168] TNA E 28/89/38.

[169] The last file is E 28/97, and is a list of military writs.

enough to show that Priors continued to serve as a councillors at least until 1527.[170] The payments on the issue rolls and *The Crowland Chronicle Continuations* show that Prior Langstrother attended the king's council in 1469 and 1471 in his capacity as treasurer. Given his attendance in 1463 and association with Warwick, it is likely that he would have attended as Prior as well, had his period of office not coincided with conflict between Edward IV, the duke of York and Warwick, in which Langstrother was embroiled.[171] Virtually no council records exist for the short time that Priors Tornay (1471–74) and Multon (1474–76) held office and, not surprisingly, there is no evidence that they attended king's council.[172] A printed extract from the Ellesmere manuscript 2654 in the Huntington Library lists Prior John Weston as attending council in 1487, but with 39 lords in attendance it is clearly a great council in session, breaking for the weekend and reassembling the following Monday.[173]

MS Lansdowne 160 contains attendance lists (but few details) from 1491 to 1498 and then 1521 to 1530.[174] Judging from the size of the meetings (eight or under), most were king's councils, but four appear to be great council meetings.[175] Luckily details do exist for the 1494 meeting from two separate sources and, as the days interlink, it is clear both sources concern the same meeting.[176] Lansdowne 160 notes that the king was present with many others on Thursday 6 and Monday 10 November 1494.[177] The *Select Cases in the Council of Henry VII* gives details of proceedings on Friday 7 and Tuesday 11 November 1494 and lists the king plus 38 lords as present. Prior Kendal is mentioned in the second item of business, where this meeting asked a group of nine councillors to debate on how to abolish corruptions and have a solution ready to put before the next parliament (October 1495).[178] This appears, most probably, to be a meeting of great council referring business to king's council, both from the break for the weekend, common during parliament and great councils (king's councils often met on Saturday), and from the referral of this much larger meeting to a group of councillors of numbers similar to those who attended contemporary king's councils.[179] A third entry notes Prior Kendal's opinion that the use of false deeds to title of land deserved harsh punishment.[180] This opinion, reminiscent in format of the recorded opinions in the 1449 parliament, was also

---

170 When one looks at the records of star chamber (TNA STAC) and court of requests (TNA REQ), it is astounding how similar they are, to the point where they should both be considered business of the king's council, see M. M. Condon, 'Ruling Elites in the Reign of Henry VII', in *Patronage, Pedigree and Power in Later Medieval England*, ed. C. D. Ross, Gloucester, 1979, 109–42.

171 TNA E 403/843; *Crowland Chronicle*, 127; Hicks, *Warwick the Kingmaker*, 277, *passim*.

172 *CPR 1467–1477*, 583, mentions one king's councillor, the keeper of the rolls of chancery.

173 *Select Cases in the Council of Henry VII*, ed. C. G. Bayne and W. H. Dunham, Selden Society LXXV, London, 1958, 13. As with *POPC*, the printed star chamber and court of requests examples confuse great council with king's council meetings.

174 BL MS Lansdowne 160, ff. 307–312v.

175 BL Lansdowne 160, ff. 307–308v. I suggest that the meetings of 10 February 1491, 3 July 1493, 6–11 November 1494 and 28 April 1496 were great councils.

176 *Select Cases in the Council of Henry VII*, 28–9.

177 BL MS Lansdowne 160, f. 307v.

178 *Select Cases in the Council of Henry VII*, 28–9. The eight mentioned are named as councillors.

179 The king's attendance also suggests a great council, as kings rarely attended king's council.

180 *Select Cases in the Council of Henry VII*, 29.

probably given at the great council, rather than king's council, where normally only decisions were recorded.

Despite the confusion of the records of the great council intermixed with king's council, the records both of the star chamber and the court of requests show that Prior Kendal and Prior Docwra attended king's council throughout their periods of office, although the lack of detailed records means we cannot confirm how regularly. However, there is a note of 12 February 1494 listing 17 councillors who were to sit in the court of requests until the end of October, and Prior Kendal was to sit continually from 15 days after Easter (Monday 14 April) until August, a period of three and a half to four months.[181] Bishops, knights and officials served continually, but the lay lords served for set periods of two to four months. Rather than being a new decree, it was most probably a previous precedent for the Prior to serve in the spring and summer months, and helps explain why most of the attendance records that exist for Prior Botyll are between the months of April and August (see Figures 19–23). The precedent continued for the remaining other dates for Kendal, three days noted in May 1495, 20 April 1497, 28 May 1498 and 11 March 1500.[182]

The first surviving record for Prior Docwra attending king's council was on 8 July 1508, when he was one of nine councillors who ruled in favour of the abbot of Shrewsbury against the bailiffs of that town over a title of land.[183] He also served in October and November 1509, when attendance was high (16+) due to the start of the new reign.[184] Business at the 14 November meeting concerned the abolition of by-courts, commission of oyer and terminer at Westminster for the poor to have counsel without paying, for Dr Dunstal to be admitted to king's council regarding his diplomatic mission, and referral of a case to ordinary court for testimony.[185] Docwra attended in the following years, for example 1510, 1516, and 1517 and, as with November 1509, the business covered was both administrative and diplomatic.[186] Docwra continued to attended in his later years as Prior, the last evidence of which is his signature (and four others) authorising the expenses of Wolsey and 'others of the king our sovereign lords most honourable council' on 16 May 1523.[187] Neither he nor William Weston is mentioned in the list of those sworn of the council during 18th year of Henry VIII (22 April 1526–21 April 1527), but this

---

[181] TNA REQ 1/1/1.

[182] BL Lansdowne 160, ff. 308. 6, 20 and 30 May 1495; TNA REQ 1/1/23d, 62d; TNA REQ 1/2/96.

[183] *Select Cases before the King's Council in the Star Chamber 1477–1509*, ed. I. S. Leadam, Selden Society XVI, 1903, 187–8.

[184] B. P. Wolffe, *The Crown Lands 1461 to 1536*, London, 1970, 162–3, reproduces Ellesmere MS 2655 for 11 October and 14 November 1509; see also *EHD 1485–1558*, V, 516, where he was one of eight councillors in 1509 to decide that William Flatman should have no general pardon for murder.

[185] This gives details of more items of business than the documents printed in Wolffe, *Crown Lands*, which only mentions the abolition of by-courts, BL MS Lansdowne 639, f. 28.

[186] *Ibid.*, ff. 33–49. Again some of these meetings, such as 10 June 1510 when 31 attended, were probably great councils.

[187] BL MS Lansdowne 160, ff. 310v–311 notes he attended between 1521and 1523; BL MS Additional 54226, f. 249.

was the period during which Prior Docwra fell ill and died, and Weston had not yet returned to England.[188]

Evidence of William Weston serving as a councillor is not as clear as for his predecessors, but there are indications that he did serve in his early years as Prior. He was, for example, one of 14 'councillors' appointed to the court of requests to hear 'poor men's causes' between 4 December 1528 and 28 January 1529.[189] In the latter year, on 19 October, he was one of 32 lords assigned to sit in star chamber on Tuesdays, Thursdays and Saturdays and deal with a variety of subject matter.[190] However, examination of the star chamber and court of requests proceedings between 1527 and 1540 reveals only one case in which the Prior was involved, that of Alison v. Cleche and others.[191] This case, concerning disputes dating back to at least 1516, was brought by Richard Alison against those who had tried to stop him practising as a surgeon in Holloway, St Giles in the Field and Islington. Prior Docwra had also been commissioned to hear the dispute before his death.[192] During the summer of 1529, Prior Weston and John Skewes, esquire, were commissioned to examine those involved in the case the following Easter (1530).[193] A signed copy of their report exists and helps to place the role of Weston's commission in these star chamber records.[194] In this report, addressed to the king and his council, Weston and Skewes stated that they had called both parties before them and that while some of the defendants (such as Edward Cleche) had appeared, others (such as Thomas Titilton) had not. After reviewing the case and examining the witnesses, they found Cleche guilty and ordered him to compensate Alison. Cleche refused and requested referral to a common law court. Because of this and Titilton's failure to appear, Weston and Skewes referred the case back to king's council.

A number of conclusions can be made from this commission. Firstly, this was a referral of a local dispute from the king's council to the local lord, Prior Weston. Such referrals, as Guy has commented, were an innovation by Wolsey and were common after 1520, Prior Docwra having served intensively in 1521 and 1522.[195] Secondly, Weston was assisted by a crown servant, John Skewes, who had been in royal service for many years.[196] Thirdly, although it does not state so in the report,

---

[188]   BL Lansdowne 160, f. 311v. At least 46 were councillors sworn to the king, probably more including attorneys and solicitors, but not all attended each meeting. For example, attendance between 1527 and 1529 ranged between three and six councillors on any one day.

[189]   TNA REQ 1/5/43d.

[190]   BL MS Lansdowne 1, f. 108v. Not all 32 sat simultaneously.

[191]   TNA STAC 2/1/136, 141–7.

[192]   TNA STAC 2/1/141.

[193]   *Ibid.* The month is obscured, so it is difficult to date exactly, but it was the sixth day of an identified month, 21 Henry VIII, before Wolsey's fall, so the commission was issued on either 6 May, 6 June, 6 July, 6 August or 6 September 1529 (Wolsey surrendered the great seal on 29 September).

[194]   *Ibid.*, m. 136.

[195]   J. A. Guy, 'Wolsey, the Council and the Council Courts', *EHR*, XCI, 1976, 481–505 at 494–5; J. A. Guy, *The Cardinal's Court: The Impact of Thomas Wolsey in Star Chamber*, Trowbridge, 1977, 38.

[196]   TNA SC 12/4/30; STAC 2/13/156. Skewes also served other members of the nobility. He was, for example, one of the executors of Edward Courtenay, earl of Devon's will, TNA C 1/471/20.

it is probable that proceedings were held at the Hospitallers' Priory at Clerkenwell, as had a previous local case that Skewes and the king's sergeant of the larder dealt with on 29 January 1527.[197] This in turn suggests that Clerkenwell Priory was used for state business not only for the convenience of the Prior, but also as a base for the crown. It may also explain why an increasing number of crown servants were becoming tenants of the Priory at this time.[198] While the report is not evidence that Weston served on the council itself, it does show that he worked closely with it, at least in the late 1520s and early 1530s. Nevertheless, the lack of reference to him from this point on suggests that he played a minor role compared to his predecessors, a trend replicated by a lack of diplomatic commissions or appointment as a trier of petitions in parliament.

Conclusion

Finally, it remains to dispel a few myths about the political role of the Prior in late medieval England that are found in crusading histories. Field has claimed that the Prior had 'access to the king' due to his place in the House of Lords and 'the royal council'.[199] However, attendance in the Lords at parliament did not guarantee access to the king, especially as the king often attended only on the first and last day of a parliamentary session. Additionally, Tyerman has asserted that the Prior 'was automatically a royal councillor' and 'the premier baron of England, ranking above all other lay barons'.[200] The second statement has been dealt with in the section on precedence above, and the first can be dismissed for the simple reason that no one was automatically a royal councillor, that is a member of the king's council, because each king chose and dismissed his councillors as and when he pleased. The Prior can only be construed as an 'automatic' royal councillor in the broad sense that he was regularly called to great council, where magnates offered their advice to the king, but summons to the great council does not imply the same intimacy or depth of service as was expected of those on the king's council. It has also been suggested that the enrolment of Langstrother's oath of fealty to Edward IV in 1469 was 'virtually unprecedented', having not been required since the reign of Richard II.[201] However, although we know of only two other Priors before Langstrother, John Pavely (in 1354) and John Radington (in 1382), who swore oaths of fealty to the crown, it is possible that other Priors swore fealty but because they did not protest, no record was kept.[202] Furthermore, Priors swore general allegiance

---

[197] TNA REQ 2/1, bundle 41 (documents in REQ 2/1 were loose and not numbered when I consulted them).
[198] Skewes was a paid Hospitaller official in 1526 (BL Cotton Claudius E VI, f. 286), and at least one sergeant of the king's larder, James Mitchell (1536, 1539), leased land from the Prior, TNA LR 2/62, ff. 131–131v, 181v–182.
[199] Field, 'Sir Robert Malory', 249; P. J. C. Field, *The Life and Times of Sir Thomas Malory*, Cambridge, 1993, 68, where he repeats his 1977 claim verbatim.
[200] Tyerman, *England and Crusades*, 355.
[201] O'Malley, *English Knights Hospitaller*, 130.
[202] *CCR 1354–1360*, 54; *CCR 1381–1385*, 208.

to the crown in common with other lords, such as those oaths performed in the parliaments of 1455, 1459 and 1471.[203] Langstrother's oath should not be regarded as unusual, given the upheaval at that time. Henry VI obtained a similar one from him the following year.[204]

In summary, a number of conclusions can be made on the Prior's political role. Firstly, it appears that the Prior was summoned to parliament and great councils from the mid-thirteenth century at least, and any lack of his summons thereafter is explained by absence abroad. Nevertheless, from the 1330s the Prior received summonses more frequently, suggesting that he remained in the realm more often. This appears to have coincided with the outbreak of the Hundred Years War. Secondly, the Prior attended all parliaments and great councils when in the realm, regardless of where they took place, making him one of the few lords who always chose to obey the summons. Thirdly, those Priors who remained in the realm for long periods became more involved in English politics. This was a process that started with Prior Pavely's appointment as a trier of petitions and progressed by 1451 to Prior Botyll's attendance on the king's council. This was a long process of integration that might have happened more quickly, but was drawn out by the lengthy absences abroad of Priors Radington, Grendon, Hulles and Malory. Records of Prior Botyll's service on king's council between 1451 and 1463 indicate that he was acceptable to Henry VI, Richard, duke of York, and Edward IV, which suggests that he was considered both a neutral political figure and a valuable member of government, so valuable that by 1459 his presence was considered 'full necessary for many causes' and he was not allowed to leave the realm.[205] The records in the council files also reveal that Botyll's attitude was that he was willing to serve any monarch who brought stability to the realm. As illustrated in the previous chapter, this trend of service in internal politics was mirrored by the Prior's increasing role as an English diplomat from the late fourteenth century. The Prior's more regular attendance at parliament and involvement in politics led to his designation as the premier baron in parliament, but this status was not assigned until the first half of the fifteenth century, when precedence was first discussed. The Prior remained active in English politics until the late 1520s. Prior William Weston appears to have taken less part in English politics, not serving as a trier of petitions or directly on king's council. This was because most of his term of office coincided with the Reformation Parliament of 1529–36 and the Dissolution of the Monasteries between 1536 and 1540.

[203] *Rot. Parl.*, V, 282–3, 351–2; VI, 234.
[204] *CCR 1468–1476*, 161.
[205] *POPC*, VI, 301.

**Figure 10: Summonses and attendance at Parliament
and Great Council, 1295–1389**[206]

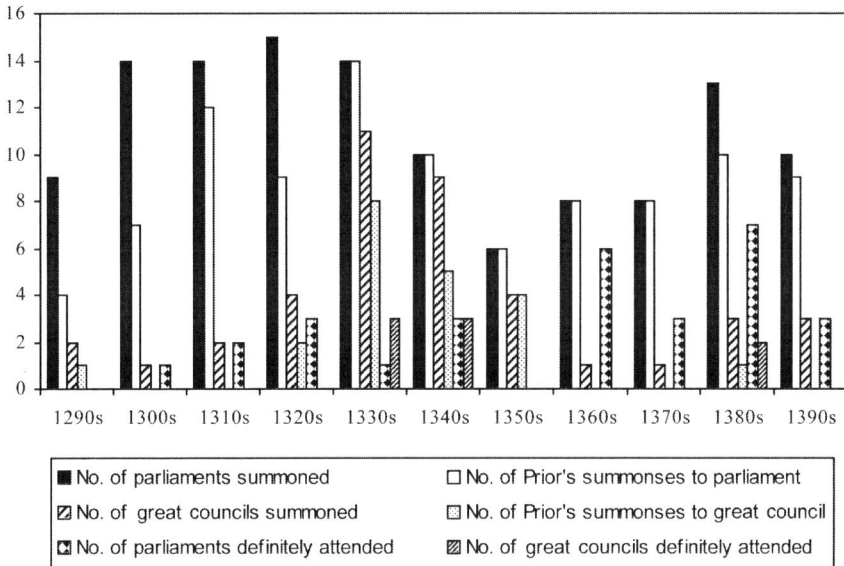

Source: *Rot. Parl., CCR, RDP, Parl. Writs.*

**Figure 11: Summonses and attendance at parliament
and great council, 1400–1539**[207]

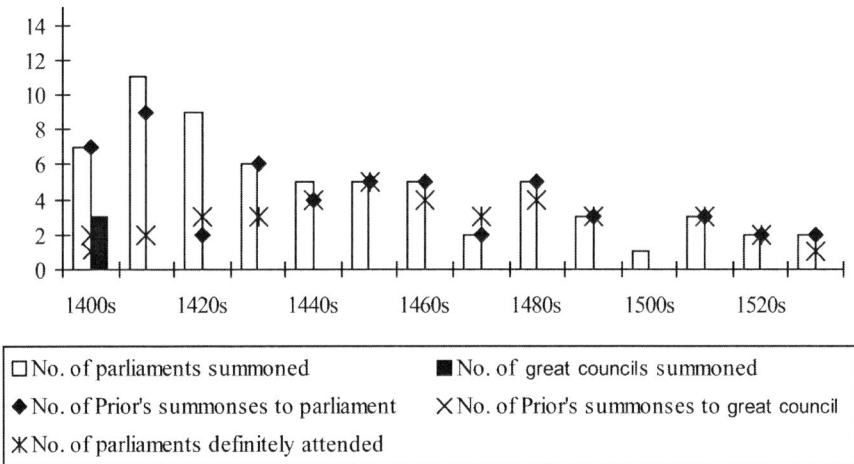

Source: *Rot. Parl., CCR, RDP, Lords Journals, L&P H VIII.*

---

[206] Attendance at parliament (until the 1360s) and great council was not normally known during this period.

[207] While attendance at parliament was normally known, attendance at great council was not normally recorded.

Figure 12: Daily attendance at parliament, February to March 1515[208]

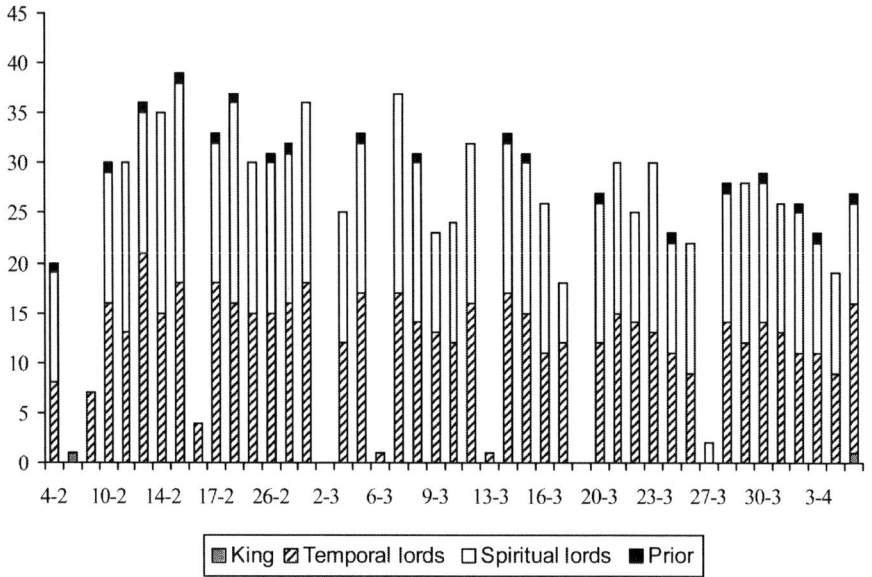

**Figure 13: Daily attendance at parliament,
November to December 1515**

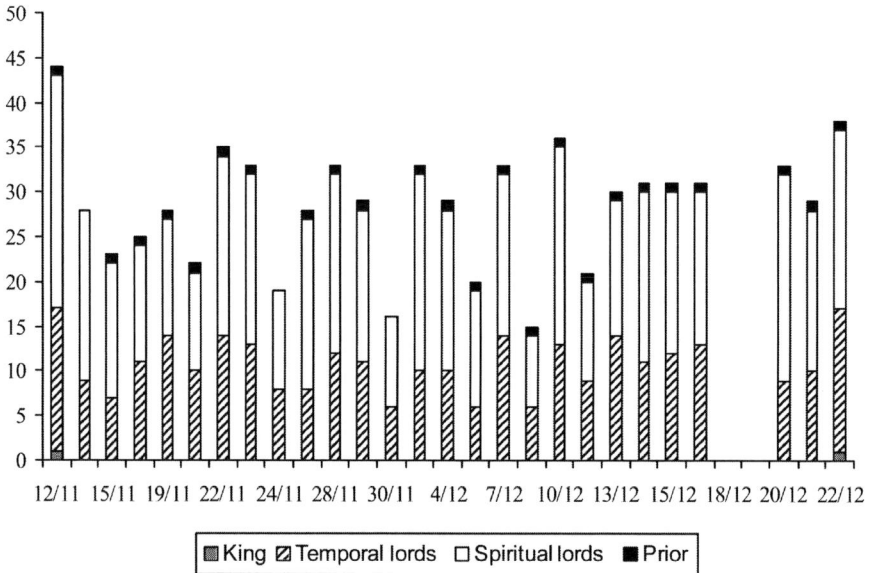

[208] Attendance at parliament in Figures 12 to 15 is taken from *Lords Journals*, I, *passim*.

Figure 14: Daily attendance at parliament, 1534

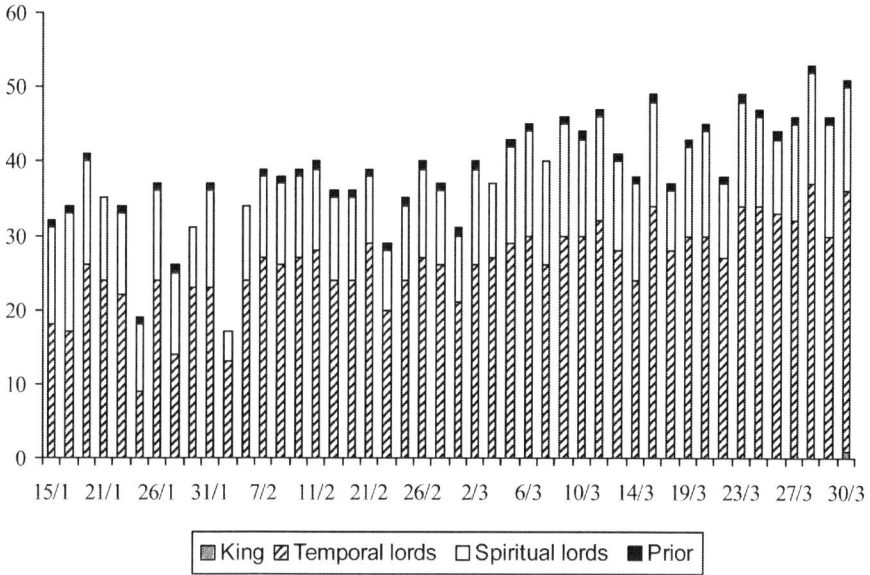

Figure 15: Daily Attendance at parliament, June to July 1536

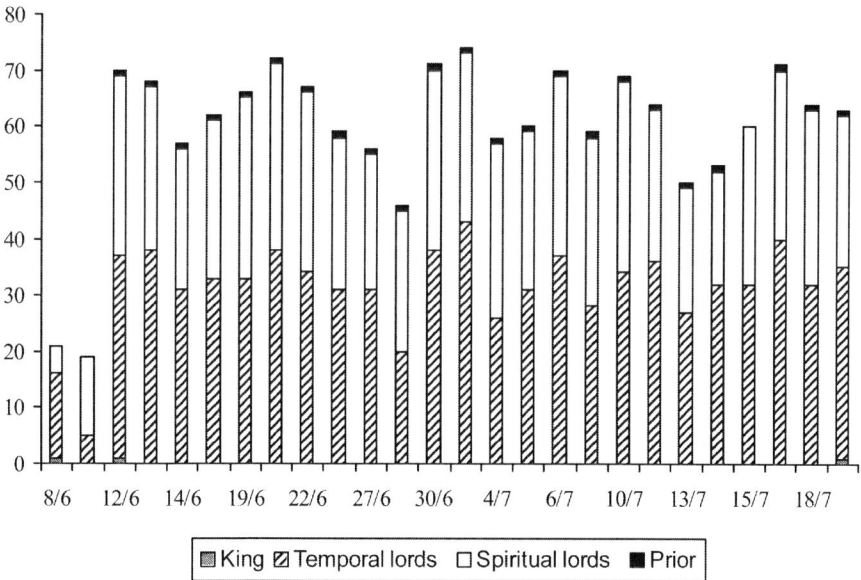

Figure 16: Triers of overseas petitions in Parliament, 1362–9[209]

Year	Category	Triers of petitions
1362	Overseas	Bishops of Salisbury, Chester, Chichester, abbot of Evesham, Prior of St John, earls of Suffolk and Salisbury, Lord Manny, Henry le Scrope, knight, John Mowbray, knight, John Knivet
1363	Overseas	Bishops of Durham, Hereford, Rochester, St David's, Chichester, abbots of Waltham and Evesham, Prior of St John, earls of Stafford, Salisbury and Anjou, Lords Dispenser and Roos, Walter Manny, Henry le Scrope, Roger Beauchamp, John Mowbray, knights, Thomas Ingleby
1365	Overseas	Bishops of Durham, Hereford, Worcester, St David's, abbots of St Edmund's, Reading, Abingdon, Prior of St John, earls of Stafford, Salisbury, Devon and Anjou, Lord Despenser, Walter Manny, Henry le Scrope, Roger Beauchamp, John Mowbray, Thomas Ingleby, knights
1366	Overseas	Bishops of Durham, Hereford, Worcester, St David's, abbots of St Edmund's, Glastonbury, Reading, Prior of St John, earls of Stafford, Salisbury, Devon and Anjou, Lord Despenser, Walter Manny, Roger Beauchamp, John Mowbray, Thomas Ingleby, William Wichingham, knights
1368	Overseas	Bishops of Durham, Hereford, Worcester, St David's, abbots of St Edmund's, Prior of St John, earls of Stafford, Devon and Anjou, Walter Manny, Roger Beauchamp, John Mowbray, Thomas Ingleby, William Wichingham, knights
1369	Overseas	Bishops of Durham, Hereford, Chichester, St David's, abbots of St Albans, St Edmund's, Peterborough, Evesham, Prior of St John, earls of Stafford, Devon and Anjou, Roger Beauchamp, John Mowbray, Thomas Ingleby, William Wichingham, knights

Source: *Rot. Parl.*, II

---

[209] The triers of petitions in Figures 16 to 18 are listed in the order in which they appear in *Rotuli Parliamentorum*.

Figure 17: Triers of overseas petitions in Parliament, 1378–80

Year	Category	Triers
1378 Gloucester	Overseas	Archbishop of York, bishops of Durham, Lincoln, Bath and Wells, Hereford, Rochester, Worcester, St Asaph, Bangor, abbot of Westminster, Prior of St John, earls of Cambridge, Buckingham (constable), Salisbury, Suffolk, Lords Lestrange of Knockin, Fitzwater, John Montague, John Arundel (marshall), Robert Tresillian, Roger Fulthorpe, Henry Asty, John Deverose, knights
1379	Overseas	Archbishop of York, bishops of Durham, Lincoln (also trier for England), Bath and Wells, Chichester, Hereford, Rochester, St Asaph, abbots of Westminster, Waltham, earl of Buckingham (constable), duke of Brittany (earl of Richmond), Prior of St John, earls of Stafford and Suffolk, Lords Lestrange of Knockin, Bardolf, John Montague, Robert Tresillian, Roger Fulthorpe, Henry Asty, knights
1380	Overseas	Archbishop of York, bishops of Durham, Bath and Wells, Chichester, Hereford, Rochester, abbots of St Austin at Canterbury, Gloucester, Waltham, earl of Buckingham (constable), Prior of St John, earls of Stafford and Suffolk, Lords Lestrange of Knockin, Bardolf, John Montague, Robert Tresillian, Henry Asty, knights

Source: *Rot. Parl.*, III

Figure 18: Triers of overseas petitions in Parliament, 1383–5

Year	Category	Triers
1383	Overseas	Bishops of Lincoln, Norwich, St David's, Exeter, Hereford, abbots Westminster, Glastonbury, earls of Cambridge, Buckingham (constable), Stafford, Salisbury, Lord Fitzwater, Prior of St John, John Cobham of Kent, William Skipwith, Roger Fulthorp, David Hammer, knights
1384 April	Overseas	Bishops of Lincoln, Hereford, abbot of Hyde, Prior of St John, earls of Oxford, Salisbury, John Cobham of Kent, William Skipwith, David Hammer, knights
1384 Nov.	Overseas	Bishops of Lincoln, Norwich, St David's, Exeter, Hereford, abbots of Westminster, Glastonbury, earls of Cambridge, Buckingham, Stafford, Salisbury, Lord Fitzwater, Prior of St John, John Cobham of Kent, William Skipwith, Roger Fulthorp, David Hammer, William Burgh, knights
1385	Overseas	Archbishop of York, bishops of Exeter, Hereford, Durham, abbots of Westminster, Glastonbury, dukes of York, Gloucester, earls of Stafford, Salisbury, Lord Fitzwater, Prior of St John, John Cobham of Kent, Roger Fulthorp, David Hammer, William Burgh, knights

Source: *Rot. Parl.*, III

Figure 19: Attendance at king's council, 1451–2[210]

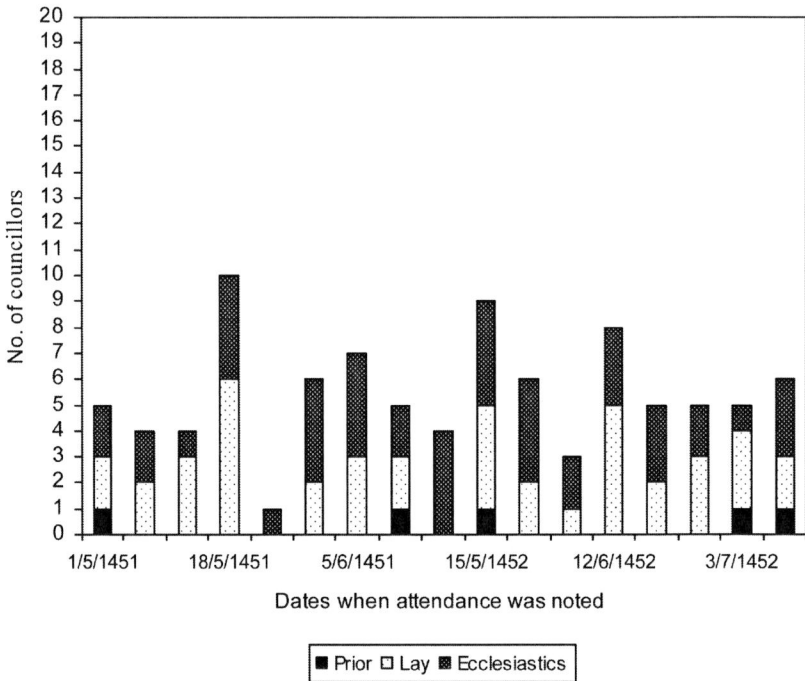

Dates when attendance was noted

■ Prior □ Lay ▨ Ecclesiastics

Source: TNA E 28/81–2

---

[210] In Figures 19 to 23, the Prior is marked separately in order to recognise him easily, but he should be considered as one of the lay lords.

Figure 20: Attendance at king's council, 1453

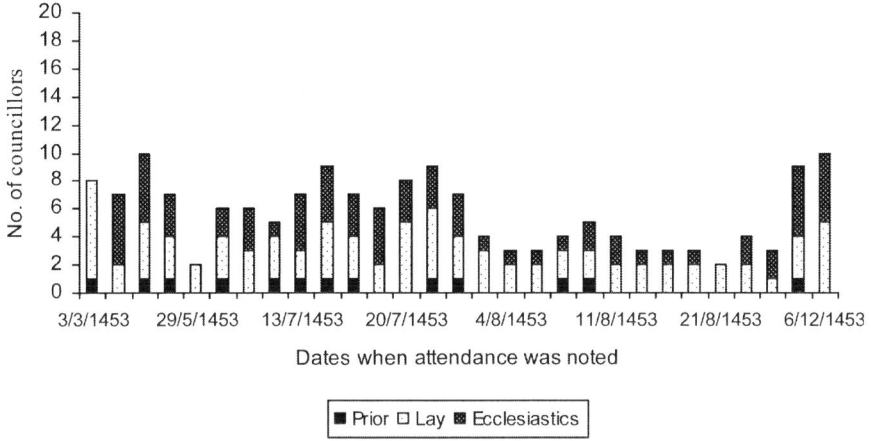

Dates when attendance was noted

Prior □ Lay ▓ Ecclesiastics

Source: TNA E 28/83, *POPC*

Figure 21: Attendance at king's council, 1454

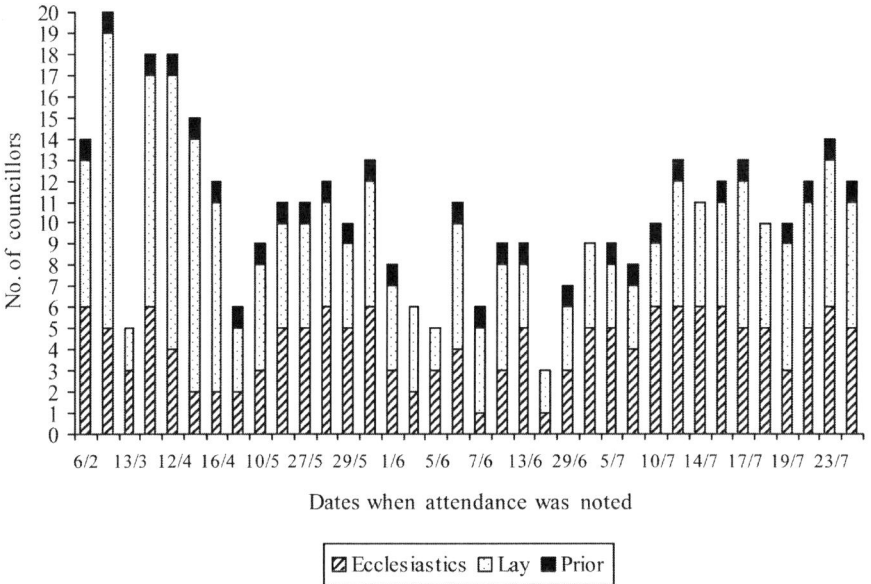

Dates when attendance was noted

▨ Ecclesiastics □ Lay ■ Prior

Source: TNA E 28/84–5, *POPC*

Figure 22: Attendance at king's council, 1455

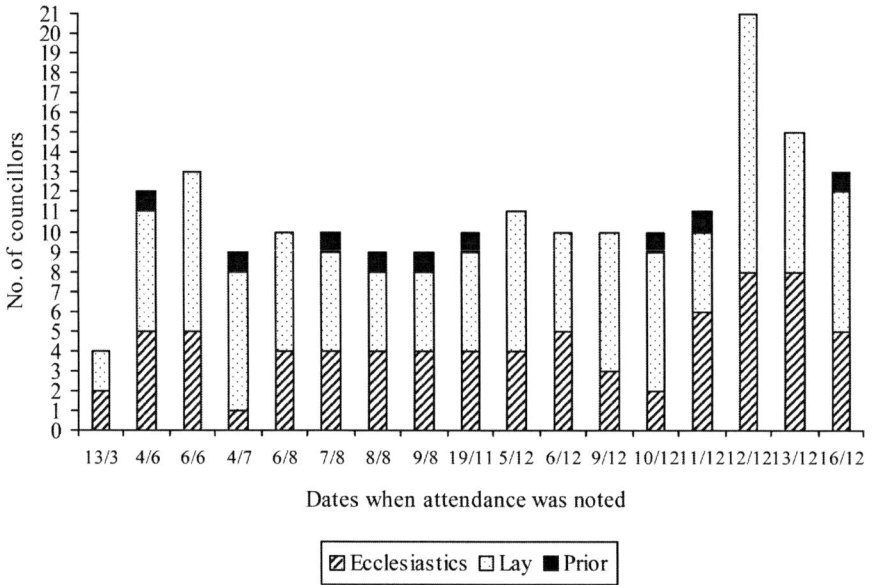

Dates when attendance was noted

☒ Ecclesiastics ☐ Lay ■ Prior

Source: TNA E 28/86–7

Figure 23: Attendance at king's council, 1456–63

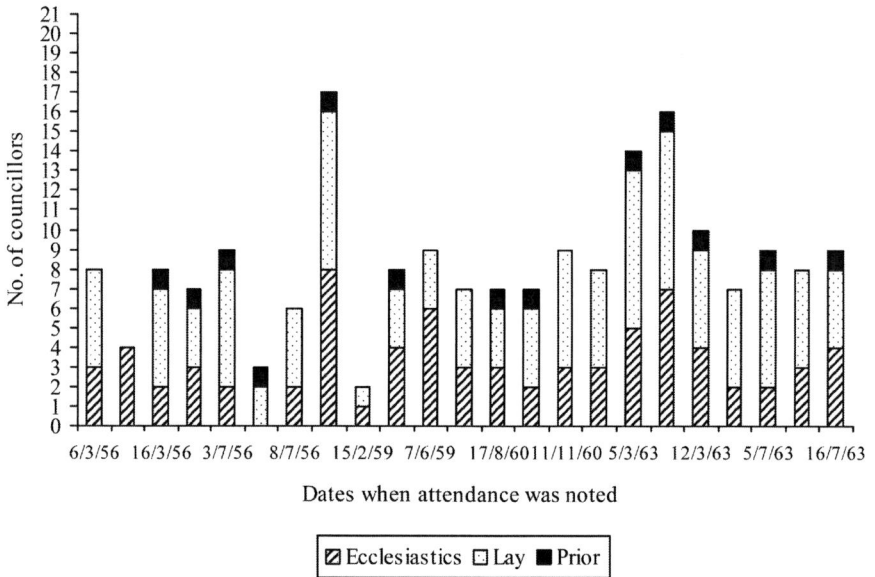

Dates when attendance was noted

☒ Ecclesiastics ☐ Lay ■ Prior

Source: TNA E 28/87–9

6

The Prior and the Secularisation of the Order in England

From their inception, the military orders had an ambiguous status that led contemporaries to confuse whether they were secular or monastic, and this still perplexes historians today. Anthony Luttrell has pointed out that although professed members were religious and the brethren took vows of poverty, chastity, and obedience, and followed a rule approved by the papacy, they were not strictly speaking monks or canons. Neither, he continues, were they knights in the secular sense. Knight-brethren were always a minority of the total membership.[1] He concludes that there is 'no tidy classification of a military order'.[2] Recent research by Cunich, moreover, has challenged the traditional view that monks took vows of poverty, chastity and obedience, as they do today. Those vows were principally taken by mendicant friars, and the majority of monks and regular canons took vows only of stability, conversion of life and obedience.[3] The Rule of Hospitaller Master Raymond de Puy (1120–60) had committed all brethren to chastity, obedience (that is, to obey whatever their superiors commanded), and to live without property of their own.[4] Yet even at this early stage in the Order's existence, there was provision for exception to the Rule. For example, the Rule stated that those who fornicated in secret should do penance in secret, a penance they imposed on themselves. It was only those who broke their vow of chastity with public knowledge, and thus brought dishonour on the Order, who were punished.[5] There was also provision in the Rule for brethren to have private property, if disclosed to the master, on the understanding that it would pass to the Order on their death: a statute of 1295 seems to confirm this.[6] The vow that appears to have become the most important, both from the Rule and the later statutes that were built on it, was that of obedience. For instance, a statute of 1283 did not explicitly mention holding possessions or breaking chastity as reasons for

[1] A. Luttrell, 'The Military Orders: Further Definitions', *Sacra Militia*, I, 2000, 7.
[2] *Ibid.*, 12.
[3] P. Cunich, 'Dissolution and De-Conversion: Institutional Change and Individual Response in the 1530s', *International Medieval Research*, V, 1998, 25–42.
[4] *The Rule, Statutes and Customs of the Hospitallers 1099–1310*, ed. E. J. King, London, 1934, 20.
[5] *Ibid.*, 23.
[6] *Ibid.*, 25; *The Thirteenth Century Statutes of the Knights Hospitallers*, ed. E. J. King, Order of St John of Jerusalem Historical Pamphlet 6, London, 1933, 40.

brethren to lose their habit, but it did mention desertion, disloyalty or surrender in battle without the Master's permission.[7] This emphasis on obedience is understandable given the increasing military role that the Hospitallers assumed from the twelfth century onwards.

Such complexities of definition acknowledged, it is still possible to conduct an analysis of the 'secularisation' of the Prior and English Hospitallers. Although Priors were part lay, they were also part ecclesiastic. When one talks of 'secularisation' in this context, what is meant is the Prior's loss of control of possessions to lay persons. This chapter will deal with the secularisation of the English Priory mainly by looking at the Prior's leases of property over the 50 years prior to the Dissolution. Although the 1442 report records a handful of leases from the foundation of the Order in England until the date of that report, indentures of leases only survive consistently and in enough quantity for analysis from 1492. Unlike the Templars or the monastic orders, the Hospitallers were already leasing out a substantial proportion of their property in England from an early stage.[8] Since Hospitaller land was largely dispersed, leasing was the most efficient way of farming it.[9] Unfortunately, it is not possible to say that more property was leased out in the 1530s than was in the 1330s by comparing the lease books to the 1338 Survey. There are two reasons for this. Although the 1338 Survey does indicate some leasing of property, especially *camerae* and ex-Templar possessions, it is more concerned with income and expenditure than with the details of the actual leases. Secondly, since no proper reorganisation of the English Priory had been made by the time of the 1338 Survey to incorporate and merge the Templar possessions, any comparison may well give the wrong impression of greater leasing in the 1530s. Thus Upleadon (Hereford) was a separate preceptory in 1338, but by the 1530s it had been demoted to the status of a manor of Dinmore preceptory (Hereford) and was being farmed out.[10] One might think that this was evidence of greater leasing, but it is an illusion. The only way to judge any trend to greater leasing is by analysing the indentures recorded in the provincial chapter meetings, commonly called the 'lease books', extant from 1492 to 1539.[11] These reveal that leasing was widespread by the late fifteenth century. Given that demesne farming had been in retreat throughout England since the fourteenth century and was all but complete by the early fifteenth century, this is to be expected.

The records of the provincial chapters for the three last Priors of England have been used in order to detect any changes in leasing patterns. These cover the years 1492–1501, under Prior Kendal, 1503–26, under Prior Docwra, and 1529–39,

---

7   It does forbid plunder on the battlefield and sodomy, but these could have been forbidden for practical military reasons rather than religious ones, *ibid.*, 29.
8   Examples include TNA DL 25/320, under Prior Ralph Dineham (1178–81); TNA E 40/2416, under Prior Robert Dineham (1223–34); TNA DL 25/3275, under Prior Chauncy (1273–80); TNA E 329/55, under Prior Tothale (1295–1315).
9   M. Gervers, 'Pro defensione Terre Sancti: The development and Exploitation of the Hospitallers' Landed Estates in Essex', in *The Military Orders: Fighting for the Faith and Caring for the Sick*, ed. M. Barber, Aldershot, 1994, 3–20 at 17.
10   1338 Survey, 195–6; TNA LR 2/62, ff. 150v–151, 185–185v.
11   BL MS Lansdowne 200, 1492–1501; BL MS Cotton Claudius E VI, 1504–26; TNA LR2/62, 1529–39.

under Prior Weston. There are 1,340 individual indentures in total for the whole of the English Priory.[12] Using a relational database, these records have been filtered to concentrate on the properties that the Prior had influence over, most of which refer to Clerkenwell, but also including other priorial *camerae*, which by the 1490s were Cressing, Sampford, Balsall and Melchbourne.[13] The *camera* of Peckham and its members was under the control of the Grand Master, but he usually awarded it to the Prior. Concentration on the Prior's indentures gives a good indication of what was happening in the English Priory as a whole, as of the 1,340 entries covering 1492 to 1539, 832 (62 per cent) relate to the Prior. This increases to 63.5 per cent, if one counts indentures for Priors Docwra and William Weston when they were preceptors, and 68 per cent if preceptor-brethren related to the Prior are included. The provincial chapters record not only the leases of land, but also appointments of officials, confraters, grants of presentations, manumissions and annuities. All of these categories have been included in the sample because they all indicate the extent of the Prior's patronage. Three main questions are addressed in the following sections. Firstly, who was the Prior leasing to? Secondly, how much land passed totally out of the Prior's control? Thirdly, in conclusion, how, if at all, did the suppression of the English Priory fit into the Dissolution of the Monasteries?

Although Priors and preceptors had to take decisions on a day-to-day basis, the main business of the Priory was dealt with, and ratified at, the provincial chapter. If there was not a lot to discuss or quick decisions had to be made, then an assembly was held. If the Prior was absent for a long period, as was the case for Prior Docwra in 1503 and 1504, then his lieutenant held the meeting. These meetings tended to be quite short, and dealt with limited, urgent business. For example, those of 1503–04 only authorised the anticipation of incomes for preceptors who had been called for service on Rhodes.[14] Proper chapters were not held until Docwra returned to England, as indicated by his coat of arms inscribed at the start of the first chapter he presided over in 1505.[15] Yearly chapters were held under Prior Kendal between 1492 and 1501. Under Prior Docwra, this trend continued from 1503 until 1519, after which three more were held in 1522, 1524 and 1526. Under Prior Weston, meetings were less frequent, with six meetings in 1529, 1531, 1533, 1536, 1537 and 1539. That provincial chapters were not held in other years is indicated in a letter written by Richard Lister to Lord Darcy in October 1521, in which he comments that no chapter was kept at St John's because the Prior was at Calais.[16] Indentures were written out before the meetings, inferred by the occasional entry when there is a gap where the name should be. Although only the decisions, not the discussions, are recorded, what we find in the lease books is a good representation of the business that was carried on at the chapter. It is, not surprisingly, very similar to the

---

[12] There are an additional seven indentures of maintenance at Clerkenwell for service granted at the provincial chapter on 23 June 1481 presided over by Prior John Weston. These are listed after the 1526 provincial chapter, and notes in the margin indicate those who were deceased.

[13] Cressing, Sampford and Melchbourne appear from at least 1381, NLM 321, ff. 145–145v; Balsall from at least 1433, NLM 345, ff. 126–7.

[14] BL MS Cotton Claudius E VI, ff. 3–7v.

[15] *Ibid.*, f. 8.

[16] *L&P HVIII 1521–1523*, III, 696.

business conducted by the English Hospitallers at their headquarters in Viterbo and then Malta, illustrated by the deliberations of the English tongue.

Leasing-out of Possessions

Indentures made at the provincial chapters were approved by the Prior and the brethren present there.[17] Approval by the provincial chapter for the Prior's indentures meant that they were valid beyond the life of any one Prior. Preceptors needed to get the Prior's approval for significant indentures that were made, as the Prior held the freehold of all Hospitaller property in the English Priory. This is clear from a legal case in 1388 involving the prioress of Buckland (the defendant), who claimed that although the two Hospitaller houses at Buckland were one preceptory, jointly ruled by the preceptor and prioress, they were subject to the Prior of England, who held the freehold and against whom any legal action should be taken.[18]

Apart from getting the approval of the brethren at the provincial chapter, the English Prior (and preceptors) had virtual autonomy when it came to making indentures from the Hospitaller headquarters on Rhodes or Malta. Specific permission to lease was only required in two circumstances. Firstly, preceptors needed to have the Grand Master's approval, in the form of a magisterial bull, to lease their preceptories (though they could still lease individual manors without permission), and this was granted in advance for the period, normally three years, that they did service in the East. Secondly, the Prior needed the Grand Master's approval to lease the magisterial *camera* of Peckham, although by the late 1530s this no longer seemed necessary. Through analysis of the lease books from 1492 to 1539, we can identify four distinct groups with whom the Prior made indentures: (a) hereditary tenants (those to whom the lease passed in succession), (b) Hospitaller servants, (c) the Prior's kin and (d) crown servants. As we shall see, crown servants became an increasingly significant group leasing from the Prior.[19]

During Kendal's priorship, farms were the overwhelming form of indenture, as they were under all three Priors (see Figure 24), although under Weston there appears to be a reduction in the number of farms from that of his predecessor. That is not surprising, as Docwra held office for much longer (26 years) than Kendal (12 years), or Weston (13 years), so more leases expired during his priorship than he was able to reallocate. The other aspect that stands out is the large increase in the granting out of the temporary rights of presentations to Hospitaller-controlled churches under Prior Weston. The possible reasons for these variations will be discussed later in this chapter, but first, the types of indentures will be analysed in relation to the four

---

[17] Minor indentures that do not appear in the lease books also appear in a few surviving manor court rolls, for example, Shakespeare Birthplace Trust Records Office, DR18/30/4/1–5 for Balsall; TNA SC 2/153/31 for Melchbourne. It appears that these did not require the approval of the provincial chapter.

[18] *Year Books of Richard II, 12 Richard II, 1388–1389*, ed. G. F. Deiser, Ames Foundation VI, Cambridge, MA, and London, 1914, 152–3.

[19] TNA LR 2/62, ff. 12v–13, 14–14v, 56v–57, 72, 78–79, 91, 103–103v, 132, 133v, 164.

categories of persons that these indentures were made with. As will be seen, there was some crossover between categories.

Farms

There are two main ways to discover which category tenants fitted into: either from their family name, which tends to indicate hereditary tenancies or tenancies to the Prior's kin, or through the title, where given, which indicates Hospitaller servants, either described as 'servant' or as *dilectus nobilis in Christo* (henceforth DNC), the term generally used to describe lay members of the local community who were offering some sort of service to the Order, or crown servants. Analysing farm indentures under Prior Kendal (see Figure 25), those with no title and those referred to by profession, as esquires, gentlemen or by place of origin (81 per cent of the total categorised by title), seem to indicate hereditary tenancies, and a fair proportion of leases (38 per cent) were clearly stated as joint tenancies, for life, with wives and children, which indicates that they were grants in survivorship. Even those that were indentures made with single persons infer that they were being passed on. One illustration of this is the indentures with the Evinger family, beer brewers, who leased tenements in Charing Cross Street. At the June 1492 provincial chapter, John Evinger leased two cottages that had previously been let to a John Horsley from the time of Prior Tornay (1471–74).[20] At the July 1494 chapter, he was allowed to lease a further four cottages that Horsley had rented.[21] By September 1498, his son Andrew had taken on the tenancy and the following year was leasing these with his sister Margaret along with a further tenement (the Beerhouse) to the west of the six cottages.[22] John Evinger had leased the Beerhouse from at least 1483 (perhaps from 1479), as is clear from the alien subsidy roll of that year.[23] Although the leases did not specify that they were for life, they were very long leases, those to John being for 79 to 80 years, and those to his son Andrew from 71 to 75 years. Furthermore, an Ellen Evinger, widow, was leasing the Beerhouse in 1537 for a term of 60 years.[24] Five of the nine indentures made with Evinger family members were single tenancies, though it is apparent that it was expected that these leases would pass from husband to wife to children. The above categories illustrate automatic consecutive leases, with no sign of special patronage other than that they had leased from the Prior for generations.

The other categories, and some of those without a title, however, reveal a deeper level of patronage, even nepotism, and this becomes even clearer when one combines it with the information from family names. For example, one alderman of London

[20] BL MS Lansdowne 200, ff. 3, 21v.

[21] Horsley rented nine cottages in total. The implication is that he was subletting to Evinger, *ibid.*, ff. 21v–22.

[22] *Ibid.*, ff. 53–53v, 59v–60.

[23] *The Alien Communities of London in the Fifteenth Century. The Subsidy Rolls of 1440 and 1483–4*, ed. J. L. Bolton, Richard III and York History Trust, Stamford, 1998, 51.

[24] TNA LR 2/62, ff. 160v–161.

was Hugh Pemberton, a family associated with the Hospitallers in this period. In 1494 he was allowed (with the assent of the Grand Master) to farm the magisterial *camera* of Peckham for three years, and this was renewed for a further three years in 1496.[25] Another example was the 20-year lease in 1496 of Burgham rectory, Kent, to the archdeacon of Northampton, Peter Hussey, another surname associated with the Hospitallers.[26] It seems appropriate here to mention that Kendal gave preference to his relatives. Although no one with the name Kendal is mentioned, he was related to both the Tong and the Hussey families.[27] In 1492, a John Tong, gentleman, was granted the lease of a tenement in St John's Street, Clerkenwell, adjacent to tenements that he already held there, and was granted a further two cottages there in 1499, both leases for 50 years.[28] Kendal allowed his fellow Hospitaller kin, John Tong, preceptor of Mount St John and Ribston, to have a life-lease of Temple Dinsley (Herts.) in 1498.[29] The following year, he leased Fletchampstead manor (Warwick, part of Balsall) to George Tong, gentleman, for life.[30]

Although all of the Prior's tenants were considered his servants to one extent or another, quite a few are mentioned directly as such, denoted either as DNC or 'our servant'. Some were granted farms of land, such as William Yolton, gentleman, DNC, and wife Agnes, who were granted a tenement in St John's Street for life in 1493.[31] In 1495, Richard Baily was granted a tenement in St John's Street for 80 years and had the right to enjoy hospitality in Clerkenwell Priory.[32] Finally, in 1499 Richard Pasmere, servant of the Prior, and his wife Joanne had two indentures for lands that were part of Rainham manor (Rainham Berwick, Essex) for 99 years, one rented for the nominal amount of a ruby rose, the other for 6s. 8d. These leases were renewed the following year, on Richard's death, to Joanne alone, on the same terms.[33] Evidently the Prior wanted his servants close at hand and in charge of important manors, such as Rainham Berwick, where John Weston liked to spend the summer and where Kendal held the September 1496 provincial chapter, under his direct control. Such long leases, presumably with their aggregated entry fines, could also indicate that the Prior maximised his own profits at the expense of his successors.[34]

There is also some evidence of leases to those with government connections (see Figure 26). In 1493, Kendal granted a 90-year lease of a tenement in Fleet Street to Thomas Roche, a baron of the exchequer.[35] Roche was very active in the government administration and legal issues around this time, and could certainly

[25] BL MS Lansdowne 200, ff. 18, 37.

[26] *Ibid.*, f. 39.

[27] We know the Tongs and Husseys were related, and thus both kin of Kendal, from a later reference to a Thomas Tong, 'alias Hussey', in 1533, TNA LR 2/62, f. 109–109v.

[28] BL MS Lansdowne 200, ff. 6, 71.

[29] *Ibid.*, f. 54–54v.

[30] *Ibid.*, ff. 66–67v.

[31] *Ibid.*, f. 15.

[32] *Ibid.*, f. 26–26v.

[33] *Ibid.*, ff. 74–74v, 83–83v.

[34] We cannot be certain whether entry fines were charged, as such revenues were considered the Prior's personal income and are therefore not stated in the indentures, but it seems likely.

[35] BL MS Lansdowne 200, f. 11.

have helped Kendal in various ways.[36] A more high-profile lease was that in 1495 of Hampton Court manor for 80 years to Giles Lord Daubeney, who held important offices throughout Henry VII's reign (e.g. lieutenant of Calais, king's chamberlain), and who had gone on the 1492 embassy to France with Kendal.[37] Such a contact at the heart of government would have been most useful, especially in 1495, when Kendal had faced accusations of involvement in the Perkin Warbeck conspiracy.

In summary most of Prior Kendal's farms were leased to hereditary tenants or servants. Only a small proportion were clear examples of new patronage. This may be explained because a Prior was normally appointed towards the end of his career and thus did not have time to apportion much patronage before his death, especially when awaiting the expiry of existing leases. Kendal was only Prior for 12 years, when indentures made by Priors Tornay and John Weston were still valid and, due to their length, only occasionally expiring. There is even one example of a hereditary lease, originally granted by Prior Tothale and the English brethren at the Melchbourne provincial chapter in June 1311, which only expired in 1515.[38]

Thomas Docwra, however, was Prior for 26 years. Did he personally distribute more patronage than his predecessor? As with Prior Kendal, the vast majority (76 per cent) indicate hereditary tenancies. Again, as with Kendal, Docwra's servants, such as Francis Bell, who leased Peckham for 21 years, William Warde and Guthlac Overton, auditor general of Priory, were rewarded for their efforts, although Overton, at least, did not work exclusively for the Prior.[39] Docwra, like Kendal, leased lands to his kin and those related to other Hospitallers. In 1511, he leased Edgware (Middx.) and Theydon Bois (Essex) manors to George Dalison esquire (possibly a relative of Docwra and certainly of the Dalison Hospitaller brethren) after the lease made by John Weston in 1486 had expired. This was followed up three years later by a grant of the reversion of tenements in St John's Street, Clerkenwell, after the death of Joanne Sutton.[40]

There is indisputable evidence of preferment under Docwra towards his kin. In 1506, Prior Docwra farmed two tenements in St John's Street on 40-year leases to John Docwra (d. 1511), clerk, prebendary of Blewbury (Wilts.), a position Prior Docwra had him appointed to in 1503.[41] At the same chapter, John leased land in Somerset on a 60-year lease from preceptor Lancelot Docwra.[42] In 1526, another John Docwra (d. 1536), also appointed by the Prior as prebendary of Blewbury in

---

[36] TNA E 101/518/4 (1494); TNA E 326/178 (1496).

[37] BL MS Lansdowne 200, f. 30–30v; for Daubeney's appointment as lieutenant of Calais in 1486, see TNA E 41/419.

[38] Lands in Stanley, farmed by Tothale in June 1311 to John and Walter, sons of William Hamerton, and their heirs forever, for 8s. per annum, then by Docwra to Thomas Knawsburgh and his heirs forever in January 1515 for 11s. per annum, BL MS Cotton Claudius E VI, ff. 138, 141–141v.

[39] *Ibid.*, ff. 92, 151v, 165v, 191v–192 for Warde; *ibid.*, ff. 132–132v, 202v–203v for Bell; *ibid.*, ff. 87–87v, 95, 189–189v for Overton; Overton was solicitor for Sir John Sharpe and was training his nephew as an auditor. It is not possible to say whether he was related to Richard Overton, the turcopolier and preceptor of Eagle in the 1370s, TNA C 1/551/49.

[40] BL MS Cotton Claudius E VI, ff. 87v–88; *ibid.*, ff. 142–143.

[41] All indentures mentioned in this paragraph (except the two noted) were made between Prior Docwra and his relatives, *ibid.*, f. 46–46v; *Fasti Ecclesiae Anglicanae*, III, 38.

[42] BL Cotton Claudius E VI, f. 29–29v.

1524, was granted the lease of land in Rainham (Essex) from the Prior on a 29-year lease.[43] A further John Docwra, gentleman, son and heir of James the brother of Prior Docwra, farmed Hetherington manor (Northants.) for 40 years in 1508. In 1514 he farmed Sutton-at-Hone manor (Kent) for 50 years, and in 1516 he farmed Battisford preceptory for three years (from Brother Thomas Golin). Finally, in 1519, he farmed Temple Dinsley (Herts.) for 50 years and in 1522 the lease was extended for a further three years.[44]

Three other Docwra relatives gained grants of leases from Prior Docwra. In 1508, Miles Docwra, gentleman, and his wife Katherine farmed a cottage and garden in St John's Street, which they held for life. The following year Miles was granted the joint lease (with a John Sougax) of Morehall manor (Essex), again for life.[45] The same year (1509), Martin Docwra, gentleman of Balsall, was granted the farm of Fletchampstead manor for life and by 1515, he had been appointed seneschal of Balsall for life and was farming that manor on a 26-year lease in 1526. In the same year, he was also granted the farm of Greenham manor for life, which he held with his wife Isabel and son Edward.[46] Finally, in 1514 John Docwra, gentleman, son and heir of Thomas of Kirkby Kendall, Westmoreland, held the farm of tenements in St John's Lane, immediately outside the door of Clerkenwell Priory, for 60 years, as well as being granted maintenance in Clerkenwell for life, for his service to the Prior. The same year, he held the farm of Blewbury prebendary jointly with Miles Docwra and Christopher Green. Then in 1524, he farmed an additional messuage with tenements and stables in St John's Lane, on a 60-year lease.[47]

Although the Order was an undying corporation, such extensive nepotism suggests that it could be partially transformed into, and beyond, a monarchy. Approval by the provincial chapter for these indentures meant that leases extended after the life of the individual Priors who made them. This caused problems for the incoming Prior, as Prior Weston found after 1527. For example, Weston had to take legal action against John Docwra (son of Thomas of Kirkby Kendall), who was accused of taking bonds, jewels, plate and chattels belonging to the Hospitallers while Prior Docwra lay dying.[48] These relatives saw the goods as their own and sued for their return, as was the case with Thomas Chicheley, esquire of Wimpole, who had married one of Prior Docwra's nieces, and who took legal action against Prior Weston for seizing plate that had been given to him by Prior Docwra.[49] The most difficult situations, however, occurred when a relative both farmed lands and had been appointed to an office, as illustrated by Martin Docwra, who both leased Balsall and was seneschal of that manor. Soon after his return to England, Weston

43   *Fasti Ecclesiae Anglicanae*, III, 38; BL MS Cotton Claudius E VI, ff. 270v–271.
44   *Ibid.*, ff. 66v–67, 118v–119, 159–159v, 202–202v, 219–219v; *L&P HVIII 1540–1541*, XVI, 423–4.
45   BL MS Cotton Claudius E VI, ff. 65v–66, 73v–74.
46   *Ibid.*, ff. 72v–73, 87, 265–267. Additionally in 1526 he was granted the next presentation to Risley church, *ibid.*, f. 288v.
47   *Ibid.*, ff. 143v–144, 129v–130, 131–131v, 240v–241.
48   TNA C 1/598/7.
49   TNA C 1/392/56. Chicheley had been present at Clerkenwell on 3 November 1526, as one of the witnesses at the marriage of John Docwra (son of Thomas of Kirkby Kendall) and Elizabeth Turpin, BL MS Lansdowne 200, f. 1.

sued Martin Docwra for detention of deeds concerning Balsall and its members.[50] Docwra counter-sued (c. 1532) against Weston and Sir George Throckmorton, who had orders to take possession of the manor.[51] This had some success and Throckmorton does not appear in the lease books as seneschal of Balsall until 1539, after Martin Docwra's death.[52] However, disputes continued after Martin's decease. For example, his widow, Isabel, now married to Giles Forster, was accused by Weston of waste within the manor, though this did not stop them from getting an extension of the lease in 1539.[53]

The trend to lease to crown officials and those connected with government appears to have increased during Docwra's priorship, perhaps due to his own close connections formed on crown business (see Figure 27). Although only two minor officials are mentioned in the lease books specifically as crown servants (William Malhom and Anthony Lowe), others have been identified. John Cutte, knight, receiver general of the duchy of Lancaster, was renting Chaureth manor in Essex in 1505. The Hospitallers were not the only religious order from which he farmed. In 1511, he was also leasing lands from the prior of the London Charterhouse.[54] Other, minor, crown administrative and household servants, such as John Tayler (in 1511), Henry VIII's chaplain, and later master in chancery, William Malhom (in 1512), chancery clerk, and Antony Lowe (in 1519), of the king's household, farmed lands controlled by the Prior.[55] In addition, there is evidence of greater leasing to those whom Docwra knew from serving on the council and on diplomatic duty. For example, in 1505, Giles Lord Daubeney's lease was extended, on surrender of his previous indenture.[56] After the deaths of Daubeney (d. 1508) and of his heirs, the lease expired and Docwra farmed Hampton Court manor to Thomas Wolsey in 1515, previously Henry VII's chaplain, recently appointed archbishop of York and chancellor of England.[57] Hampton was a prime manor, excellently located to be near the court whether it was in London or the Thames Valley palaces. Both Daubeney and Wolsey entertained ambassadors and royalty there.[58] The lease of Hampton Court manor is also an example of how the crown had long regarded certain Hospitaller manors as if they were its own. Although officially Hospitaller property, the king sent his retired servants to be housed and receive pensions at Hampton Court manor from at least 1316 and then throughout the fourteenth century.[59] Occasionally the king himself lodged there, as in 1353.[60] By the late

---

[50] The exact date is not given, TNA C 1/588/36.

[51] TNA C 1/627/11; TNA C 1/778/30–33.

[52] TNA LR 2/62, f. 188–188v.

[53] TNA C 1/925/35; LR 2/62, ff. 179–181. Lease extended from 1552 to 1563. Isabel, who outlived Giles, was still farming Balsall in the 1540s, after the dissolution of the Order in England, TNA C 1/797/27–29; TNA C 1/1250/45–46.

[54] BL MS Cotton Claudius E VI, f. 13–13v; TNA E 328/267.

[55] BL MS Cotton Claudius E VI, ff. 94v–95; ibid., f. 109–109d; ibid., f. 193.

[56] Ibid., f. 8–8v.

[57] Ibid., f. 139–139v.

[58] S. Thurley, 'The Domestic Building Works of Cardinal Wolsey', in Cardinal Wolsey: Church, State and Art, ed. S. J. Gunn and P. G. Lindley, Cambridge, 1991, 76–102 at 87.

[59] CCR 1313–1318, 447; CCR 1341–1343, 660; CCR 1354–1360, 393; CCR 1360–1364, 244; CCR 1374–1377, 524; CCR 1377–1381, 141.

[60] CPR 1350–1354, 417.

fifteenth century, as noted above, crown servants and confidants (Daubeney, Wolsey) had long leases of the manor.[61] Finally, Prior Weston granted the revenues of a number of properties including Hampton Court to Wolsey, and within two years of Wolsey's fall in 1529, Henry VIII took formal possession of the manor himself.[62]

Other crown servants leased property from Docwra. In 1516, the Prior leased Temple Warwick manor to Sir Edward Belknapp, of the king's council, general surveyor of crown lands, and later (1519) to serve with Docwra on diplomatic duty.[63] In 1519, he leased Wilbraham manor (Cambs.) to Sir Thomas Boleyn (father of Anne), the queen's chamberlain, future earl of Wiltshire, and who served with Docwra on diplomatic duty in 1521.[64] Finally, in 1522, Docwra leased Sutton-at-Hone manor (Kent) for 60 years to Sir Richard Wingfield, who had gone on the diplomatic mission with him and Boleyn the previous year.[65] Docwra seems to have been giving favour to those who could either smooth (or potentially disrupt) administrative matters for the Hospitallers, who were perhaps of commercial value, or had the king's ear.

Finally, for farms, we come to Prior William Weston's leases. Deducting those to the Prior's servants of varying sorts, 70 per cent were hereditary leases, still the majority, but significantly lower than in Kendal's or Docwra's time. Another considerable difference was the drop in the number of leases to ecclesiastics to just two, one clerk (held jointly with one of Weston's servants) and one chaplain.[66] The greatest difference, however, is the increased number of farms to crown servants, 1.1 per cent under Kendal, 3.5 per cent under Docwra, but 8.5 per cent under Weston (see Figure 28). Many of the leases to crown servants were to those who also had Hospitaller links, for example, two leases (both concerning Temple Court manor, Surrey, 1529, 1531) to Richard Weston, William's brother, the treasurer of Calais at this point, and one (a tenement in St John's Lane, 1533) to Thomas Tong alias Hussey, keeper of the king's alms.[67] The examples of Weston and Tong indicate the intricate relationship between Hospitaller possessions and their movement into the lay realm through kinship ties. That Tong, a crown servant, was leasing a tenement in St John's Lane, within the outer section of Clerkenwell Priory, which was normally reserved for Hospitaller servants (as opposed to St John's Street, which was without the Priory, though part of its possessions), neatly illustrates this. Other kin under Kendal and Docwra had leased tenements within the outer Priory before, but none had been crown servants. This extra dimension is significant. As Hospitaller kin became ever more employed by the lay government, the crown was alerted to the potential for its other servants to lease Hospitaller lands. That this should happen more under Prior Weston is comprehensible when one realises that his father had been a crown official on Jersey since Henry VII's reign and his brother

---

[61] BL MS Lansdowne 200, f. 30–30v; BL MS Cotton Claudius E VI, ff. 8–8v, 139–139v.

[62] *L&P HVIII 1529–1530*, IV, 2473; *L&P HVIII 1531–1532*, V, 120–33; TNA E 41/152; TNA LR 2/62, f. 69–69v.

[63] BL MS Cotton Claudius E VI, f. 172v; TNA E 41/267.

[64] BL MS Cotton Claudius E VI, ff. 176v–177.

[65] *L&P HVIII 1521–1523*, III, 713–16.

[66] TNA LR 2/62, ff. 7v–8, 189.

[67] *Ibid.*, ff. 9d–10v, 69v, 109–109v.

Richard had been in royal service for many years and indeed helped him to obtain the priorship.[68] Richard had previously leased Baddesley and Mayne preceptory from his brother in 1516 and then for a further three years in 1519, though in both cases a bull of the Grand Master was needed to do so.[69]

Of the other crown servants, two are notable because of their role in the Dissolution. Firstly, Richard Rich, appointed chancellor of the court of augmentations in 1537, was granted the reversion of Broxbourne manor (Herts.) in 1539, once the current lease expired (1553).[70] Secondly, Prior Weston made three separate indentures with Thomas Cromwell, which illustrate how, as Cromwell grew in importance, he was granted leases in the hope that he would act in the Order's favour. In 1531 Cromwell, gentleman, was leased Temple Dartford and Sutton-at-Hone manors for 70 years at £50 a year.[71] In 1536, Cromwell, esquire, the king's chief secretary and recently appointed vicegerent, leased Highbury manor for 99 years at £34 1s. per annum[72] Finally, in 1537 Cromwell, knight and lord privy seal, leased the magisterial *camera* of Peckham for 60 years for a red rose (virtually nothing).[73] The leasing of Peckham is an apt illustration of the secularisation of the English Priory between the 1490s and 1530s. In 1494, Prior Kendal, by a magisterial bull dated 4 August 1490, leased Peckham for three years (backdated to 24 June 1493) to Hugh Pemberton, alderman of London, for £66 per annum[74] A new indenture on the same terms was made to Pemberton in 1496 for another three years, but this time no bull was cited, perhaps because the previous bull was considered sufficient.[75] Peckham next appears in the lease books in 1519, when, by authority of a magisterial bull dated 20 September 1516, Prior Docwra (also described as preceptor of Peckham) leased it to a Hospitaller servant, Francis Bell, for 21 years at £60 per annum, a slight lowering of the rent, but a substantial increase in the length of tenure.[76] By the final indenture that the lease books record for Peckham, in 1537, Prior Weston farmed the magisterial *camera* to Thomas Cromwell, without needing a magisterial bull, on the terms mentioned above.[77] This strongly suggests the liquidation of assets in the late 1530s in anticipation of the dissolution of the Priory.

As is indicated by the examples of Hampton and Peckham, there appears to have been a significant increase in the length of leases on the Prior's lands, especially those in and around London. Leases on lay estates during this period tended to be quite short, with few over 20 years in length.[78] The Prior's leases of manors

---

[68] T. Thornton, 'The English King's French Islands: Jersey and Guernsey in English Politics and Administration, 1485–1642', in *Authority and Consent in Tudor England*, ed. G. W. Bernard and S. J. Gunn, Aldershot, 2002, 197–217 at 206–7.

[69] BL MS Cotton Claudius E VI, ff. 158v–159, 186–186v.

[70] TNA LR 2/62, ff. 194v–195.

[71] *Ibid.*, ff. 74v–75.

[72] *Ibid.*, ff. 124v–125; C. J. Kitching, 'The Probate Jurisdiction of Thomas Cromwell as Vicegerent', *BIHR*, XLVI, 1973, 102–6 at 102.

[73] TNA LR 2/62, f. 160–160v.

[74] BL MS Lansdowne 200, f. 18.

[75] *Ibid.*, f. 37.

[76] BL MS Cotton Claudius E VI, ff. 202v–203v.

[77] TNA LR2/62, f. 160–160v.

[78] S. J. Gunn, 'Henry Bourchier, Earl of Essex (1472–1540)', in *The Tudor Nobility*, ed. G. W. Bernard, Manchester, 1992, 134–79 at 147.

were more akin to those on episcopal estates, where the average lease in the first years of Henry VIII's reign was between 20 and 40 years.[79] The lease of Whetstone manor (Middx.) expanded from 21 to 40 years between 1505 and 1536 and that of Temple Court (Surrey) from 50 to 70 years between 1507 and 1531.[80] The lease of Sutton-at-Hone (Kent) increased from 10 to 65 years between 1493 and 1536, that of Highbury manor (Middx.) from 21 years in 1492 to 99 years in 1536, and Peckham from three years in 1494 to 60 years in 1537.[81] Hampton Court, already leased for an 80-year term in 1495, increased to 99 years in 1505, before it passed out of Hospitaller hands forever in 1531.[82] This trend towards longer leases was replicated on the Prior's lands in other parts of the country, although changes in the length of the leases were less pronounced. The lease of Compton manor (Sussex) rose from 40 to 50 years between 1500 and 1512; that of Chaureth (Essex) from 21 to 40 years between 1499 and 1529, and Buckland (Somerset) from 30 years in 1501 to 50 years in 1539.[83]

Not all leases increased in length and indeed some decreased (see Figure 29). For example, in 1499 John Weyland leased Cranford manor (Middx.) for 60 years; his son, Richard, leased the manor for 40 years in 1533.[84] Indeed, it appears that between 1492 and 1539 the proportion of very long leases (those over 80 years) on prioral lands actually decreased, from about 11 per cent of all Prior Kendal's farms, to 3 per cent under Docwra and just over 2 per cent under Prior Weston. For the whole English Priory, out of 928 separate farm indentures between 1492 and 1539, only 36 leases (24 with the Prior, 12 with preceptors) were for 80 to 99 years, amounting to just 3.9 per cent of the total. Leases between 60 and 79 years in length formed 11 per cent of all leases under Kendal, rose to 17 per cent under Docwra, and then fell to 10 per cent under Weston. The proportion of leases for life and/or in survivorship also decreased, from 30 per cent of all prioral farms under Prior Kendal, to 11 per cent under Docwra, and 5.6 per cent under Weston. In contrast, the proportion of shorter leases (those up to 39 years in length) increased modestly, from just under 28 per cent in the 1490s to 34 per cent by the 1530s. The biggest increase in proportion of leases is noticeable on leases between 40 and 69 years in length. These increased from 19 per cent under Kendal to 33 per cent under Docwra, and 43 per cent under Weston. This corresponds to the pattern on episcopal estates in the first half of the sixteenth century, as identified by Richard Brown for the bishopric of Winchester, where leases increased from 30 or 40-year terms in the 1490s to 50- or 60-year leases by the 1520s.[85] Increasing the length of

[79] F. M. Heal, *Of Prelates and Princes: A Study of the Economic and Social Position of the Tudor Episcopate*, Cambridge, 1980, 30.
[80] BL MS Cotton Claudius E VI, ff. 14–14v, 52v; TNA LR 2/62, ff. 69v, 138v–139.
[81] BL MS Lansdowne 200, ff. 7v, 15–15v, 18; TNA LR 2/62, ff. 124v–125, 140–141v, 160–160v.
[82] BL MS Lansdowne 200, f. 30–30v; BL MS Cotton Claudius E VI, f. 8–8v; TNA LR 2/62, f. 69–69v.
[83] BL MS Lansdowne 200, ff. 58v–59, 80, 84–84v; BL MS Cotton Claudius E VI, ff. 108d–109; TNA LR 2/62, ff. 17–18, 182–183v.
[84] BL MS Lansdowne 200, f. 59–59v; TNA LR 2/62, f. 98–98v.
[85] R. Brown, 'Bastard Feudalism and the Bishopric of Winchester, 1282–1530', unpublished PhD thesis, King Alfred's College, Winchester, 2002, 266–7.

leases made sense to the Prior at a time when prices were stagnating or falling; it was not obvious to anyone until the late 1520s that there was a firm upwards trend.

Quite often leases were submitted for renewal long before they were due to expire, normally because the tenant wished to extend the length of the lease. Such was the case for John Gage at Compton Manor, Richard Weston at Temple Court, Henry Thornton at Buckland and Giles Lord Daubeney at Hampton Court.[86] Priors normally took the opportunity of a new lease to increase the rent. John Cutte paid £15 per annum for the farm of Chaureth in 1505, but his widow had to pay £17 per annum in 1522, as she had not been included on the 1505 indenture.[87] John Verney paid £93 6s. 8d. per annum in 1501 for Buckland, whereas Henry Thornton paid £103 6s. 8d. per annum in 1516.[88] The farm of Whetstone manor rose from £8 in 1505 to £11 7s. 6d. per annum in 1536 and Highbury from £8 in 1492 to £34 1s. in 1536.[89] It appears that Priors Docwra and Weston curbed the number of exceedingly long leases (and life grants), making the occasional exception for crown officials, and sometimes (but not always) loyal servants and kin. Instead, they opted for mid-range leases that guaranteed an assured level of income in case of future drops in rents, whilst not being long enough for the Prior to lose complete control of their manors or for the value of land to increase so dramatically that it could not be anticipated in the rent. Furthermore, such large increases of rent precluded increases in entry fines. Whereas enhanced entry fines were to the benefit of the current Prior, rent increases ensured inflation-proofed income to future Priors. They indicate that Priors Docwra and Weston had the future well-being of their office and order at heart.

Exchanges

Although the Prior granted leases of land to those he thought would be of use in government, very little passed out of Hospitaller hands completely or forever. There are three instances of exchanges, one to John, duke of Bedford, in 1433, former protector and at that point chief councillor of England with Humphrey, duke of Gloucester, during Henry VI's minority, and the other two to Henry VIII in the 1530s. On 8 July 1433, permission was given at parliament for the duke of Bedford to grant the advowson of Cheshunt church (Herts.) to Prior Malory in exchange for lands in Southwark and Lambeth, which the duke held by the demise of the late Prior Hulles. Malory had licence to appropriate Cheshunt on endowing a vicar.[90] The second example was the manor of Hampton Court which passed to the Henry VIII in 1531, that is, during the Reformation Parliament. Previously leased by Giles

---

[86] BL MS Lansdowne 200, f. 30–30v; BL MS Cotton Claudius E VI, ff. 8–8v, 52v, 108v–109, 168v–169v, 190–191; TNA LR 2/62, ff. 69v, 87–87v.
[87] BL MS Cotton Claudius E VI, ff. 13–13v, 217–217v.
[88] BL MS Lansdowne 200, f. 84–84v; BL MS Cotton Claudius E VI, ff. 168v–169v.
[89] BL MS Lansdowne 200, f. 7v; BL MS Cotton Claudius E VI, f. 14–14v; TNA LR 2/62, ff. 124v–125, 138v–139.
[90] *Rot. Parl.*, IV, 461; *CPR 1429–1436*, 296; NLM 348, 118v.

Lord Daubeney (1495, 1505) and Wolsey (1515) on long leases (80 then 99 years for Daubeney, and 99 years for Wolsey), it was exchanged, with the assent of parliament, for the former Stanesgate Priory (Essex), which had been dissolved by Wolsey in 1525.[91] The third exchange took place in May 1536. The Prior was granted the recently dissolved Kilburn Priory (Middx.) and in return granted the king Paris Garden and Wykes manors, which were then used as part of Jane Seymour's endowment.[92] That the exchange took place just a few days after the execution of the Prior's nephew Sir Francis Weston (d. 17 May 1536) must have been a bitter pill for the Prior to swallow and could suggest that it was granted to avoid further reprisals against the Weston family. Nevertheless, even this exchange could be viewed as an appropriate redistribution of monastic wealth, given the expectation at the time that the resources of the dissolved monasteries would be used for educational purposes and the relief of the poor.[93] Furthermore, in the later two exchanges the Prior gained lands in Middlesex and Essex, where he already had a concentration of lands. For example, besides the former Stanesgate Priory, part of the exchange for Hampton Court manor included gaining control of Rainham vicarage (valued at £10 per annum), where the Prior already held Rainham manor.[94]

It is clear from analysis of the farm indentures between 1492 and 1539 that, although there was an increasing tendency to lease to crown servants, this was a small percentage of the total number of farms. Leases were the bread-and-butter income of the Priory and this was defended rigorously by the Prior, even against the king himself, as indicated by the negotiations made by his solicitors Guthlac Overton and William Aprice over compensation for the loss of Paris Garden and Wykes manors.[95] Income and not patronage was the first priority of farming indentures. Nevertheless, the significant increase in leases of farms to crown servants in Weston's priorship indicates both the pressure the prior was put under by the crown, and a clear attempt, in acquiescence, to win favour in a period of political uncertainty.

Appointments and Annuities

A much clearer pattern of patronage and bastard feudal relations is visible from the indentures of annuities and appointments. Many of the appointments were to established local gentry, such as the Wrothe and Windsor families of Middlesex, who also had property in other counties where the Prior held lands.[96] In this section those in receipt of annuities or described as *feodatus* (*feodarius*) have been included,

---

[91] *Ibid.*, f. 69–69v; *VCH Essex*, II, 140–1.

[92] For background on Kilburn, see *VCH Middlesex*, I, 1969, 181; TNA LR 2/62, ff. 124–124v, 158–9.

[93] J. J. Scarisbrick, *The Reformation of the English People*, Oxford, 1984, 77.

[94] R. Newcourt, *Repertorium or an Ecclesiastical History of the Diocese of London*, 2 vols, London, 1708–10, II, 480.

[95] These two were well rewarded for their service, TNA LR 2/62, f. 124–124v.

[96] J. Freeman, 'Middlesex in the Fifteenth Century: Community of Communities?' in *Revolution and Consumption in Late Medieval England*, ed. M. A. Hicks, Woodbridge, 2001, 89–103 at 96–9.

as these people were given maintenance and a stipend not just for past services, but also for future duties to be performed for the Prior. The indentures were thus a form of contractual appointment.[97] Appointments and annuities were both ways of rewarding those who served the Prior, whether they were a knight for 'favour and advice', a custodian of an estate, or a simple launderer.[98] The benefits of appointment to these offices were more than the fee received; for example, seneschals and custodians had control over the workforce, and the fact that they were appointed for life (and in survivorship) meant that they (and their heirs) could exercise considerable patronage over lesser leases. During Kendal's priorship, 40 indentures of appointment were made, all for life, of which 28 were for maintenance for 'good and diligent service'.[99] Service and maintenance went together, such as the maintenance granted in Clerkenwell to Richard Baily, bailiff of Highbury manor, in 1493, and that to master Thomas Davy, DNC, seneschal of Clerkenwell, in 1498.[100] These men swore fealty to the Prior in return for maintenance and a stipend, usually between £2 and £3 6s. 8d. per annum, depending on their duties and status. The agreement was for life. For instance, in 1497, a Robert Wadyluff, chaplain, was granted maintenance in Melchbourne and a five-mark (£3 6s. 8d.) stipend.[101] We hear no more of him in the lease books, but he is mentioned 33 years later as the seneschal of Melchbourne in the manorial court rolls of 28 and 29 April 1530, his main duties being to arrange leases of minor lands and receive tenants' rents.[102]

There is some evidence that the Prior's lay tenants influenced these appointments, even if they were officially granted by the Prior and provincial chapter. For example, in 1500 Alexander Verney, chaplain, DNC, was given maintenance in Bodmiscombe manor for life, and a generous stipend of 8 marks (£5 6s. 8d.) per annum[103] Bodmiscombe was part of the possessions of Buckland Prioris, which was leased from Prior Kendal by John Verney, esquire.[104] In his will of 1506, witnessed by the prioress of Minchin Buckland and a brother-chaplain of Buckland Prioris, John Verney requested that his lease of Buckland Prioris pass to his two younger sons, though they do not appear to have continued the lease.[105] Verney had been

---

97   For example, John Clementson, yeoman and servant, was granted maintenance in 1519 for past and future service, BL MS Cotton Claudius E VI, f. 195v.

98   Roger and Alice Harrison, for example, were confirmed launderers for Clerkenwell for life in 1529, were allowed a tenement rent-free for repairs they had done on it and were allowed to wear livery as for yeomen and have meat and drink at the Priory, TNA LR 2/62, ff. 63v–64.

99   This included maintenance in Clerkenwell for a Robert Malory, gentleman, perhaps a relative of the late Prior Malory, BL MS Lansdowne 200, f. 44v.

100 Davy appeared in 1492, described as a gentleman and renting a cottage in St John's Street, *ibid.*, ff. 11v–12, 56–56v.

101 *Ibid.*, f. 49v. In 1495, one of his kin, William Wadyluff, had been granted the next presentation to Little Stockton Church, Bedfordshire, and under control of Melchbourne, *ibid.*, f. 23v.

102 TNA SC 2/153/31–31d.

103 Most received between £2 and £3 6s. 8d. per annum, BL MS Lansdowne 200, f. 79v.

104 Alexander was not John Verney's son. These were named in his will as Robert, his heir, John and George. He was, perhaps, son of his brother, Richard, *ibid.*, f. 84–84v.

105 By 1508 it had passed out of the Verney family's hands, perhaps quitclaimed, BL MS Cotton Claudius E VI, ff. 56v–57; *Somerset Medieval Wills*, ed. F W Weaver, Somerset Record Society, XIX, London, 1903, 103.

a patron of Buckland Prioris, leaving money for his own burial in the church there, next to his wife. Moreover, his daughter, Joanne, was a sister in the nearby nunnery.[106] Given these factors, it is highly likely that John Verney arranged for Alexander to be granted maintenance by the Order. The survival of John Verney's will, combined with the evidence in the lease books, reveal just how secularised the Priory had become by the early sixteenth century. While it still received the income from its properties (though depleted by extravagant stipends and annuities), it had lost physical possession of many of them and even the the right to appoint minor officials.

The remaining appointments made by Kendal were to offices such as bailiffs, custodians, seneschals and an auditor. These were also for life and most were to Hospitaller servants, granted on the death of the previous holder. Seven of the 12 appointments were made during 1495–6, at a time when the Prior was under suspicion of involvement in the Perkin Warbeck affair, and may have felt the need to increase retainers. These included the appointment of Sir Thomas Tyrell, for service, as seneschal of Witham and Cressing in 1495, and Sir Reginald Bray as head seneschal for the whole English Priory the following year, though both could exercise these offices through deputies.[107] Another interesting appointment was that of Thomas Lucas as seneschal of Chippenham in 1499, as he was described both as the king's solicitor and as DNC, and therefore a servant of both the Prior and the crown.[108] None of the officers appointed, who were mostly gentlemen, was paid highly, the standard rate being £2 per annum For example, a Robert Rochester, gentleman, was paid £2 per annum as seneschal of Cressing and Witham, the same amount paid to the seneschal there in 1338.[109] His successor, Tyrell, was paid slightly more at a rate of £2 13s. per annum, though this was perhaps because he was a knight, rather than a gentleman.[110] The exception was Sir Reginald Bray, who as head seneschal of the English Priory, received £10 per annum[111] It is no coincidence that Bray (d. 1503) held this position. At this time, he was chancellor of the duchy of Lancaster, king's councillor and 'one of the few with ready access to the person and mind of the king himself'.[112] With Bray on the payroll, and with Daubeney, Henry VII's chamberlain, farming a prime manor, Kendal ensured he had access to the king through two of the most influential men in England.

Due to the slightness of administrative records of the English Hospitallers, when

---

[106] Although by 1506 the nunnery was semi-autonomous, it was still linked with the English Priory, which was obliged to maintain chaplains to provide divine service for the nuns, as they had in 1338, 1338 Survey, 19; *Somerset Medieval Wills*, 102–5.

[107] Bray was head seneschal of England, except for Witham and Cressing, which Tyrell held, BL MS Lansdowne 200, ff. 23, 36.

[108] *Ibid.*, f. 64v.

[109] BL MS Lansdowne 200, f. 2, appointed after the death of Sir Thomas Montgomery; 1338 Survey, 169.

[110] BL MS Lansdowne 200, ff. 2, 23, 64v, 77v.

[111] *Ibid.*, f. 36.

[112] Bray possibly had a Hospitaller connection before this, through marriage (1475–8) to Katherine Hussey, co-heir of Nicholas, former victualler of Calais, M. Condon, 'From Caitiff and Villain to Pater Patriae: Reynold Bray and the Profits of Office', in *Profit, Piety and* Professions, 137–68 at 137–8.

these offices were created is unclear. No head seneschal of England was mentioned in the 1338 Survey, though there was a general procurator of the Priory's privileges, William Whitby. He, the survey states, had been paid a stipend of £2 per annum since Prior Archer's time, and had a room and various benefits in Clerkenwell. He also received a joint-pension of 20 marks with Sir Walter Daniel, but Whitby's share was cancelled out by the 10 marks' rents he paid for lands leased of the Priory in Leicestershire.[113] His grants do not compare to the £10 awarded to Bray, and there is no evidence of Whitby having a link to crown service. However, one other office, the seneschal of Chippenham in 1499, is also noted as paid by grant of Prior Archer.[114] Presumably, it had been unpaid before Archer's time, the position perhaps being part of the duties of the preceptor, and this might suggest that Archer created these posts in order to placate the resistance he was facing to the transfer of Templar lands to the Hospitallers. This seems to be supported by pensions still being paid in 1338 to 24 crown officials in order to gain control of the Templar lands.[115] Of the other appointments, it is difficult to know when they were created between 1338 and the 1490s. In one case, Melchbourne, there had been a seneschal in 1338 (paid 33s. 4d.), but by the 1490s there was a separate office of custodian, in addition to that of seneschal (both paid £2 per annum).[116] This could indicate multiplication of offices under Prior Kendal, but there is too little evidence to say conclusively.

There were 67 appointments during Docwra's priorship, of which 50 were annuities and maintenance for service of one sort or another, and 17 were custodians or seneschals. As with the farms, we see Docwra's relatives are rewarded: Martin Docwra, DNC, appointed seneschal of Balsall in 1511 on wages of £4 per annum, and John Docwra (son of Thomas of Kirkby Kendal), gentleman, granted maintenance in Clerkenwell in 1514 for his generous service.[117] We also see the first mention of Guthlac Overton, DNC, who was made general seneschal of England in 1512 and was later a solicitor and auditor of the Priory.[118] Unlike his predecessor or successor, Docwra's appointments were all to his servants, most of whom were gentlemen or tradesmen. They show he rewarded loyalty: for example, the annuities given in 1512 and 1515 to George Nigir, a servant of the Prior since Docwra had been captain of St Peter's castle, near Halicarnassus (modern-day Bodrum), in the 1490s.[119] There is an indication that offices were being duplicated. For example, in 1522, Andrew Windsor, knight, and his son Edmund Windsor, esquire, were appointed the joint seneschals of Temple Wycombe (Bucks.) for their lives and paid 26s. 4d. per annum wages.[120] Wages for these appointments were common. The custodian of Melchbourne and seneschal of Chippenham, both appointed in 1524 were paid £2 per annum, the same as in 1495 and 1499 respectively.[121] The big

[113] 1338 Survey, 97, 178, 206, 208.
[114] Again the wage of 40s. was the same in 1499 as it had been in 1338, *ibid.*, 79; BL MS Lansdowne 200, f. 64v.
[115] 1338 Survey, 203–4.
[116] *Ibid.*, 71; BL MS Lansdowne 200, ff. 27v, 77v.
[117] BL MS Cotton Claudius E VI, ff. 87, 129v–130.
[118] *Ibid.*, f. 108v.
[119] *Ibid.*, ff. 111, 153v.
[120] *Ibid.*, f. 229.
[121] *Ibid.*, f. 256v.

difference was in the amount paid to the general seneschal of England. In 1495 Bray had been paid, £10 per annum, but Guthlac Overton, appointed in 1512, was only granted £2 per annum, the usual amount for other seneschals.[122]

Under Prior Weston, there were 67 appointments, all made for life, of which 42 were maintenance for service, including prominent servants such as William Aprice, Constantine Bennet, William Denys, and Weston's servant from Rhodes and Malta, Franchesco Galliardello.[123] Family members were also employed. One of Weston's first appointments in 1529 was to make his brother, Sir Richard Weston (already a confrater), head seneschal of the English Priory. This was revised in June 1533, when Richard's son Francis (executed 1536) became joint head seneschal with his father, less than a month after he was knighted as part of the celebrations for Anne Boleyn's coronation.[124] Of the other appointments, quite a few were not long-term Hospitaller servants or relations. Robert Radcliff, earl of Sussex, was joint seneschal with his son Sir Henry Radcliff (Lord FitzWalter) of Witham manor in 1536 (paid £2 3s. 4d. per annum). Richard Leyton, archdeacon of Buckinghamshire and a commissioner for the Dissolution of the Monasteries, was made legal conservator in England of the Hospitallers in 1536, and paid a considerable £50 per annum. Lord Mauduit was appointed seneschal of Melchbourne (£2 per annum) in the same year, and his son, John, was joint seneschal with his father in 1537.[125]

There were considerably more joint appointments under Weston than under Kendal or Docwra. Apart from those mentioned above, Robert Wrothe, esquire, was appointed joint seneschal (£3 6s. 8d. per annum) of Clerkenwell and other manors in Middlesex and Surrey in 1529 with Richard Hawke, esquire, and again in 1533 with John Coke, gentleman.[126] John Bowles, gentleman, was appointed seneschal (26s. 8d. per annum) for Hertfordshire with John Swift, gentleman; John Coke was re-appointed seneschal of Clerkenwell (£3 6s. 8d. per annum) with Thomas Wrothe, gentleman; George Throckmorton, knight, and his son, Robert, were made seneschals of Balsall (£4 per annum), all in 1539.[127] These later appointments took place from 1536 onwards, after the execution of Prior Weston's nephew Francis, and at the beginning of the Dissolution of the smaller and larger monasteries, when the need for favour increased due to uncertainty over the future. The granting of these offices for life and in survivorship also indicates that Weston was anticipating the Dissolution.

---

[122] Ibid., f. 108v.
[123] TNA LR 2/62, ff. 56v–57, 61, 91, 120v, 122v. Also receiving maintenance in Clerkenwell in 1536 was a Thomas Docwra (perhaps of Kirkby Kendall), ibid., f. 148–148v.
[124] Ibid., ff. 64v–65, 100v.
[125] Ibid., ff. 147v–149, 166.
[126] Ibid., ff. 63–63v, 122v.
[127] Ibid., ff. 187, 188–188v.

Presentations

As the bishops' registers confirm, the Prior officially presented to all Hospitaller churches. Only when the Prior was overseas did his lieutenant present in his place. Having said that, it is likely that preceptors had some influence in the appointments to churches. For example, it was surely on the recommendation of Brother John Sutton, preceptor of Beverley (Yorks.), that Nicholas Sutton, gentleman, gained presentation to Beeford church (York diocese) in 1537.[128] As with appointments and annuities, the Prior occasionally granted the right of presentation to others, but for a single presentation only. Between 1492 and 1501, Prior Kendal granted two of these temporary rights of presentation. Both grants were joint presentations, the first in 1495 to four yeomen, who were allowed the next presentation to Little Stockton church (Beds.). The second was to Dean church (Lincoln diocese) in 1501 to two Hospitaller servants, Thomas Hobson (DNC) and William Yolton, gentlemen.[129] One of those granted the presentation to Little Stockton was a William Wadyluff, whose kin, Robert Wadyluff was given maintenance at Melchbourne (Beds.) in 1497 and was seneschal of Melchbourne in 1530.[130] However, this was not a case of locals gaining control, even if temporarily, of the right of presentation, as Wadyluff and his co-presentors were all from Yorkshire. This may be indicative of a deliberate policy by Priors aimed at preventing local families from gaining a claim to presentation rights. If so, then the policy was at least partially abandoned during Docwra's office, with locals granted presentation rights in at least seven, perhaps eight, out of 12 cases, which could indicate that Docwra was involved in the trafficking of ecclesiastical appointments in order to maximize his profits.[131] The other four grants were to Hospitaller kin, including one to Preceptor Lancelot Docwra (1519) and another to Martin Docwra (1526).[132]

Both Kendal's and Docwra's temporary grants of presentation rights were on a small scale and were not to people of great influence, but mainly to loyal Hospitaller servants and employees, corresponding to the farms and appointments they made. For Prior Weston, the situation was different, at least with regard to scale. Compared with Kendal's two and Docwra's 12 (eight of which were in 1526), Weston granted 48 grants of next presentation rights (36 held jointly) between 1529 and 1539.[133] As with the granting of offices, this further suggests Weston was anticipating the Dissolution and the liquidation of assets. This period corresponds with a marked drop in presentations by the Prior, as recorded in the bishops' registers, numbering

---

128 *Ibid.*, f. 164v.
129 BL MS Lansdowne 200, ff. 23v, 88v–89.
130 *Ibid.*, f. 49v; TNA SC 2/153/31–31d.
131 One grant does not state where the presentor comes from. Ten of the twelve were joint presentations, BL MS Cotton Claudius E VI, ff. 80v, 152v–153, 286v–288v.
132 Apart from Brother Lancelot Docwra and Martin Docwra, members of the Babington and Pole families were also granted temporary rights of presentation, *ibid.*, ff. 80v, 152v–153, 195v–196, 286v–288v.
133 TNA LR 2/62, ff. 51v–53v, 64v–65, 70v, 94–95v, 119–120, 146–146v, 153–153v, 163v–165, 189–189v, 192–2.

just three between 1528 and 1540,[134] including presentations to churches, such as Stebbing (£12 per annum), to which Priors traditionally presented their own and Hospitaller kin. For example, Prior Botyll presented Robert Langstrother (1440) and John Botyll (1450) to Stebbing, and soon after taking office, Thomas Docwra presented John Docwra.[135] In contrast, Weston granted away the right of presentation to Stebbing in 1533 and 1536, though in both cases it was to those associated with the Priory.[136] Docwra presented to Cardington vicarage (Hereford) in 1524 and 1526, but at the 1529 provincial chapter, Prior Weston granted the temporary right of presentation to four people.[137] The 48 grants were chronologically equally distributed during his priorship with 24 before the Reformation Parliament and 24 from 1536 onwards. What is perhaps surprising is that virtually none were granted to crown servants or those close to court, except Prior Weston's brother, Richard, and one to Christopher Hales, later master of the rolls.[138] Only three knights (William Barton in 1531, Richard Weston in 1533, and Andrew Windsor, Lord Windsor, in 1539) and the archdeacon of Buckinghamshire, Richard Leyton in 1536, were granted temporary rights of presentation, although the latter two had the sole right, whereas Barton and Weston had to share the right of presentation with the Prior's servants.[139] Most of the presentation rights went to Hospitaller kin and to servants (in many cases they are both) who had some degree of standing in the local community – Humphrey Babington, William and John Cordall, Franchesco Galliardello and Guthlac Overton, to name a few.[140] In the case of John Cordall, he continued to manage the Clerkenwell estate after the suppression of the Hospitallers, chasing up rent arrears and repairs. Another ex-Hospitaller servant, Constantine Bennett, was still living in St John's Street and a leading representative of Clerkenwell parish in the early 1570s.[141] Why the sudden rise in grants of presentation under Prior Weston? It is possible that Weston was maximizing his income. It was illegal to sell livings, but not the right of next presentation.

[134] One in 1530 and two in 1534, *The Registers of Thomas Wolsey, Bishop of Bath and Wells, 1518–1523, John Clerke, Bishop of Bath and Wells, 1523–1541, William Knyght, Bishop of Bath and Wells, 1541–1547, and Gilbert Bourne, Bishop of Bath and Wells, 1554–1559*, ed. H. Maxwell-Lyte, Somerset Record Society, vol. LV, Frome and London, 1940, 64, 71.

[135] Newcourt, *Repertorium*, II, 557.

[136] To Franchesco Galliardello and William Ermstead in 1533, and Guthlac Overton, Edward Overton and Robert Browne in 1536, TNA LR 2/62, ff. 119–119v, 153v.

[137] *The Register of Charles Bothe*, ed. A. T. Bannister, Hereford, Cantilupe Society, XX, 1921, 338–9; TNA LR2/62, f. 52v.

[138] *Ibid.*, f. 146v. Hales is here described as esquire, but was later knighted when master of the rolls, TNA C 147/161.

[139] TNA LR 2/62, ff. 94, 119, 191, 146v.

[140] *Ibid.*, ff. 64v, 119v–120 for Babington; *ibid.*, ff. 95v, 119v, 153 for the Cordalls; *ibid.*, ff. 119–119v for Galliardello; *ibid.*, ff. 146–146v, 153v for Overton.

[141] TNA C 1/1416/39–41 for Cordall; TNA SP 46/29/61, C 147/230 for Bennett.

Conclusion

Certain conclusions become apparent from analysis of the lease books from 1492 to 1539. Firstly, very little was granted away forever and thus the Prior could not lose ultimate control of his possessions. Nevertheless, in contrast to secularisation on monastic lands, which took place after the Dissolution, secularisation on the English Hospitallers' lands, already at an advanced stage by the 1490s, accelerated in the years prior to the Dissolution. In common with other large ecclesiastical estates, such as those of the bishopric of Winchester, much property was farmed out for rents to local gentry and was not under the direct control of the Prior.[142] However, the Prior continued to be overlord, whether grants were hereditary or for life. Farms were leased to all sections of society, including merchants. The Stonor family were leasing Hospitaller property from at least the 1330s, and, in the case of Warpesgrove, still held it in 1483.[143] John Evinger, was not just a beer brewer, but a merchant who still owned property in his native Antwerp.[144] The Prior and the preceptors still held manorial courts, such as those held in the names of Prior Docwra and Prior Weston for Balsall in 1505 and 1534, for Prior Weston and Giles Russell, preceptor of Dingley, at Great Weldon (Northants.) in 1529, or that held by the Prior's representatives at Melchbourne and Sharnbrook (Beds.) in 1530.[145] Secondly, possessions that left the Prior's hands forever went to the crown and happened simultaneously with the Reformation. The Prior did get compensation in the form of other lands, benefiting both from Wolsey's suppressions in the 1520s and from the suppression of the lesser monasteries. Thirdly, with regard to annuities, appointments and presentations, again most were granted to those associated with the Prior and the Hospitallers. Giving such positions and favours to Hospitaller kin and servants, that is, to those the Prior trusted, helped ensure the efficient management of his estates.

There was a gradual increase in the Prior's grants to those more associated with the crown than the Hospitallers, especially between 1529 and 1539. This increase was an attempt to buy favour, but it was the usual favour shown to crown servants that had existed under Kendal, Docwra and, presumably, all English Priors. It is also symbolic of the pressure that the English Priory as a whole was under to satisfy royal will: in 1515 Henry VIII supported Brother Richard Neville's appointment to the next vacant preceptory, despite Neville's having only recently completed his initial five-year service on Rhodes. Normally brethren, following the Hospitaller policy of appointment according to seniority, might have to wait at least a decade before becoming a preceptor. Henry VIII's appeal to the Pope, overriding the Grand Master's decision, ensured Neville was a preceptor by 1519.[146]

---

[142] Brown, 'Bastard Feudalism and the Bishopric of Winchester', 294.

[143] The Stonor family were leasing Warpesgrove and Easington manors in 1336, *Kingsford's Stonor Letters*, II, 159.

[144] Bolton, *Alien Communities*, 51.

[145] Shakespeare Birthplace Trust Records Office, Stratford-upon-Avon, DR18/30/4/2; DR18/30/4/4; TNA SC 2/195/91; TNA SC 2/153/31–31d.

[146] *L&P HVIII 1515–1516*, II, 195; BL MS Cotton Claudius E VI, f. 206–206v.

It is very difficult to judge the mentality of Priors Kendal, Docwra and Weston, that is, whether they regarded themselves as lay or ecclesiastc. There is no firm evidence that they were as laicised as the preceptor of Torphichen, William Knollis, who is known to have fathered a son, even if it may be suspected.[147] The portraits of Kendal (as turcopolier) and Prior Docwra show them in more lay attire than Prior Langstrother, even though Langstrother has his armour on under his habit.[148] Docwra acted frequently as a crown servant, especially on diplomatic duty, but this need not mean he put the concerns of the lay local authorities over those of the Order. It is possible that he served the crown because he wished to maintain a high international profile in the West in order to enhance his bid to be Grand Master, which he nearly achieved in 1521. Prior Weston appears to have served the crown less than his predecessors, but whether this was his choice or he was excluded is not clear. He was certainly concerned with the spirituality of the English brethren, as is shown, for example, in the deliberations of the English tongue, which records the decision of the 1529 provincial chapter to fund chaplains to minister to the brethren on Malta.[149] Inscriptions on his sarcophagus also indicate his devotion to the Virgin Mary.[150] Additionally Weston, as is apparent from Henry VIII's letters and papers, did not always give in to the requests of crown servants for prime appointments in the English Priory. For example, in September 1536 William Cavendish asked Cromwell to use his influence to gain him the auditorship of the Priory. Weston honestly replied that it had already been granted to William Aprice, a Hospitaller servant for over 30 years.[151]

As regards legal issues, the English province had a great deal of autonomy from both ecclesiastical and civil authorities, and preserved it longer than in other provinces, such as Castile, Navarre, Italy or Portugal, where the king imposed his brother as prior of Crato in 1528.[152] When one looks at other states where the Reformation was taking effect, the English province managed to survive until fairly late in comparison. The Prussian branch of the Teutonic Order was secularised in 1525 and the Hospitallers were dissolved or secularised by protestant rulers (of which Henry VIII was not really one) in Sweden (1527), Norway (1532) and Denmark (1536).[153] Clerkenwell Priory, at least, maintained its independence from ecclesiastical authority up until its suppression, as indicated by the record of a dispensation for marriage without banns in January 1540 between John Cordall (Prior's servant)

---

[147] John Knollis gained a dispensation in 1506 to become a cleric, even though born illegitimately of a Hospitaller brother and an unmarried woman, *CPL 1503–1513*, 479; O'Malley, *English Knights Hospitaller*, 109.

[148] King, *Knights of St John*, facing 72, 87, 92.

[149] *Book of Deliberations of the Venerable Tongue of England 1523–1567*, ed. H. P. Scicluna, Valletta, 1949, 14–16.

[150] W. Pinks, *The History of Clerkenwell*, ed. E. J. Wood, London, 1881, 38–9.

[151] *L&P HVIII 1536*, XI, 166, 170, 5 and 7 September 1536.

[152] C. Barquero Goñi, 'The Hospitallers and the Castilian-Leonese Monarchy: the Concession of Royal Rights, Twelfth to Fourteenth Centuries', in *The Military Orders: Fighting for the Faith and Caring for the Sick*, ed. M. Barber, Aldershot, 1994, 28–33; Barquero Goñi, 'The Hospitallers and the Kings of Navarre'; A. Luttrell, 'Change and Conflict Within the Hospitaller Province of Italy after 1291', in *Mendicants, Military Orders, and Regionalism in Medieval Europe*, ed. J. Sarnowsky, Aldershot, 1999, 185–99.

[153] Luttrell, 'The Military Orders 1312–1798', 347–50.

and Isabella Overton, who are noted as being under the jurisdiction of the Hospital of St John of Jerusalem.[154]

Sanctuary was also an issue. In the later middle ages, there were two main types of sanctuary, temporary, for 40 days (which could not be sought by those accused of sacrilege or high treason), and permanent, which only a few places that had the right to grant.[155] The Hospitaller Priory at Clerkenwell claimed to be one of the latter. In 1516, Prior Docwra and the abbot of Westminster both made claims to grant sanctuary and this led to a debate in star chamber on 10 November 1519, at which the king was present.[156] The Hospitallers' case had arisen because John, son of Sir John Savage, had taken refuge in Clerkenwell after a murder in June 1516. The Hospitallers and Westminster Abbey claimed to have the privilege of sanctuary, although the Hospitallers' claim was dismissed on the grounds that they did not have a charter granted by the king. The star chamber discussions ended with the decision that the creation of a sanctuary was the king's prerogative, and that anyone who relied on a papal grant was guilty of treason by way of praemunire.[157] This decision has previously been interpreted to mean that in practice Clerkenwell had lost the privilege of sanctuary by 1520.[158] Yet, despite the council's conclusion, no decision was sanctioned, as parliament did not meet (except for the short 1523 session) until 1529. Discussions on sanctuaries and privileged places were a regular theme in parliament in the 1530s and as late as 1539 there were complaints that people were avoiding ordinary jurisdiction by going to the Hospitallers and other religious houses.[159] It was only with the suppression of the English Priory that its sanctuaries were finally abolished.[160]

Clerkenwell Priory, like the Hospitaller quarter (the *collachium*) on Rhodes or on Malta, was never exclusively occupied by brethren alone. It was more integrated into lay society than houses of other religious orders.[161] The 'secularisation', if that is the appropriate term, of the Prior and Priory was a separate matter and did not necessarily lead to the suppression of the Priory, let alone make it part of the Dissolution, which itself was not a foregone conclusion.[162] It was not clear at all, until the last moment, that complete Dissolution was the intention. As late as 1537, the emphasis was on reformation of monasteries for educational and other good causes and this was backed up by parliamentary discussion.[163] The Prior even seemed to benefit from the first round of monastic suppressions, gaining Kilburn

154 *Faculty Office Registers 1534–1549: A Calendar of the First Two Registers of the Archbishop of Canterbury's Faculty Office*, ed. D. S. Chambers, Oxford, 1966, 205.

155 I. D. Thornley, 'The Destruction of Sanctuary', in *Tudor Studies*, ed. R. W. Seton-Watson, London, 1924, 182–207 at 182–3.

156 *Ibid.*, 200–1.

157 P. Gwyn, *The King's Cardinal. The Rise and Fall of Thomas Wolsey*, London, 1990, 54, 133. Savage was pardoned in 1520. Praemunire was later used in the 1530s, when papal authority in England was refuted.

158 O'Malley, *English Knights Hospitaller*, 175.

159 *Lords Journals*, I, 87–8 for 17 June 1536; *L&P HVIII 1539*, XIV, 407.

160 *SR*, III, 780–1.

161 A. Luttrell, *The Town of Rhodes 1306–1356*, Rhodes, 2003, 81; A. Luttrell, 'Hospitaller Birgu: 1530–1536', *Crusades*, II, 2003, 134–5.

162 J. J. Scarisbrick, *Henry VIII*, 2nd edn, New Haven, CT, and London, 1997, ix.

163 Scarisbrick, *Reformation*, 77.

Priory in 1536. Then in July 1537, Henry VIII confirmed to Weston, amongst other privileges, the right to receive new brethren into the Order, to go abroad without a licence except a writ of passage, and to give vacant possession of Hospitaller possessions to those whom the Grand Master and Convent appointed.[164] This appeared to be more than a confirmation of existing Hospitaller rights and the worthiness of their existence, and additionally that they were not affected by the Dissolution. Even as late as April 1539, at the last provincial chapter, the Prior was making the usual leases and appointments.[165] Indeed, it should be pointed out that the English Priory was not dissolved by acts concerning the lesser (1536) and greater (1539) monasteries, but that a separate act (April 1540) was drawn up especially for them. Although some had proposed in 1534 that the Prior's revenue should be curbed and all his possessions should go to the king on his death, this was not translated into an act at the parliament of that year or the next two parliaments, though some of the recommendations found their way into the final act of suppression in 1540.[166]

It is worth looking at the statute dissolving the English and Irish Priories, drawn up in the third session of the 1539–40 parliament, as it clarifies just why the Priory was dissolved. Three reasons were given for dissolving the Order in England (and Ireland). Firstly, the Prior and brethren were accused of supporting the Pope, supposedly unnaturally and contrary to their duty and allegiance, simply by sending responsions abroad for their own maintenance, some of which it was alleged went to the Pope. It was then argued that their dissolution was necessary to extinguish any remnant of the Pope's authority in England. Finally, it cites the loss of Rhodes as another reason, because their purpose was now defunct, and the revenues could be used instead for the defence of the realm.[167] Behind the premise of religious reform, the real concern was the loss of potential revenue to the crown, clear from the continual references to the 'great sums of money' that were 'craftily exhausted' out of the country.[168] This, however, was a trumped-up charge as, since the fourteenth century, it had been necessary for the Prior to gain a licence to export responsions, and even then most that was exported was done through bills of exchange, rather than ready cash. Nevertheless, brethren in England were given until 1 July 1540, in Ireland until 30 September and those abroad until 1 February 1541 to renounce their habit and religion or face punishment, it is implied, for contravening the Statute of Praemunire.[169] Praemunire, originally devised in the mid-fourteenth century to protect crown rights from papal interference, was in the 1530s used aggressively.[170] The papacy was now regarded by the English crown in the same way as a secular state enemy.

[164] *L&P HVIII, 1537*, XII, 167.
[165] TNA LR 2/62, ff. 179–200.
[166] *L&P HVIII 1534*, VII, 515; J. Youings, *The Dissolution of the Monasteries*, London, 1971, 145–7. Both are referring to BL MS Cotton Cleopatra E IV, ff. 174–5.
[167] *SR*, III, 778.
[168] *Ibid.*
[169] *Ibid.*, 779.
[170] R. Houlbrooke, 'The Decline of Ecclesiastical Jurisdiction under the Tudors', in *Continuity and Change: Personnel and Administration of the Church in England 1500–1642*, ed. R. O'Day and F. Heal, Leicester, 1976, 339–258 at 240–2.

The suppression of the Hospitallers was contemporary with the general Dissolution, but it was not completely part of it. As Scarisbrick has argued for the Dissolution of the Monasteries, it appears that the main motives for the suppression of the Hospitallers were political and economic not religious, but the analogy can go no further.[171] The provision for the transfer of Hospitaller lands to the officers for the court of augmentations was to be 'in like manner, form, fashion and condition as the possessions of the lands of the abbeys, monasteries or priories suppressed or surrendered', but this very wording implies that although the mechanics of suppression were similar, the English Hospitallers' suppression was separate.[172] It was the dissolution of a secular, as opposed to a monastic, religious order. Although some monasteries resisted suppression, the Hospitallers had the added dimension of having trained knights who could potentially organise resistance to their dissolution. That is why so much emphasis was put in the statute on their allegiance to the king, and why those abroad had until 5 June 1541 to return and declare themselves the king's 'true and loyal subjects'.[173] Despite this ultimatum, nine brethren (out of 31 in 1540) of the English tongue were still active on Malta in the 1540s, of which five were mentioned in the statute.[174] As a secular order, the English Priory should have been reformed rather than suppressed, as were the secular clergy under the control of their bishoprics, but the international nature of the Order, with its headquarters adhering to the Pope, so long its strong point, provided the English crown with a perfect excuse for its dissolution.

---

[171] Scarisbrick, *Reformation*, 62; Scarisbrick, *Henry VIII*, xvii–xviii.

[172] *SR*, III, 781.

[173] *Ibid.*

[174] Those five being Giles Russell, Oswald Massingberd, Nicholas Upton, Henry Gerard and Dunstan Newdigate.

**Figure 24: Numerical breakdown of types of indenture
with the Prior, 1492–1539**

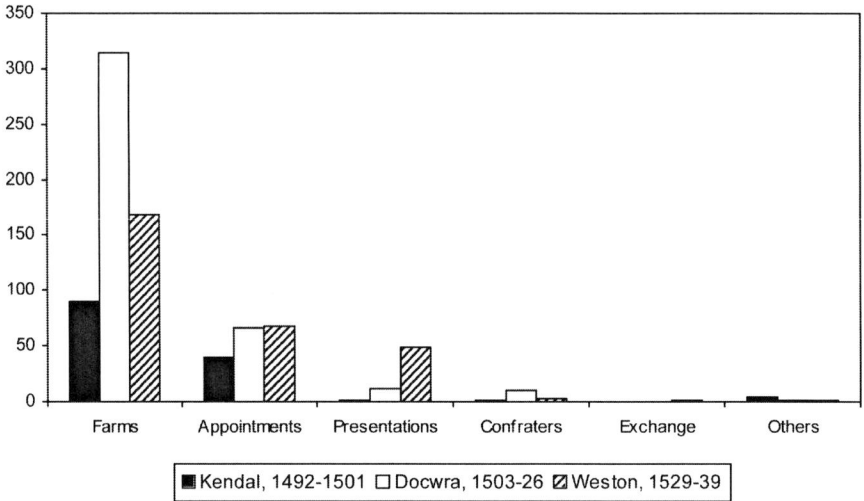

Farms   Appointments   Presentations   Confraters   Exchange   Others

■ Kendal, 1492-1501   □ Docwra, 1503-26   ▨ Weston, 1529-39

Source: BL MSS Lansdowne 200, Cotton Claudius E VI; TNA LR2/62

**Figure 25: Percentage breakdown by appellation of those farming
the Prior's lands, 1492–1539**

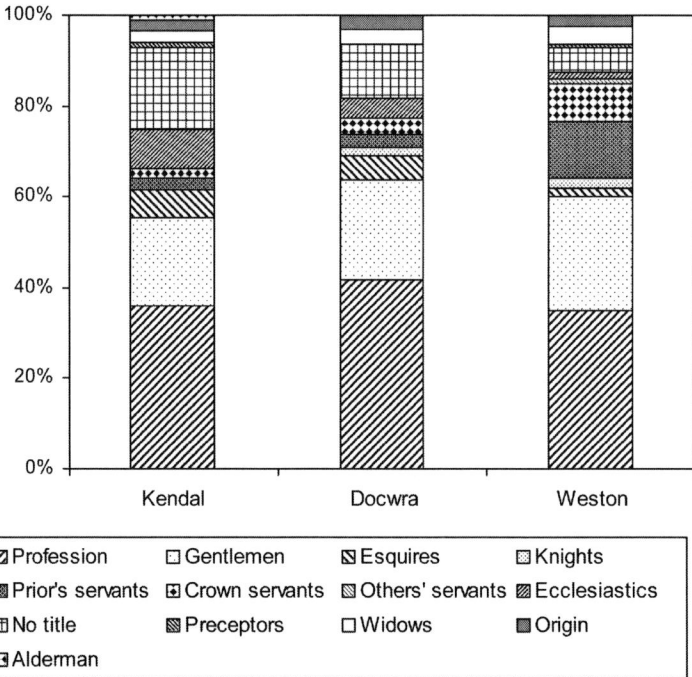

Kendal   Docwra   Weston

▨ Profession   □ Gentlemen   ▨ Esquires   ▨ Knights
▨ Prior's servants ⊞ Crown servants ▨ Others' servants ▨ Ecclesiastics
⊞ No title   ▨ Preceptors   □ Widows   ▨ Origin
⊡ Alderman

Source: BL MSS Lansdowne 200, Cotton Claudius E VI; TNA LR2/62

Figure 26: Crown servants leasing Prior's lands, 1492–1501

Year	Family name	First name	Title/crown office	Lease	Lease length (years)
1493	Roche	Thomas	Baron of exchequer	Fleet Street, tenement	90
1495	Daubeney	Giles, Lord	king's chamberlain	Hampton Court manor	80
1499	Belknapp	Edward	Knight of the body, later surveyor of the king's prerogative	Hardwick manor	25

Source: BL MS Lansdowne 200

Figure 27: Crown servants leasing Hospitaller lands, 1503–26 (all leased from the Prior except those marked *)

Year	Family name	First name	Title/crown office	Lease	Lease length (years)
1505	Cutte	John	Receiver general of duchy of Lancaster; Under-treasurer of Exchequer	Chaureth manor	30
1505	Daubeney	Giles, Lord	king's chamberlain	Hampton Court manor	99
1508	Rich	Richard	Later chancellor of augmentations	Carlton and Thurlow manors	20
1511	Tayler	John	Clerk of parliament and royal chaplain	Chancery Lane, 3 cottages	60
1512	Gage	John	Esquire of the body, later comptroller of king's household	Compton manor	50
1512	Malhom	William	Of chancery	Fleet Street, tenement	65
1514	Warcop	Leonard	Sergeant at arms	Kirkby Fleetham rectory*	16
1515	Wolsey	Thomas	Chancellor, archbishop of York	Hampton Court manor	99
1516	Belknapp	Edward	Surveyor of the king's prerogative	Temple Warwick manor	40
1516	Thornton	Henry	king's sergeant at arms	Buckland Preceptory	40
1516	Weston	Richard	Knight of the Body	Baddesley and Mayne preceptory*	3
1518	Boleyn	Thomas	Keeper of exchange at Calais and foreign exchange in England. Later earl of Wiltshire. Father of Anne.	Wilbraham manor	21
1519	Gage	John	Esquire of the body, later comptroller of king's household	Compton manor	50
1519	Thornton	Henry	king's sergeant of arms	Buckland preceptory	40
1519	Thornton	Henry	king's sergeant of arms	Tenement outside New Temple bar, London	40

1519	Lowe	Anthony	Of king's household	Charing Cross Sreeet, tenement	60
1519	Weston	Richard	Knight of the Bath, deputy master of wards	Baddesley and Mayne preceptory*	3
1522	Wingfield	Richard	Knight, diplomat	Sutton-at-Hone	60

Source: BL MS Cotton Claudius E VI

Figure 28: Crown servants leasing Hospitaller lands, 1529–39 (all leased from the Prior except that marked *)

Year	Family name	First name	Title/crown office	Lease	Lease length (years)
1529	Gage	John	Vice-chamberlain of household	Sutton-at-Hone manor	60
1529	Smith	John	Of exchequer	Witham and Cressing manors	29
1529	Weston	Richard	Knight	Temple Court manor	49
1531	Cromwell	Thomas	King's councillor, supervisor of king's legal and parliamentary affairs	Dartford and Sutton-at-Hone manors	70
1531	Smith	John	Of exchequer	St John's Sreet, tenement	40
1531	Weston	Richard	Knight	Temple Court manor	70
1531	Thornton	Henry	King's sergeant of arms	Buckland preceptory	40
1533	Hales	Christopher	Attorney general	Peckham, lands*	29
1533	Tong	Thomas	Keeper of alms	St John's Lane, tenement	50
1536	Cromwell	Thomas	King's secretary, Vicegerent	Highbury manor	99
1536	Mitchell	James	Sergeant of larder	Havingsfield manor	40
1536	Whorwood	William	Solicitor general	Halston preceptory	3
1537	Cromwell	Thomas	Lord Cromwell, keeper of privy seal	Magisterial *camera* (Peckham, Stallsfield, Rodmersham)	60
1537	Ladesman	Henry	King's servant	A parcel of 'Commanders Mantell'	29
1537	Warcop	Leonard	Sergeant at arms	Kirkby Fleetham rectory*	
1539	Mitchell	James	Sergeant of larder	Havingsfield manor	40
1539	Rich	Richard	Chancellor of augmentations	Broxbourne manor	29
1539	Whorwood	William	Solicitor general	Halston preceptory	5

Source: TNA LR 2/62

Figure 29: Length of leases on prioral lands, 1492–1539

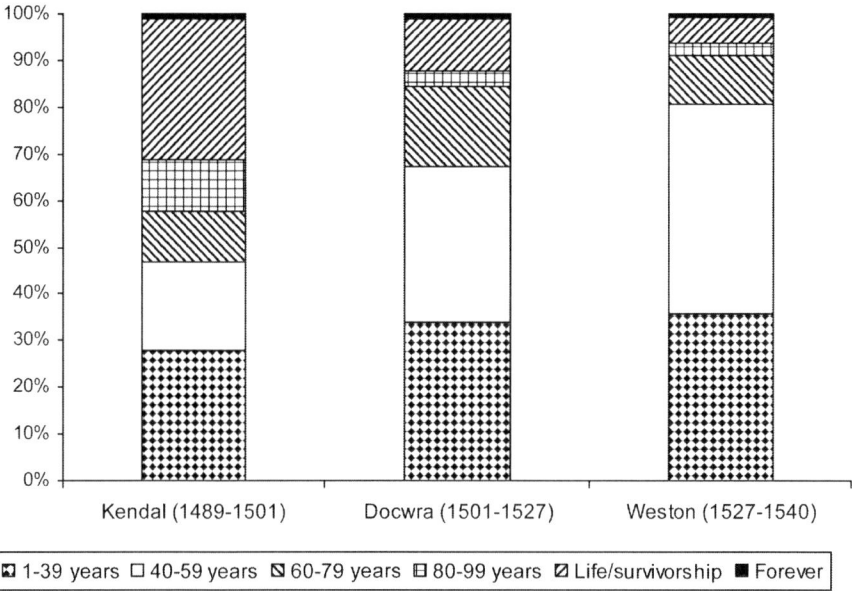

Source: BL MSS Lansdowne 200, Cotton Claudius E VI, TNA LR2/62

7

Conclusion

The introduction of this book, amongst other things, presented the current state of understanding on the Prior of St John in England. It drew attention to a number of current orthodoxies derived from general assumptions about the Hospitallers' role in Western Europe which this book has tested through thematic studies on the Priors' crown roles. Crusade historians are universally agreed that the main role of a provincial prior was to govern his priory well on behalf of the Order and to maximise its contributions to maintain brethren serving in the East. It is further supposed that the Priors of England always had a close relationship with the English crown. Finally, the current historical orthodoxy is that the Priors were in constant battle to fulfil their Hospitaller duties, especially over the payment of responsions, and commentaries by modern historians present the crown–Hospitaller relationship as one of friction. All these assertions contain elements of truth, but they need qualification and refinement. The individual chapters of this book have challenged these orthodoxies and indicated how they need to be reviewed.

The chapters are arranged to mirror the chronological development of the Prior of St John's role in service to the crown. The English Priors probably always had a financial role in England, both as a source of income to the crown as a provider of loans, and as a collector and keeper of both lay and ecclesiastical taxation. In the thirteenth century, they generally took a back seat to the Templars in financial relations with the crown (Chauncy's appointment as treasurer of England being the exception), but after the suppression of the Templars, the Hospitallers inherited not only the Templars' possessions but also their responsibilities and duties. Two further Priors became treasurers of England, a position no master of the Templars had held.

Priors also had military duties to the crown, but the nature of these duties changed during the fourteenth century. At first, in common with all spiritual and temporal lords, they were required to provide funds, transportation and victuals, and to array troops. These duties continued throughout the period under examination. From the 1330s, however, they started to hold official, paid positions. For most of the period, these tended to be defensive military roles, as keeper of Southampton, as admirals of the southern fleet and as deputy keeper of the Scottish marches, but by the early sixteenth century, we find Prior Docwra participating in offensive military manoeuvres into foreign territory on the continent.

A few examples of the Prior on diplomatic service for the crown are known from the twelfth and thirteenth centuries, but such service was rare; the master of the Templars was more often chosen as an envoy, though even he gave only occasional service. A more regular pattern of service starts to emerge in the late fourteenth century, but then, for nearly half a century, the Prior was not involved in crown diplomatic activity, though he performed this role to various powers on behalf of the Hospitallers. The Prior was a regular crown envoy from the 1440s up until the death of Prior Docwra in 1527; even thereafter Weston, though not an envoy, entertained foreign dignitaries who were visiting England.

Evidence of the activity of the Priors indicates a development of their political duties within England in clear stages over nearly 250 years. The Prior's right to attend parliament was not assured until the fourteenth century, his place on king's council not automatic, nor even demonstrable until 1451. While attending court for specific occasions, he did not stay there, often retiring to his Priory after an event, such as when John Weston returned from diplomatic duty in 1480, reported to Edward IV at Eltham palace, and then rode back to Clerkenwell the same night.[1] In the first half of the fourteenth century, the Prior's 'duty', in common with that of other lords, was to attend parliament and great councils. This was something Priors needed to do in order to protect their order's interests. From the 1360s, we see him appointed by parliament as a trier of petitions, an appointment that Priors continued to hold up until the late 1520s. Then from 1451, the Prior started to attend the king's council and was paid for doing so. This indicates that, from this point, he was one of those sworn of the council, an official position.

What overall conclusions and questions are raised by this study? Firstly, it is clear that, bountiful though the Hospitaller archive on Malta is, it provides only a partial view of the Prior's role in England, and a view from the organisation's centre-outwards. This study demonstrates how essential local archive deposits are in order to obtain a more rounded view of the Prior's role, both as a Hospitaller and as a local lay lord. It provides a view from the province to the centre. The local archives are not as user-friendly as those in Malta. There are no sections where one can be guaranteed to find information on the Prior, whereas the Hospitallers records devote specific sections to each tongue. However, this book testifies to the worth of searching through the various classes in the National Archives, which reveal a gradual development of service over the late Middle Ages, rather than constant service since the eleventh century. It also makes visible an increased secularisation of the Order, especially from the last decade of the fifteenth century. Secondly, whereas from early on the Prior had been involved in some sort of service to the crown, whether as a judge on oyer and terminer courts (a task that in the thirteenth century Priors paid to be exempt from), supplying provisions for military campaigns, or attending parliament, as the later Middle Ages progressed the type of service became more intimate and regular, especially from the mid-fourteenth century. The Prior's greater involvement in secular affairs coincides with the outbreak of the Hundred Years War and the gradual emergence of an English identity.

Did Priors have a choice on whether to serve the local ruler? In short, the answer is yes. Once one transcends the superficial argument of constant friction between

---

[1] *Cely Letters*, 95–6.

Prior and monarch, one can perceive the Prior in the role of lay lord, bargaining and protecting to the advantage of his estate, and obtain a sense of his crown service in the changing conditions as the later Middle Ages progressed. It was a trend that was developing in other parts of the English province at an earlier stage, as the example of the Prior of Ireland (Kilmainham) indicates. Between 1284 and 1413, six Priors of Kilmainham served as lord deputies of Ireland, many undertaking more than one term of office, and in the case of Prior Roger Outlaw on seven separate occasions between 1324 and 1341.[2] Furthermore, three Priors of Kilmainham were appointed chief governors of Ireland between 1328 and 1422.[3] In Scotland Hospitaller service to the Scottish crown occurred later than in Ireland or England, starting with William Knollis, Prior of Torphichen, who held the office of treasurer twice between 1469 and 1492.[4] English Priors could still choose to limit their involvement in secular affairs, as the examples of Priors Radington, Grendon, Hulles and Malory show. Even later Priors who became intimately involved in the government of England, such as Botyll and Docwra, were able to put their order first when required, especially at the beginning of their term of office. There is even a possibility that Prior William Weston's lack of service may have been his choice, the result of a decision to focus back on Hospitaller duties, though, if so, it was a disastrous choice. A Prior's own career interests within the Order might be enhanced through serving secular rulers. Prior Docwra must have been aware that his frequent diplomatic duties for the crown helped to maintain his international profile and therefore promote his bid (which almost became reality in 1521) to become Grand Master.

Was service to the crown for or against the interests of the Order in general? In England after the start of the Hundred Years War, it seems that the best way to serve the Order's interests was for the Prior not only to interact with the secular state, but to integrate into it. Once appointed a provincial prior, the focus of a brother's action changed from active service in the East to efficient running of their priory. To become actively involved in the government of a country undoubtedly aided this task. English Priors who involved themselves in state affairs were the ones who managed to win benefits for the Hospitallers. Hales gained acceptance from the Good Parliament of 1376 to send responsions to the East at a time when there was much resistance in England to funds being sent abroad. Radington did the same in 1385. Botyll, at the height of his involvement on king's council, obtained permission to collect indulgences in aid of Rhodes. Docwra ensured that English brethren continued to be sent for service in the East, despite pressure for them to remain in England. After the loss of Rhodes, perhaps anticipating questions as to the value and purpose of the Order, he commissioned an English translation of the account of the 1522 siege in order to show the bravery of the knights and the continuing relevance of the struggle to protect Christendom. The Order recognised the value of working with the local ruler. Nicholson suggests that during the Great Schism, the Order developed a 'hands-off approach' to the problems of the English Priory, which was caught between the Order that supported Avignon and the crown

2   *HBC*, 165–6.
3   *Ibid.*, 162–3.
4   *Ibid.*, 187–8.

that favoured Rome.[5] In the fifteenth century, the headquarters followed a similar strategy, to the extent that they instructed their representatives to accept the final decision of the English king in disputes over the Priory, in the cases of Langstrother versus Woodville and Weston versus Multon. Despite the headquarters' preference for Prior, what mattered most was the co-operation of the state authorities for the smooth running of the province.

Service to the crown by the Prior resulted in other Hospitaller brethren doing the same. Sometimes it was in a supporting role for the Prior. When Prior Thame was keeper of Southampton, he had other brethren collecting and distributing troops' wages. On other occasions, brethren were involved separately in crown service, such as when, in March 1379, Brother Tilman Nidek (preceptor of Trebeigh and Prior's attorney 1370–90) was paid for his service as the king's nuncio to William, duke of Juliers (Low Countries).[6] This occurred while Prior Hales was on the minority council: it is probable that he recommended Nidek for the mission and highly likely that he used his influence to accelerate payment for Nidek's duties. Future Priors themselves, such as Kendal, served the crown. William Weston, when petitioning Henry VIII to accept his appointment as Prior, even asked him to take into account his long record of service to the crown.[7]

The Prior's service to the crown led not only to Hospitaller brethren and kin serving the crown, but also, in the sixteenth century at least, to crown servants coming into Hospitaller service and farming Hospitaller lands. Two examples of this trend are Guthlac Overton and John Skewes. In November 1508, Henry VII confirmed Overton as one of the two auditors of the duchy of Cornwall, a position he had held since that Michaelmas.[8] From then on, he was in demand by others, including the Prior.[9] Overton was general seneschal of the English Priory in 1512, its auditor general in 1519 and was still associated with the Priory in 1536.[10] In this last year, apart from farming various lands, we find him granted the next presentation to three churches; in two cases he held this right jointly with his son, Edward, and Robert Browne, a nephew of one of his customers (John Sharpe, knight), whom he had trained as an auditor.[11] Skewes had also served the king and other members of the nobility before his association with the Prior. In 1511, he was involved in the execution of the will of Edward Courtenay (d. 1509), earl of Devon, whose son William was married to one of Edward IV's daughters.[12] In 1520, he was employed by Henry VIII and compiled a lists of rents received from crown lands.[13] Then, in 1529, he worked with Weston on a commission of the king's council.[14] By that time he had entered the Prior's service, as we find him as a seneschal for the Hospitallers

5   Nicholson, 'Hospitallers in England', 43.
6   NLM 323, f. 144v; TNA E 403/471, m. 21, 31 May 1379, when he was paid £53 6s. 8d.
7   *L&P HVIII 1526–1527*, IV, 1461, 30 June 1527.
8   *CPR 1494–1509*, 285.
9   TNA C 1/551/49. He was, for example, the solicitor of Sir John Sharp.
10 BL MS Cotton Claudius E VI, ff. 108v, 189–189v; TNA LR 2/62, ff. 126v–127.
11 TNA LR 2/62, ff. 146–146v, 153v; TNA C 1/551/49.
12 TNA C 1/471/20.
13 TNA SC 12/4/30.
14 STAC 2/1/136.

in Bristol in 1526.[15] The use of Hospitaller servants by the crown, and crown servants by the Hospitallers, illustrates how integrated into lay society the Priory had become by the sixteenth century. Furthermore, the example of Overton presenting with other laymen indicates how the Priory became further secularised: once members of the laity gained privileges from the Prior, they then sought privileges for their kin and others, such as their servants and those with whom they did business. There are indications that the crown treated certain Hospitaller properties as its own from a far earlier date, as the example of Hampton Court indicates. Although only a few properties were affected, they were indicative of a growing trend. Crown use of Hospitaller property and the blurring of the distinction between crown and Hospitaller servants both indicate the extensive secularisation of the English Priory in the years prior to the dissolution of the Order in England.

In conclusion, although the main role of a provincial prior, as far as the Hospitallers were concerned, was to govern his priory well and to maximise its income, the English Hospitaller Prior developed another, just as important, role as a lay lord who owed service to his king and became a significant political figure in England. English Priors were dependent on the goodwill of the crown in order to perform their Hospitaller duties, and this was so in other western provinces. Service to the crown ensured that Priors were better able to defend Hospitaller interests and decisions. Even William Weston, Prior at a critical stage, did not concede to Cromwell's preference for auditor of the Priory.[16] Finally, although there were periods of friction, mostly about the payment of responsions, these disputes have been overemphasised: most of the time the Prior negotiated with the crown to the advantage of the Hospitallers, and co-existed with it.

The Hospitallers in the later medieval and early modern period have often been portrayed as an anachronism in a changing world. This study of the English Prior's role to the crown suggests that they were aware of and responded appropriately to these changing conditions. A Europe revolving more around national identities required more involvement in national politics. This was a successful strategy with relatively few casualties during the Reformation, of which the English Priory was one. Although William Weston went to great lengths to placate Henry VIII, it was beyond his power (and perhaps beyond his will) to alienate the English Priory from the rest of the Order, which was loyal to the papacy. It was the Hospitallers' very success in remaining a truly international order that brought about their downfall in England.

---

[15] BL MS Cotton Claudius E VI, f. 286.
[16] *L&P HVIII 1536*, XI, 166, 170.

Appendix 1

Diplomatic Duties of the Prior for the Crown

1380 to Scotland
John of Gaunt, Duke of Lancaster, Alexander Neville, Archbishop of York, Thomas Beauchamp, earl of Warwick, William Ufford, earl of Suffolk, Prior Robert Hales, Master Richard le Scrope, Master John Waltham

1386 to Cyprus and Rhodes
Prior John Radington special nuncio

1389 to Genoese merchants
Walter Skirlaw, bishop of Durham, John Gilbert, bishop of St David's, Prior John Radington, John Lovell, knight, John Devereaux, knight, Edward Dalingrugge, knight, William Neville, knight, Master John Barnet

1391 to Teutonic Knights
John of Gaunt, Prior John Radington, Thomas Percy, knight

1392 to France
John of Gaunt, Prior John Radington

1394 to Scotland
Walter Skirlaw, bishop of Durham, Henry Percy, earl of Northumberland, Prior John Radington, William Lord Roos of Hamlock, Ralph Lord Neville, Henry Percy, knight, Ralph Percy, knight, Richard Stury, knight, Gerard Heron, knight, Master Thomas Stanley, Master Alan Newark, John Mitford, esquire

1406 to Teutonic Knights
Edmund Stafford, bishop of Exeter, Henry Bowet, bishop of Bath and Wells, Prior Walter Grendon, Lord Hugh Burnell, William Rickhill, William Hankford, William Esturmy, knight, Master John Kingston, William Brompton, citizen of London

1447 to Pope
Prior Robert Botyll, Master Vincent Clement, Master Thomas Candour

1447 to France
Walter Lyhert, bishop of Norwich, Prior Robert Botyll, John Sutton, Lord Dudley, Master Vincent Clement, Master Thomas Kent, Master Thomas Candour

1451 to Teutonic Knights

Prior Robert Botyll, Master Thomas Kent, Master William Witham, Henry Beringham, knight, John Stokkey, citizen of London

1453 to Burgundy

Prior Robert Botyll, Master Richard Caunton, Master William Toby, Master Thomas Kent

1458 to Burgundy

Richard Neville, earl of Warwick and captain of Calais, Richard Beauchamp, bishop of Salisbury, Henry Viscount Bourchier, Prior Robert Botyll, Lord Henry Scrope of Bolton, Master Vincent Clement, papal collector in England, William Bourchier, knight, Lord Thomas Neville, Lord John Neville, Lord Humphrey Bourchier, Lord John Wenlock, John Stratton, Robert Hall, Thomas Chippenham, Thomas Vaughan, John Thirsk, mayor of the staple of Calais, Master Louis Galet, William Pirton, lieutenant of Guînes castle, John Williamson of Louthe, Richard Whethill, John Wodehouse, William Obery

1461 to Burgundy

Prior Robert Botyll, John Wenlock, captain of the seas, Master Peter Taster, dean of St Severin

1462 to Earl of Ross

Lawrence Booth, bishop of Durham, John Tiptoft, earl of Worcester, Prior Robert Botyll, Lord John Wenlock, Master Robert Stillington

1465 to Brittany

Prior Robert Botyll, Master Thomas Kent, Master Henry Sharp

1466 to Burgundy

Richard Neville, earl of Warwick, Robert Stillington, bishop of Bath and Wells, Richard Wydeville, Lord Rivers, Prior Robert Botyll, William Lord Hastings, Master Peter Taster, John Fogge, knight, Master Thomas Kent, John Say, knight, Thomas Colt

1467 to Brittany

Prior Robert Botyll

1470 to Spain

Prior John Langstrother, Master Henry Sharp

1471 to France

George Neville, archbishop of York and chancellor, George, duke of Clarence, John Hales, bishop of Coventry and Lichfield, Robert Tully, bishop of St David's, Richard Neville, earl of Warwick, Henry Bourchier, earl of Essex, Prior John Langstrother, Master John Russell, Master Henry Sharp

1480 to France

Prior John Weston, Master Thomas Langton

1486 to Scotland

John Alcock, bishop of Worcester, John Russell, bishop of Lincoln, Prior John Weston, John Lord Dynham, Thomas Lovell, knight, Master Henry Ainsworth

1487 to Pope

Prior John Weston

1488 to Castile

Prior John Weston, Master John Gunthorpe, Master Christopher Urswick, Master Thomas Savage, Master Henry Ainsworth

1492 to France

Richard Fox, bishop of Bath and Wells, Giles Lord Daubeney, captain of Calais, Prior John Kendal, William Hussey, knight, Chief Justice, James Tyrell, captain of Guînes, Master Henry Ainsworth

1495 to Philip the Fair

Richard Fox, bishop of Durham, John Viscount Wells, Prior John Kendal, Master William Wareham, Master Christopher Urswyk, Master John Risley

1506 to Philip the Fair

William Wareham, archbishop of Canterbury, Richard Fox, bishop of Winchester, Prior Thomas Docwra, Master Nicholas West

1507 to Archduke Charles

Richard Fox, bishop of Winchester, Thomas, earl of Surrey, Prior Thomas Docwra, Gilbert Talbot, knight, deputy of Calais, Master Nicholas West

1510 to France (2 embassies)

Prior Thomas Docwra, Master Nicholas West

1514 to France

Charles Somerset, earl of Worcester, Prior Thomas Docwra, Master Nicholas West

1516 to Scotland

Prior Thomas Docwra

1517–18 to Castile (two embassies)

Prior Thomas Docwra, Tomasso Spinelli, resident ambassador

1518 to France

Charles Somerset, earl of Worcester, Nicholas West, bishop of Ely, Prior Thomas Docwra, Nicholas Vaux, captain of Guyenne

1519 to France

Charles Somerset, earl of Worcester, Prior Thomas Docwra, Nicholas Vaux, captain of Guyenne, Edward Belknap, knight

1521 to Emperor Charles and to France

Prior Thomas Docwra, Thomas Boleyn, knight, Richard Wingfield, knight

1522–3 to Emperor Charles
Prior Thomas Docwra, Master Richard Sampson, resident ambassador

1524 to Emperor Charles
Prior Thomas Docwra

1525 to Rome
Prior Thomas Docwra

1525 to Emperor Charles
Prior Thomas Docwra, Master Richard Sampson, resident ambassador

1525 to France
Prior Thomas Docwra

Appendix 2

Hospitaller Presentations to Benefices, 1297–1540[1]

Year	Month	Day	Prior	Lieutenant	Other preceptor
1298	1	30	Tothale		
1302	3	24	Tothale		
1302	4	6	Tothale		
1302	12	15	Tothale		
1303	1	5	Tothale		
1303	3	23	Tothale		
1304	11	15	Tothale		
1306	4	11	Tothale		
1306	10	4	Tothale		
1307	2	9	Tothale		
1307	3	16	Tothale		
1307	8	27	Tothale		
1307	10	9	Tothale		
1307	12	22	Tothale		
1309	3	4	Tothale		
1309	3	12	Tothale		
1309	11	3	Tothale		
1310	1	10	Tothale		
1310	3	12	Tothale		
1310	6	20	Tothale		
1310	8	9	Tothale		
1310	10	2	Tothale		
1310	11	19	Tothale		
1311	7	7	Tothale		
1312	5	24	Tothale		
1312	7	9	Tothale		
1312	7	21	Tothale		
1312	11	7	Tothale		
1313	2	7	Tothale		
1313	7	16	Tothale		
1313	7	20			Hospitallers
1314	3	22	Tothale		

[1] This table is based on the bishops' and archbishops' registers in print, consulted at the Institute of Historical Research, Senate House, London.

Year	Month	Day	Prior	Lieutenant	Other preceptor
1314	7	19	Tothale		
1314	10	29	Tothale		
1314	12	11	Tothale		
1315	2	10	Tothale		
1315	4	26	Tothale		
1315	7	16	Tothale		
1316	8	21	R. Pavely		
1316	11	23	R. Pavely		
1317	3	28	R. Pavely		
1317	11	11	R. Pavely		
1318	4	20	R. Pavely		
1318	5	27	R. Pavely		
1318	5	30	R. Pavely		
1318	7	11	R. Pavely		
1318	10	7		R. Leicester	
1319	3	5	R. Pavely		
1319	5	15	R. Pavely		
1319	7	5	R. Pavely		
1319	11	29	R. Pavely		
1320	12	21	Archer		
1321	1	1		R. Leicester	
1321	5	4	Archer		
1321	5	14	Archer		
1321	12	21	Archer		
1322	3	26	Archer		
1322	9	22	Archer		
1323	2	14	Archer		
1323	4	12	Archer		
1323	6	11	Archer		
1323	8	3	Archer		
1323	12	28	Archer		
1324	1	13	Archer		
1324	5	16	Archer		
1324	6	19	Archer		
1324	7	8	Archer		
1324	7	30	Archer		
1324	7	31	Archer		
1324	10	23	Archer		
1324	11	4	Archer		
1324	11	11	Archer		
1325	4	19	Archer		
1325	10	20	Archer		
1325	12	3	Archer		
1326	1	18	Archer		
1326	7	24	Archer		
1327	1	20	Archer		
1328	5	8			Hospitallers
1328	10	5	Archer		

Year	Month	Day	Prior	Lieutenant	Other preceptor
1329	9	22	Archer		
1329	10	1	Archer		
1329	11	11	Archer		
1329	12	30	Archer		
1330	8	5	Archer		
1330	8	15	Archer		
1330	11	27		R. Leicester	
1330	11	29		R. Leicester	
1331	1	21		R. Leicester and Tibertis	
1331	4	27	Tibertis		
1331	7	28	Tibertis		
1331	8	28		R. Leicester	
1331	12	17	Tibertis		
1332	4	27	Tibertis		
1332	5	6	Tibertis		
1332	9	28	Tibertis		
1333	6	30	Tibertis		
1333	9	17	Tibertis		
1334	1	6	Tibertis		
1334	2	18	Tibertis		
1335	1	5	Tibertis		
1335	2	22	Thame		
1336	10	30	Thame		
1340	7	21	Thame		
1341	8	3	Thame		
1342	12	15	Thame		
1343	2	14	Thame		
1344	9	25	Thame		
1344	10	4	Thame		
1345	2	9	Thame		
1345	10	3	Thame		
1346	5	30	Thame and preceptor of Temple Bruer		
1346	7	4	Thame		
1347	4	26	Thame		
1348	2	3	Thame		
1348	2	16	Thame		
1348	2	20	Thame		
1348	2	25	Thame		
1348	4	22	Thame		
1348	12	12	Thame		
1349	2	16	Thame		
1349	3	12	Thame		
1349	4	22	Thame		
1349	5	14	Thame		
1349	5	26	Thame		
1349	5	28	Thame		

Year	Month	Day	Prior	Lieutenant	Other preceptor
1349	6	16	Thame		
1349	6	20	Thame		
1349	6	22	Thame		
1349	6	27	Thame		
1349	6	28	Thame		
1349	7	20	Thame		
1349	7	23	Thame		
1349	7	24	Thame		
1349	8	28	Thame		
1350	3	12	Thame		
1350	4	5	Thame		
1350	11	13	Thame		
1350	12	15	Thame		
1351	2	27	Thame		
1351	6	25	Thame		
1351	7	2	Thame		
1351	8	16	Thame		
1351	10	12	Thame		
1354	2	18			Hospitallers
1354	5	30	J. Pavely		
1355	8	17	J. Pavely		
1355	9	22	J. Pavely		
1358	1	9	J. Pavely		
1359	1	24	J. Pavely		
1361	2	8	J. Pavely		
1361	4	9	J. Pavely		
1361	12	5	J. Pavely		
1362	1	21	J. Pavely		
1362	4	26	J. Pavely		
1363	5	7	J. Pavely		
1363	5	17	J. Pavely		
1363	6	11	J. Pavely		
1363	7	31	J. Pavely		
1363	10	22	J. Pavely		
1363	10	27	J. Pavely		
1364	12	12	J. Pavely		
1365	2	8	J. Pavely		
1366	7	6	J. Pavely		
1367	4	23	J. Pavely		
1367	5	3	J. Pavely		
1367	8	6	J. Pavely		
1369	8	12	J. Pavely		
1369	11	22	J. Pavely		
1369	12	1	J. Pavely		
1372	4	22	Hales		
1372	7	20	Hales		
1373	5	6	Hales		
1373	11	19		J. Noble	

Year	Month	Day	Prior	Lieutenant	Other preceptor
1375	6	6	Hales		
1375	12	23	Hales		
1376	5	3	Hales		
1378	7	31	Hales		
1380	3	10	Hales		
1380	3	19	Hales		
1382	3	19	H. Inge (president)		
1382	10	9	Radington		
1382	12	1	Radington		
1383	12	4	Radington		
1383	12	25	Radington		
1384	2	17	Radington		
1385	6	23	Radington		
1385	10	4	Radington		
1386	6	23		H. Inge	
1386	7	23		H. Inge	
1386	9	7		H. Inge	
1386	10	30		H. Inge	
1387	5	22		H. Inge	
1387	12	10		H. Inge	
1388	3	13		H. Inge	
1388	10	4	Radington		
1388	10	16	Radington		
1388	11	13	Radington		
1388	11	21	Radington		
1389	4	17	Radington		
1389	7	28	Radington		
1389	8	13	Radington		
1389	9	12	Radington		
1390	5	8		H. Inge	
1391	5	19		H. Inge	
1391	7	17		H. Inge	
1391	9	7		H. Inge	
1391	10	6		H. Inge	
1392	2	7		H. Inge	
1392	4	12		H. Inge	
1392	5	10		H. Inge	
1392	9	9		H. Inge	
1392	9	18		H. Inge	
1393	1	14		H. Inge	
1393	1	20		H. Inge	
1394	3	13	Radington		
1398	2	6		R. Normanton	
1398	5	7		R. Normanton	
1399	5	17		R. Normanton	
1399	10	25		R. Normanton	
1400	7	17		R. Normanton	
1400	7	23		R. Normanton	

Year	Month	Day	Prior	Lieutenant	Other preceptor
1400	9	20		R. Normanton	
1400	10	4		R. Normanton	
1400	10	5		R. Normanton	
1401	4	1		R. Normanton	
1401	8	8	Grendon		
1401	8	15	Grendon		
1401	8	18	Grendon		
1401	11	26	Grendon		
1402	2	14		R. Normanton	
1402	11	8		R. Normanton	
1402	11	9		R. Normanton	
1404	2	16		R. Normanton	
1404	6	16		R. Normanton	
1405	3	14		R. Normanton	
1405	4	17		R. Normanton	
1405	5	29	Grendon		
1406	2	2	Grendon		
1406	10	22	Grendon		
1406	11	4	Grendon		
1406	11	17	Grendon		
1407	1	7	Grendon		
1407	2	20	Grendon		
1408	1	17	Grendon		
1408	3	29	Grendon		
1408	7	1	Grendon		
1408	7	14		J. Brisley	
1408	10	8	Grendon		
1408	12	16	Grendon		
1408	12	19	Grendon		
1409	1	15	Grendon		
1409	4	24	Grendon		
1409	5	23	Grendon		
1409	7	28	Grendon		
1409	9	15	Grendon		
1409	11	4		J. Brisley	
1409	12	1	Grendon		
1409	12	10	Grendon		
1410	2	7	Grendon		
1410	2	13	Grendon		
1410	5	14	Grendon		
1410	9	13	Grendon		
1410	9	23	Grendon		
1411	2	8	Grendon		
1411	4	30	Grendon		
1411	6	7	Grendon		
1411	8	22	Grendon		
1411	9	13	Grendon		
1412	10	24	Grendon		

Year	Month	Day	Prior	Lieutenant	Other preceptor
1412	12	2	Grendon		
1413	2	13	Grendon		
1413	2	22	Grendon		
1413	6	3	Grendon		
1413	8	12	Grendon		
1413	10	8	Grendon		
1414	3	26	Grendon		
1414	8	14	Grendon		
1414	10	23	Grendon		
1414	12	7	Grendon		
1415	2	11	Grendon		
1415	6	14	Grendon		
1415	6	25	Grendon		
1416	2	16	Grendon		
1416	3	4	Grendon		
1417	3	20	Grendon		
1417	8	4	Hulles		
1418	4	15		J. Bromston	
1418	5	17		J. Bromston	
1418	8	9		J. Bromston	
1420	4	26		H. Crounhale	
1420	10	4		H. Crounhale	
1420	10	25		H. Crounhale	
1420	11	6		H. Crounhale	
1420	11	19		H. Crounhale	
1421	1	17		H. Crounhale	
1421	3	22		H. Crounhale	
1421	5	25		H. Crounhale	
1421	5	31		H. Crounhale	
1421	7	10		H. Crounhale	
1421	12	8		H. Crounhale	
1422	1	29		H. Crounhale	
1422	2	4		H. Crounhale	
1422	3	10		H. Crounhale	
1422	8	13		H. Crounhale	
1422	8	20		H. Crounhale	
1422	9	1		H. Crounhale	
1423	1	20		H. Crounhale	
1423	3	29		H. Crounhale	
1423	6	16		H. Crounhale	
1423	6	17		H. Crounhale	
1423	7	26		H. Crounhale	
1423	8	10		H. Crounhale	
1423	10	20		H. Crounhale	
1423	11	5		H. Crounhale	
1424	7	25		H. Crounhale	
1424	8	14		H. Crounhale	
1424	8	25		H. Crounhale	

Year	Month	Day	Prior	Lieutenant	Other preceptor
1424	9	22		H. Crounhale	
1424	10	6		H. Crounhale	
1424	12	9		H. Crounhale	
1425	1	20		H. Crounhale	
1425	2	7		H. Crounhale	
1425	2	18		H. Crounhale	
1425	3	1		H. Crounhale	
1425	3	3		H. Crounhale	
1425	3	5		H. Crounhale	
1425	6	15		H. Crounhale	
1425	6	18		H. Crounhale	
1425	8	15		H. Crounhale	
1425	11	9		H. Crounhale	
1426	4	16		H. Crounhale	
1426	12	18	Hulles		
1428	2	21	Hulles		
1428	8	27	Hulles		
1428	10	23	Hulles		
1429	3	11	Hulles		
1429	3	31	Hulles		
1429	7	11	Hulles		
1429	7	26	Hulles		
1429	8	12	Hulles		
1430	6	28	Hulles		
1430	7	26	Hulles		
1430	12	21	Hulles		
1431	1	3	Hulles		
1431	9		Hulles		
1432	11	3	Malory		
1433	1	12	Malory		
1434	3	23	Malory		
1435	2	11	Malory		
1435	10	13	Malory		
1437	2	2		R. Paule	
1437	2	19			J. Ellum
1437	11	4	Malory		
1438	1	17			J. Ellum
1438	6	28	Malory		
1439	5	2	Malory		
1440	10	12	Botyll		
1441	3	15	Botyll		
1441	8	12		T. Weston	
1443	1	1			Preceptor
1444	12	31	Botyll		
1445	2	20	Botyll		
1446	10	15	Botyll		
1447	3	16		W. Langstrother	
1447	5	27	Botyll		

Year	Month	Day	Prior	Lieutenant	Other preceptor
1448	2	28		W. Langstrother	
1449	6	20	Botyll		
1450	8	11	Botyll		
1450	8	23	Botyll		
1453	3	27		W. Langstrother	
1453	9	28	Botyll		
1453	10	25	Botyll		
1453	12	22	Botyll		
1454	7	19	Botyll		
1456	2	5	Botyll		
1456	2	12	Botyll		
1456	3	15	Botyll		
1456	8	4	Botyll		
1456	10	21	Botyll		
1457	12	22	Botyll		
1458	4	13	Botyll		
1459	4	26	Botyll		
1460	3	27	Botyll		
1460	8	24	Botyll		
1460	11	20	Botyll		
1464	1	13	Botyll		
1465	2	19	Botyll		
1466	3	22	Botyll		
1466	9	11	Botyll		
1467	8	22	Botyll		
1468	11	21	President		
1471	10	17	Tornay		
1471	11	6	Tornay		
1472	1	9	Tornay		
1473	9	2	Tornay		
1473	12	2	Tornay		
1474	5	24	Multon		
1474	9	29	Multon		
1475	6	2			J. Boswell
1476	1	22	Multon		
1476	7	31	Multon		
1476	8	23	Multon		
1476	11	6	Multon		
1477	10	17	J. Weston		
1479	10	20	J. Weston		
1479	10	28			J. Boswell
1480	1	22	J. Weston		
1480	4	10	J. Weston		
1480	11	2	J. Weston		
1482	2	17		W. Weston	
1486	5	1			T. Docwra
1487	6	28		R. Egilsfeld	
1487	7	30		R. Egilsfeld	

Year	Month	Day	Prior	Lieutenant	Other preceptor
1487	9	13		R. Egilsfeld	
1489	7	8			R. Thornburgh
1490	6	27		R. Egilsfeld	
1491	5	2	Kendal		
1491	8	30		R. Egilsfeld	
1492	9	13	Kendal		
1493	3	29	Kendal		
1494	10	9	Kendal		
1495	9	25	Kendal		
1495	3	3	Kendal		
1495	11	13	Kendal		
1496	1	15	Kendal		
1496	1	22	Kendal		
1496	6	27	Kendal		
1498	10	13	Kendal		
1498	10	28	Kendal		
1499	1	4	Kendal		
1502	3	24	T. Newport (president)		
1502	8	31		T. Newport	
1503	1	19		T. Newport	
1504	3	15		T. Newport	
1506	1	23	Docwra		
1506	3	10	Docwra		
1506	3	24	Docwra		
1506	10	26	Docwra		
1509	5	5	Docwra		
1516	7	17	Docwra		
1517	5	25	Docwra		
1521	9	4	Docwra		
1523	6	8	Docwra		
1523	11	9	Docwra		
1524	4	20	Docwra		
1524	9	28	Docwra		
1526	2	20	Docwra		
1530	10	30	W. Weston		
1534	6	2	W. Weston		
1534	6	17	W. Weston		

Bibliography

Manuscript sources

Bodleian Library, Oxford
MS Ashmole 1137
MS Rawlinson, Essex 11

British Library, London
MSS Additional 54226, 6165, 40631, 41476–97, 70511
Egerton Charter 208
MS Cotton Claudius E VI
MSS Cotton Cleopatra E IV, F III, F IV
MS Cotton Galba B VII
MSS Cotton Nero B II, C IX, E VI
MS Cotton Otho C IX
MS Harley 158
MSS Lansdowne 1, 160, 200, 639, 979
MS Royal 13 B XI

Centre for Kentish Studies, Maidstone
U451 Temple Dartford and Sutton-at-Hone deeds

National Library of Malta, Valletta
Archives 73–4   Books of the Council, 1459–72
Archives 280–7   Chapter Generals, 1330–1548
Archives 316–95 Book of Grand Master's Bulls, 1346–1504

Order of St John Museum and Library, London
Butler Papers

The National Archives, Public Record Office, Kew
C 1 Chancery, Early Chancery Proceedings
C 47 Chancery Miscellanea
C 49 Chancery, Parliamentary and Council Proceedings
C 54 Chancery, Close Rolls
C 55 Chancery, Supplementary Close Rolls
C 60 Chancery, Fine Rolls
C 61 Chancery, Gascon Rolls
C 64 Chancery, Norman Rolls
C 65 Chancery, Parliament Rolls

C 66 Chancery, Patent Rolls
C 71 Chancery, Scotch Rolls
C 76 Chancery, Treaty Rolls
C 81 Chancery, Warrants for the Great Seal
C 143 Chancery, Inquisitions Ad Quod Damnum
C 147 Chancery, Ancient Deeds, Series CC
DL 25 Duchy of Lancaster, Deeds, Series L
E 28 Exchequer, Treasury of the Receipt, Council and Privy Seal Records
E 30 Exchequer, Treasury of Receipt, Diplomatic Documents
E 39 Exchequer, Treasury of Receipt, Scottish Documents
E 40 Exchequer, Treasury of Receipt, Ancient Deeds, Series A
E 41 Exchequer, Treasury of Receipt, Ancient Deeds, Series AA
E 101 Exchequer, King's Remembrancer, Accounts Various
E 135 Exchequer, Miscellaneous Ecclesiastical Documents
E 326 Exchequer, Augmentation Office, Ancient Deeds, Series B
E 329 Exchequer, Augmentation Office, Ancient Deeds, Series BS
E 364 Exchequer, Pipe Office, Foreign Account Rolls
E 403 Exchequer, Treasury of Receipt, Issue Rolls and Registers
E 404 Exchequer, Treasury of Receipt, Warrants for Issue
LR 2 Land Remembrancer Office, Miscellaneous
LR 10 Land Remembrancer Office, Drafts and Warrants
LR 14 Land Remembrancer, Ancient Deeds, Series E
REQ 1 Court of Requests, Proceedings
REQ 2 Court of Requests, Proceedings
SC 2 Special Collections, Court Rolls
SC 6 Special Collections, Ministers' and Receivers' Accounts
SC 7 Special Collections, Papal Bulls
SC 12 Special Collections, Rentals and Surveys
SP 46 State Papers Domestic, Supplementary
STAC 1 Court of Star Chamber, Proceedings
STAC 2 Court of Star Chamber, Proceedings

Shakespeare Birthplace Trust Records Office, Stratford-upon-Avon
DR18 Balsall manorial records

Surrey History Centre, Woking
LM 791 Survey of lead belonging to St John's, Smithfield

Printed sources

Accounts Rendered by Papal collectors in England 1317–78, ed. W. E. Lunt and E. B. Graves, Philadelphia, 1968
The Alien Communities of London in the Fifteenth Century. The Subsidy Rolls of 1440 and 1483–4, ed. J. L. Bolton, Richard III and York History Trust, Stamford, 1998
The Ancient Kalendars and Inventories of the Treasury of His Majesty's Exchequer, 3 vols, ed. F. Palgrave, Record Commission, London, 1836
Anekdota Engrafa yia ti Rodo kai tis Noties Sporades apo to Archeio ton Ioanniton Ippoton (Unpublished Documents concerning Rhodes and the South-east Aegean Islands from the Archives of the Order of St John), I, ed. Z. Tsirpanlis, Rhodes, 1995

The Anglica Historia of Polydore Vergil 1485–1537, ed. D. Hay, Camden 3rd Series, LXXIV, 1950

'The Anglo-French Negotiations at Bruges, 1374–1377', ed. E. Perroy, *Camden Miscellany XIX*, Camden 3rd Series, LXXX, 1952

Annales Monastici, 5 vols, ed H. R. Luard, Rolls Series, London, 1864–9

The Anonimalle Chronicle 1333–1381, ed. V. H. Galbraith, Manchester, 1927

Book of Deliberations of the Venerable Tongue of England 1523–1567, ed. H. P. Scicluna, Valletta, 1949

Calendar of Charter Rolls preserved in the Public Record Office, 1257–1516, 5 vols, London, 1906–27

Calendar of Close Rolls preserved in the Public Record Office, 1288–1509, 45 vols, London, 1904–63

Calendar of the Entries in the Papal Registers relating to Great Britain and Ireland: Papal Letters 1198–1492, 15 vols, London, 1893–1960

Calendar of Fine Rolls preserved in the Public Record Office, 1272–1509, 22 vols, London, 1911–62

Calendar of Patent Rolls preserved in the Public Record Office, 1281–1509, 47 vols, London, 1893–1916

Calendar of State Papers and Manuscripts, existing in the Archives and Collections of Milan 1385–1618, ed. A. B. Hinds, London, 1912

Calendar of State Papers and Manuscripts relating to English Affairs existing in the Archives and Collections of Venice and in other Libraries of Northern Italy, 1202–1674, vols I–VI, ed. R. Brown and H. F. Brown, London, 1864–84

Cambridgeshire and the Isle of Ely Lay Subsidy for the Year 1327, ed. J. J. Muskett and C. H. Evelyn-White, London, 1900

Cartulaire Général de l'Ordre des Hospitaliers de S. Jean de Jérusalem (1100–1310), 4 vols, ed. J. Delaville le Roulx, Paris, 1894–1905

Cartulaire du Prieuré de Saint Gilles de l'Hôpital de Saint Jean de Jérusalem (1129–1210), ed. D. le Blévec and A. Venturini, Paris, 1997

A Cartulary of Buckland Priory in the County of Somerset, ed. F. Weaver, Somerset Record Society, XXV, 1909

The Cartulary of the Knights of St John of Jerusalem in England, Prima Camera, Essex, ed. M. Gervers, Oxford, 1996

The Cartulary of the Knights of St John of Jerusalem in England, Secunda Camera, Essex, ed. M. Gervers, Oxford, 1982

Catalogue de Rolles Gascons, Normans et Francois dans les archives de la Tour de Londres, 2 vols, ed. T. Carte, London, 1743

Catalogue of the Records of the Order of St John of Jerusalem in the Royal Malta Library, 6+ vols, ed. A. Gabarretta and J. Mizzi, Valletta, 1964–

The Cely Letters 1472–1488, ed. A. Hanham, The Early English Text Society, CCLXXIII, London, 1975

The Chronicle of Adam Usk 1377–1421, ed. C. Given-Wilson, Oxford, 1997

The Chronicle of Calais in the Reigns of Henry VII and Henry VIII to the Year 1540, ed. J. G. Nichols, Camden Society, XXXV, 1846

A Chronicle of the First Thirteen Years of the Reign of King Edward the Fourth by John Warkworth, ed. J. Halliwell, Camden Society, X, 1839

'Chronicle of the Rebellion in Lincolnshire, 1470', ed. J. G. Nichols, *Camden Miscellany*, I, Camden Society, First Series, XXXIX, 1847

Chronique de la Traison et Mort de Richart Deux Roy Dengleterre, ed. B. Williams, London, 1846

Clerical Poll Taxes of the Diocese of Lincoln, 1377–1381, ed. A. K. McHardy, Lincoln Record Society, XXXVII, 1992

Close Rolls of the Reign of Henry III, 14 vols, London, 1902–38

Conti, S. dei, *Le Storie de' Suoi Tempi dal 1475 al 1510*, 2 vols, tr. F. Calabrò and D. Zanelli, Rome, 1883

The Crowland Chronicle Continuations: 1459–1486, ed. N. Pronay and J. Cox, London, 1986

Death and Dissent: Two Fifteenth-Century Chronicles. The Dethe of the Kynge of Scotis and Warkworth's Chronicle, ed. L. M. Matheson, Woodbridge, 1999

The Diplomatic Correspondence of Richard II, ed. E. Perroy, Camden 3rd Series, XLVIII, 1933

Diplomatic Documents Preserved in the Public Record Office, 8 vols, ed. P. Chaplais, London, 1964

'Documents Regarding the Fulfilment and Interpretation of the Treaty of Brétigny, 1361–1369', ed. P. Chaplais, *Camden Miscellany* XIX, Camden 3rd Series, LXXX, 1952

'Documents Relating to the Anglo-French Negotiations of 1439', ed. C. T. Allmand, *Camden Miscellany* XXIV, Camden 4th Series, IX, 1972

Dugdale, W., *Monasticon Anglicanum: A History of the Abbies and other Monasteries, Hospitals, Frieries, and Cathedral and Collegiate Churches, with their Dependencies, in England and Wales; Also of All Such Scotch, Irish, and French Monasteries, as were in any Manner Connected with Religious Houses in England*, 6 vols in 8 parts, ed. J. Caley, H. Ellis, B. Bandinel, London, 1817–30

Edward IV's French Expedition of 1475, ed. F. P. Barnard, Oxford, 1925

English Historical Documents, 12 vols, ed. D. C. Douglas, London, 1953–1977

English Medieval Diplomatic Practice, 3 vols, ed. P. Chaplais, London, 1982

Expedition to Prussia and the Holy Land made by Henry Earl of Derby (afterwards King Henry IV) in the Years 1390–1 and 1392–3, ed. L. Toulmin Smith, Camden Society LII, London, 1894

Faculty Office Registers 1534–1549: A Calendar of the First Two Registers of the Archbishop of Canterbury's Faculty Office, ed. D. S. Chambers, Oxford, 1966

The Fane Fragment of the 1461 Lords' Journal, ed. W. H. Dunham, New Haven, CT, 1935

Foedera, conventiones, literæ, et cujuscunque generis acta publica, inter reges Angliæ, et alios quosvis Imperatores, Regis, Pontifices, Principes, vel communitates, ab ineunte sæculo duodecimo, viz. ab anno 1101, ad nostra usque tempora, habita aut tractata, 2nd edn, 20 vols, ed. T. Rymer, London, 1727–35

Foedera, conventiones, literae, et cujuscunque generis acta publica: inter reges Angliae et alios quosvis imperatores, reges, pontifices, principes, vel communitates, ab ineunte saeculo duodecimo, viz. ab anno 1101. ad nostra usque tempora, habita aut tractata: ex autographis, infra secretiores archivorum regiorum thesaurarias per multa saecula reconditis, fideliter exscripta, 3rd edn, 10 vols, ed. T. Rymer, Hague, 1739–45

The Forty-First Annual Report of the Deputy Keeper of the Public Records, London, 1880

The Forty-Second Annual Report of the Deputy Keeper of the Public Records, London, 1881

The Forty-Fourth Annual Report of the Deputy Keeper of the Public Records, London, 1883

The Forty-Eighth Annual Report of the Deputy Keeper of the Public Records, London, 1887

De Gestis Concilii Basiliensis Commentariorum, ed. D. Hay and W. K. Smith, Oxford, 1967

Giustinian, S., *Four Years at the Court of Henry VIII 1515–1519*, 2 vols, tr. R. Brown, London, 1854

The Great Chronicle of London, ed. A. H. Thomas and I. D. Thornley, London, 1938

Hall's Chronicle, ed. H. Ellis, London, 1809

Historie of the Arrivall of Edward IV in England and the Finall Recouerye of his Kingdomes from Henry VI AD MCCCCLXXI, ed. J. Bruce, Camden Society, I, 1838

'The Hospitallers' Western Accounts, 1373/4 and 1374/5', ed. A. Luttrell, *Camden Miscellany* XXX, Camden 4th Series, XXXIX, 1990

Inquisitions and Assessments Relating to Feudal Aids, with Other Analogous Documents Preserved in the Public Record Office. A.D. 1284–1431, 6 vols, London, 1899–1920

Issue Rolls of Thomas Brantingham, ed. F. Devon, London, 1835

Joannis Lelandi antiquari de rebus Britannicis Collectanea, ed. T. Hearne, 6 vols, London, 1774

'John Benet's Chronicle for the years 1400 to 1462', ed. G. L. Harriss and M. A. Harriss, *Camden Miscellany* XXIV, Camden 4th Series, IX, 1972

Journals of the House of Lords, 171+ vols, London, 1802–

A Kentish Cartulary of the Order of St John of Jerusalem, ed. C. Cotton, Kent Archaeological Society, XI, 1930

Kingsford's Stonor Letters and Papers 1290–1483, 2 vols, ed. C. Carpenter, Cambridge, 1996

The Knights Hospitaller in England: Being the Report of Prior Philip de Thame to the Grand Master Elyan de Villanova for AD 1338, ed. L. B. Larking, Camden Society, LXV, 1857

'Letter from Sir Joseph de Cancy, knight of the Hospital of St John of Jerusalem, to King Edward I (1281)' and 'Letter from King Edward I to Sir Joseph (1282)' tr. W. B. Sanders in *The Library of the Palestine Pilgrims' Text Society*, V, London, 1897

The Letters of James the Fourth 1505–1513, ed. A. L. Mackie, Edinburgh, 1953

The Letters of John of Salisbury, 2 vols, ed. W. J. Millor, H. E. Butler and C. N. L. Brooke, London and Oxford, 1955–79

Letters and Papers, Foreign and Domestic of the Reign of Henry VIII, 22 vols in 37 parts, London, 1864–1929

Letters and Papers Illustrative of the Reigns of Richard III and Henry VII, 2 vols, ed. J. Gairdner, Rolls Series, London, 1861–3

Letters and Papers Illustrative of the Wars of the English in France during the Reign of Henry VI, 2 vols, ed. J. Stevenson, Rolls Series, London, 1861–4

Liber niger Scaccarii nec non Wilhelmi Worcestrii Annales rerum anglicarum, cum praefatione et appendice Thomae Hearnii ad editionem primam Oxoniae editam, 2 vols, ed. W. Richardson and J. Richardson, London, 1771

The Lisle Letters, 6 vols, ed. M. St Clare Byrne, Chicago, 1981

Members of Parliament for Northumberland 1258–1588, ed. C. H. Hunter Blair, reprint from *Archaeologis Aeliana*, 4th series, X–XII, Newcastle upon Tyne, 1933–5

Memoranda de Parliamento: Records of the Parliament Holden at Westminster 1305, ed. F. W. Maitland, Rolls Series, London, 1893

The Memoranda Roll for the Michaelmas Term of the First Year of the Reign of King John (1199–1200), ed. H. G. Richardson, Roll Series XXI, London, 1943

The Memoranda Roll of the King's Remembrancer for Michaelmas 1230 – Trinity 1231, ed. C. Robinson, Rolls Society XI, Princeton, NJ, 1933

The Merchant Taylors' Company of London: Court Minutes 1486–1493, ed. M. Davies, London, 2000

Monumenta Peloponnesiaca: Documents for the History of the Peloponnese in the Fourteenth and Fifteenth Centuries, ed. J. Chrysostomides, Camberley, 1995

Le Morte Darthur: Sir Thomas Malory's Book of King Arthur and his Noble Knights of the Round Table, 2 vols, ed. A. W. Pollard, London, 1900

Narratives of the Expulsion of the English from Normandy 1449–1450, ed. J. Stevenson, Rolls Series, London, 1863

Official Correspondence of Thomas Bekynton, Secretary to Henry VI and Bishop of Bath and Wells, 2 vols, ed. G. Williams, Rolls Series, London, 1872

Parliamentary Texts of the Later Middle Ages, ed. N. Pronay and J. Taylor, Oxford, 1980

The Parliamentary Writs and Writs of Military Summons, together with the records and muniments relating to the suit and service due and performed to the King's High Court of Parliament and the Councils of the Realm, or affording evidence of attendance given at Parliaments and Councils, 2 vols, ed. F. Palgrave, Record Commission, London, 1827–34

Paston Letters and Papers of the Fifteenth Century, 2 vols, ed. N. Davis, Oxford, 1971–6

Plumpton Correspondence, ed. T. Stapleton, Camden Society, IV, 1839

The Plumpton Letters and Papers, ed. J. Kirby, Camden 5th Series, VIII, 1996

The Politics of Fifteenth Century England: John Vale's Book, ed. M. L. Kekewich, Stroud, 1995

Proceedings and Ordinances of the Privy Council of England, 7 vols, ed. N. H. Nicolas, Record Commission, London, 1834–7

Die Recesse und Andere Akten der Hansetage von 1256–1430, 8 vols, ed. K. Koppmann, Leipzig, 1870–97

The Red Paper Book of Colchester, ed. W. G. Benham, Colchester, 1902

The Register of Charles Bothe, ed. A. T. Bannister, Hereford, Cantilupe Society, XX, 1921

The Registers of John de Sandale and Rigund de Asserio, Bishops of Winchester, 1316–1323, ed. F. J. Baigent, Hampshire Record Society, VIII, 1897

The Registers of Thomas Wolsey, Bishop of Bath and Wells, 1518–1523, John Clerke, Bishop of Bath and Wells, 1523–1541, William Knyght, Bishop of Bath and Wells, 1541–1547, and Gilbert Bourne, Bishop of Bath and Wells, 1554–1559, ed. H. Maxwell-Lyte, Somerset Record Society, vol. LV, Frome and London, 1940

Reports of the Lords Committees Touching the Dignity of a Peer of the Realm, 5 vols, London, 1820

The Roll of Arms of the Princes, Barons, and Knights who Attended King Edward I to the Siege of Caerlaverock in 1300, ed. T. Wright, London, 1864

Rotuli Litterarum Clausarum in Turri Londinensi, 2 vols, ed. T. D. Hardy, London, 1833–4

Rotuli Normanniae, 1200–1205 and 1417–18, ed. T. D. Hardy, Record Commission, London, 1835

Rotuli Parliamentorum Anglie hactenus inediti 1279–1373, ed. H. Richardson and G. Sayles, Camden 3rd Series, LI, 1935

Rotuli Parliamentorum ut et Petitiones et Placita in Parliamento, 6 vols, ed. J. Strachey, London, 1767–77

Rotuli Scotiæ in Turri Londinensi et in Domo Capitulari Westmonasteriensi Asservat, 2 vols, Record Commission, London, 1814–19

Royal and Historical Letters during the Reign of Henry the Fourth, 2 vols, ed. F. Hingeston and C. Randolph, Rolls Series, London, 1860–5

The Rule, Statutes and Customs of the Hospitallers 1099–1310, ed. E. J. King, London, 1934

The St Albans Chronicle 1406–1420, ed. V. H. Galbraith, Oxford, 1937

The Sandford Cartulary, 2 vols, ed. A. M. Leys, Oxfordshire Record Society, XIX, XXII, 1938–41

Select Cases before the King's Council in the Star Chamber 1477–1509, ed. I. S. Leadam, Selden Society XVI, 1903

Select Cases before the King's Council 1243–1482, ed. I. S. Leadam and J. F. Baldwin, Selden Society XXXV, Cambridge, 1918

Select Cases in the Council of Henry VII, ed. C. G. Bayne and W. H. Dunham, Selden Society, LXXV, 1958

Somerset Medieval Wills, ed. F. W. Weaver, Somerset Record Society, XIX, London, 1903

Statutes of the Realm 1278–1714, 9 vols, Record Commission, London, 1810–28

The Stonor Letters and Papers 1290–1483, 2 vols, ed. C. L. Kingsford, Camden 3rd series, XXIX–XXX, 1919

'Supplementary Stonor letters and papers, 1314–1482', ed. C. L. Kingsford, *Camden Miscellany* XIII, Camden 3rd series, XXXIV, 1923

Taxatio Ecclesiastica Angliae et Walliae auctoritate P. Nicholai IV circa AD 1291, Record Commission, London, 1802

The Thirteenth Century Statutes of the Knights Hospitallers, ed. E. J. King, Order of St John of Jerusalem Historical Pamphlet 6, London, 1933

Three Fifteenth Century Chronicles, ed. J. Gairdner, Camden Society 2nd Series, XXVIII, 1880

Valor Ecclesiasticus, 6 vols, Record Commission, London, 1810–1834

The Westminster Chronicle 1381–1394, ed. L. C. Hector and B. F. Harvey, Oxford, 1982

Winchester College Muniments, ed. S. Himsworth, 3 vols, Chichester, 1976–84

Wykeham's Register, vol. I, ed. T. F. Kirby, Winchester, 1896

Year Books of Henry VIII, 12–14 Henry VIII, 1520–23, ed. J. H. Baker, Selden Society CXIX, London, 2002

Year Books of Richard II, 12 Richard II, 1388–1389, ed. G. F. Deiser, Ames Foundation VI, Cambridge, MA, and London, 1914

Secondary works

Allen, D., 'The Order of St John as a "School for Ambassadors" in Counter-Reformation Europe', in *The Military Orders: Welfare and Warfare*, ed. H. Nicholson, Aldershot, 1998, 363–79

Allen, J., 'Englishmen in Rome and the Hospice 1362–1474', in *The English Hospice in Rome: The Venerabile*, XXI, Exeter, 1962, 43–81

Allmand, C. T., *Henry V*, 2nd edn, London, 1997

——, *Lancastrian Normandy 1415–1450*, Oxford, 1983

——, ed., *Society at War: The Experience of England and France during the Hundred Years War*, Edinburgh 1973

Anglo, S., *Spectacle, Pageantry and Early Tudor Policy*, 2nd edn, Oxford, 1997

Archer, R. E., ed., *Crown, Government and People in the Fifteenth Century*, Stroud, 1995

Armstrong, C. A. J., 'Politics and the Battle of St Albans, 1455', *Bulletin of the Institute of Historical Research*, XXXIII, 1960, 1–72

Arthurson, I., *The Perkin Warbeck Conspiracy 1491–1499*, Stroud, 1994

Atiya, A. S., *The Crusade in the Later Middle Ages*, London, 1938

Ayton, A., *Knights and Warhorses: Military Service and the English Aristocracy under Edward III*, Woodbridge, 1994

Baldwin, J. F., *The King's Council in England during the Middle Ages*, Oxford, 1913

Barber, M., ed., *The Military Orders: Fighting for the Faith and Caring for the Sick*, Aldershot, 1994

——, *The New Knighthood: A History of the Order of the Temple*, Cambridge, 1994

——, *The Trial of the Templars*, Cambridge, 1978

Barnie, J., *War in Medieval English Society: Social Values and the Hundred Years War, 1337–1399*, London, 1974

Barquero Goñi, C., 'The Hospitallers and the Castilian-Leonese Monarchy: the Concession of Royal Rights, Twelfth to Fourteenth Centuries', in *The Military Orders: Fighting for the Faith and Caring for the Sick*, ed. M. Barber, Aldershot, 1994, 28–33

——, 'The Hospitallers and the Kings of Navarre in the Fourteenth and Fifteenth Centuries', in *The Military Orders: Welfare and Warfare*, ed. H. Nicholson, Aldershot, 1998, 349–54

Barren, E. M., *The Scottish War of Independence*, 2nd edn, Inverness, 1934

Barron, C. M., 'The Tyranny of Richard II', *Bulletin of the Institute of Historical Research*, XLI, 1968, 1–18

Barrow, G. W. S., *Robert Bruce and the Community of the Realm of Scotland*, London, 1965

Bean, J. M. W., 'Henry IV and the Percies', *History*, XLIV, 1959, 212–27

Bennett, M. J., 'Edward III's Entail and the Succession to the Crown, 1376–1471', *English Historical Review*, CXIII, 1998, 580–609

Bernard, G. W., ed., *The Tudor Nobility*, Manchester, 1992

Bindoff, S. T. and Thomas, S., eds, *The House of Commons 1509–1558*, 3 vols, London, History of Parliament Trust, London, 1982

Binski, P., *The Painted Chamber at Westminster*, London, 1986

Bolton, J. L., *The Medieval English Economy 1150–1500*, London, 1980

Borchardt, K., Jaspert, N. and Nicholson, H., eds, *The Hospitallers, the Mediterranean and Europe: Festschrift for Anthony Luttrell*, Aldershot, 2007

Brand, P., 'Petitions and Parliament in the Reign of Edward I', in *Parchment and People: Parliament in the Middle Ages*, ed. L. Clark, *Parliamentary History*, XXIII, Special Issue, 2004, 14–38

Bronstein, J., *The Hospitallers and the Holy Land: Financing the Latin East, 1187–1274*, Woodbridge, 2005

Brown, A. L., 'The Commons and the Council in the Reign of Henry IV', in *Historical Studies of the English Parliament*, ed. E. B. Fryde and E. Miller, 2 vols, Cambridge, 1970, II, 31–60

——, *The Governance of Late Medieval England 1272–1461*, London, 1989

——, 'The King's Councillors in Fifteenth-Century England', *Transactions of the Royal Historical Society*, 5th Series, XIX, 1969, 95–118

——, 'Parliament, c. 1377–1422', in *The English Parliament in the Middle Ages*, ed. R. G. Davies and J. H. Denton, Manchester, 1981, 109–140

Brown, E. A. R., 'The Political Repercussions of Family Ties in the Early Fourteenth Century: The Marriage of Edward II of England and Isabelle of France', *Speculum*, LXIII, 1988, 573–595

Brown, R. 'The Ecclesiastical Patronage of the Bishops of Winchester, 1282–1530', *Southern History: A Review of the History of Southern England*, XXIV, 2002, 27–44

Buck, M. C., 'The Reform of the Exchequer, 1316–1326', *English Historical Review*, XCVIII, 1983, 241–60

Bullough, D. A. and Storey, R. L., *The Study of Medieval Records*, Oxford, 1971

Burgtorf, J. and Nicholson, H., eds, *International Mobility in the Military Orders (Twelfth to Fifteenth Centuries): Travelling on Christ's Business*, Cardiff, 2006

Burne, A. H., *The Agincourt War. A Military History of the Latter Part of the Hundred Years War from 1369 to 1453*, London, 1956

——, *The Crécy War. A Military History of the Hundred Years' War from 1337 to the Peace of Brétigny, 1360*, London, 1955

Butler, L., 'The Order of St John and the Peasants' Revolt', *St John Historical Society Pamphlets*, I, 1981

Calmette, J. and Périnelle, G., *Louis XI et l'Angleterre 1461–1483*, Paris, 1930

Campbell, B. M. S., ed., *Before the Black Death: Studies in the 'Crisis' of the Early Fourteenth Century*, Manchester, 1991

Carpenter, C., *The Wars of the Roses: Politics and the Constitution in England, c. 1437–1509*, Cambridge, 1997

Cartellieri, O., *The Court of Burgundy*, London, 1929

Cazelles, R., *La Société Politique et la Crise de la Royauté sous Philippe de Valois*, Paris, 1958

Chaplais, P., *Essays in Medieval Diplomacy and Administration*, London, 1981

——, *Piers Gaveston: Edward II's Adoptive Brother*, Oxford, 1994

Chrimes, S. B., *Henry VII*, 2nd edn, New Haven, CT, and London, 1999

——, Ross, C. D. and Griffiths, R. A., eds, *Fifteenth-Century England 1399–1509: Studies in Politics and Society*, 2nd edn, Manchester, 1995.

Clark, L., 'The Benefits and Burdens of Office: Henry Bourgchier (1408–83), Viscount Bourgchier and Earl of Essex, and the Treasurership of the Exchequer', in *Profit, Piety and the Professions in Later Medieval England*, ed. M. A. Hicks, Gloucester, 1990, 119–36

——, ed., *Parchment and People: Parliament in the Middle Ages*, *Parliamentary History*, XXIII, Special Issue, 2004

Clarke, M. V., *Fourteenth Century Studies*, ed. L. S. Sutherland and M. McKisack, Oxford, 1937

Clayton, D. J., Davies, R. G. and McNiven, P., eds, *Trade, Devotion and Governance: Papers in Later Medieval History*, Stroud, 1994

Clough, C., 'Late Fifteenth Century English Monarchs subject to Italian Renaissance Influence' in *England and the Continent in the Middle Ages: Studies in Memory of Andrew Martindale: Proceedings of the 1996 Harlaxton Symposium*, ed. J. Mitchell and M. Moran, Stamford, 2000, 28–34

Clowes, W. L., *The Royal Navy: A History from the Earliest Times to the Present*, 2 vols, London, 1897

Condon, M. M., 'From Caitiff and Villain to Pater Patriae: Reynold Bray and the Profits of Office', in *Profit, Piety and the Professions in Later Medieval England*, ed. M. A. Hicks, Gloucester, 1990, 137–68

——, 'Ruling Elites in the Reign of Henry VII', in *Patronage, Pedigree and Power in Later Medieval England*, ed. C. D. Ross, Gloucester, 1979, 109–42.

Contamine, P., *War in the Middle Ages*, tr. M. Jones, Oxford, 1984 (*La Guerre au moyen âge*, Paris, 1980)

Coss, P. R., 'Knights, Esquires and the Origins of Social Gradation in England', *Transactions of the Royal Historical Society*, 6th Series, V, 1995, 155–78

Coss, P. R. and Lloyd, S. D., eds, *Thirteenth Century England*, I, Woodbridge, 1986

Cowan, I. B., *Medieval Religious Houses: Scotland*, 2nd edn, London, 1976

——, Mackay, P. R. H. and Macquarrie, A., *The Knights of St John of Jerusalem in Scotland*, Edinburgh, 1983

Cruickshank, C. G., *Army Royal: Henry VIII's Invasion of France, 1513*, Oxford, 1969

Crump, C. G., 'The Arrest of Roger Mortimer and Queen Isabel', *English Historical Review*, XXVI, 1911, 331–2

Cunich, P., 'Dissolution and De-Conversion: Institutional Change and Individual Response in the 1530s', *International Medieval Research*, V, 1998, 25–42

Curry, A., ed., *Agincourt 1415: Henry V, Sir Thomas Erpingham and the Triumph of the English Archers*, Stroud, 2000

——, ' "A Game of Two Halves:" Parliament 1422–1454', in *Parchment and People: Parliament in the Middle Ages*, ed. L. Clark, *Parliamentary History*, XXIII, Special Issue, 2004, 73–102

——, *The Hundred Years War*, London and Basingstoke, 1993

——and Hughes, M., eds, *Arms, Armies and Fortifications in the Hundred Years War*, Woodbridge, 1994

Cuttino, G. P., *English Diplomatic Administration, 1259–1339*, Oxford, 1971

Cuttino, G. P., *English Medieval Diplomacy*, Bloomington, IN, 1985

Davies, R. G., 'The Episcopate and the Political Crisis in England of 1386–1388', *Speculum*, LI, 1976, 659–93

—— and Denton, J. H., eds, *The English Parliament in the Middle Ages*, Manchester, 1981

Delaville le Roulx, J. *Les Hospitaliers à Rhodes (1310–1421)*, Paris, 1913 (reprinted London, 1974)

Denton, J. H., *Robert Winchelsey and the Crown 1294–1313*, Cambridge, 1980

Dickinson, J., *The Congress of Arras 1435: A Study in Medieval Diplomacy*, Oxford, 1955

Dobson, R. B., ed., *The Peasants' Revolt of 1381*, 2nd edn, London, 1983

Dodd, G., 'The Lords, Taxation and the Community of Parliament in the 1370s and Early 1380s', *Parliamentary History*, XX, 2001, 287–310

Du Boulay, F. R. H., and Barron, C. M., eds, *The Reign of Richard II*, London, 1971

Dunham, W. H., ' "The Books of Parliament" and "The Old Record", 1396–1504', *Speculum*, LI, 1976, 694–712

——, 'Notes from the Parliament at Winchester, 1449', *Speculum*, XVII, 1942, 402–15

Dunlop, A. I., *The Life and Times of James Kennedy, Bishop of St Andrews*, Edinburgh and London, 1950

Dyer, S., 'The Weston Family and the Order of St John', *St John Historical Society Newsletter*, September 1983

Edbury, P. W., *The Kingdom of Cyprus and the Crusades 1191–1374*, Cambridge, 1991

Elton, G. R., 'The Early Journals of the House of Lords', *English Historical Review*, LXXXIX, 1974, 481–512

Ferguson, J., *English Diplomacy, 1422–1461*, Oxford, 1972

Field, P. J. C., *The Life and Times of Sir Thomas Malory*, Cambridge, 1993

——, 'Sir Robert Malory, Prior of the Hospital of St John of Jerusalem in England (1432–1439/40)' *Journal of Ecclesiastical History*, XXVIII, 1977, 249–64

Forey, A., 'Ex-Templars in England', *Journal of Ecclesiastical History*, LIII, 2002, 18–37

——, *Military Orders and the Crusades*, Aldershot, 1994

——, *The Military Orders: From the Twelfth to the Early Fourteenth Centuries*, Basingstoke, 1992

Fowler, K., 'Les Finances et la Discipline dans les Armées Anglaises en France au XIVe Siècle', *Actes du Colloque International de Cockerel, Les Cahiers Vernonnais*, IV, 1964

——, ed., *The Hundred Years' War*, London, 1971

——, *The King's Lieutenant: Henry of Grosmont, First Duke of Lancaster, 1310–1361*, London, 1969

Freeman, J., 'Middlesex in the Fifteenth Century: Community of Communities?' in *Revolution and Consumption in Late Medieval England*, ed. M. A. Hicks, Woodbridge, 2001, 89–103

Fryde, E. B. and Miller, E., eds, *Historical Studies of the English Parliament*, 2 vols, Cambridge, 1970

——, Greenway, D. E., Porter, S. and Roy, I., eds, *Handbook of British Chronology*, 3rd edn, London, 1986

Fryde, N. M., *The Tyranny and Fall of Edward II*, Cambridge, 1979

Gervers, M., *The Hospitaller Cartulary in the British Library (Cotton MS Nero E VI): A Study of the Manuscript and its Composition, with a Critical Edition of Two Fragments of Earlier Cartularies for Essex*, Toronto, 1981

——, 'Pro defensione Terre Sancti: The development and Exploitation of the Hospitallers' Landed Estates in Essex', in *The Military Orders: Fighting for the Faith and Caring for the Sick*, ed. M. Barber, Aldershot, 1994, 3–20

Gill, J., *The Council of Florence*, Cambridge, 1959

Gillingham, J., *The Wars of the Roses: Peace and Conflict in Fifteenth Century England*, London, 1981

—— and Holt, J. C., eds, *War and Government in the Middle Ages*, Woodbridge, 1984

Gilson, J. P., 'A Defence of the Proscription of the Yorkists in 1459', *English Historical Review*, XXVI, 1911, 512–25

Given-Wilson, C., *The English Nobility in the Late Middle Ages: The Fourteenth-Century Political Community*, 2nd edn, London, 1996

——, 'Richard II, Edward II, and the Lancastrian Inheritance', *English Historical Review*, CIX, 1994, 553–71

——, 'The Rolls of Parliament 1399–1421', in *Parchment and People: Parliament in the Middle Ages*, ed. L. Clark, *Parliamentary History*, XXIII, Special Issue, 2004, 56–72

——, *The Royal Household and the King's Affinity*, New Haven, CT, and London, 1986

Goodman, A., *John of Gaunt: The Exercise of Princely Power in Fourteenth Century Europe*, London, 1992

——, 'Responses to Requests for Military Service under Henry V', *Northern History*, XVII, 1981, 240–252

——, 'Richard II's Councils', in *Richard II: The Art of Kingship*, ed. A. Goodman and J. Gillespie, Oxford, 1999, 59–82

——, *The Wars of the Roses: Military Activity and English Society 1452–97*, London, 1981

—— and Gillespie, J., eds, *Richard II: The Art of Kingship*, Oxford, 1999

Grant, A., *Independence and Nationhood: Scotland 1306–1469*, London, 1984

Gras, N. S. B., *The Early English Customs System*, Cambridge, 1918

Green, J. A., *Henry I: King of England and Duke of Normandy*, Cambridge, 2006

Griffiths, R. A., 'The King's Council and the First Protectorate of the Duke of York, 1453–4', *English Historical Review*, XCIX, 1984, 67–82

——, *The Reign of King Henry VI: The Exercise of Royal Authority, 1422–1461*, Stroud, 1998

——, 'The Winchester Session of the 1449 Parliament: A Further Comment', *The Huntington Library Quarterly*, XLII, 1979, 181–91

Gunn, S. J., 'Henry Bourchier, Earl of Essex (1472–1540)', in *The Tudor Nobility*, ed. G. W. Bernard, Manchester, 1992, 134–79

Guy, J. A., *The Cardinal's Court: The Impact of Thomas Wolsey in Star Chamber*, Trowbridge, 1977

——, *The Court of Star Chamber and its Records to the Reign of Elizabeth I*, London, 1984

——, 'Wolsey, the Council and the Council Courts', *English Historical Review*, XCI, 1976, 481–505

Gwyn, P., *The King's Cardinal. The Rise and Fall of Thomas Wolsey*, London, 1990

Gwynn, A. and Hadcock, R. N., *Medieval Religious Houses: Ireland*, 2nd edn, Blackrock, 1988

Haines, R. M., *The Church and Politics in Fourteenth Century England*, Cambridge, 1978

Hanham, A., *The Celys and their World: an English Merchant Family of the Fifteenth Century*, Cambridge, 1985

Hare, C. (Andrews, M.), *The Life of Louis XI the Rebel Dauphin and the Statesman King*, London, 1907

Harriss, G. L., *Cardinal Beaufort: A Study of Lancastrian Ascendancy and Decline*, Oxford, 1988

——, ed., *Henry V: The Practice of Kingship*, Oxford, 1985

——, *King, Parliament and Public Finance in Medieval England to 1369*, Oxford, 1975

——, 'Marmaduke Lumley and the Exchequer Crisis of 1446–9', in *Aspects of Late Medieval Government and Society: Essays Presented to J R Lander*, ed. J. G. Rowe, Toronto and London, 1986, 143–78

——, 'Political Society and the Growth of Government in Later Medieval England', *Past and Present*, CXXXVIII, 1993, 28–57

——, 'Preference at the Medieval Exchequer', *Bulletin of the Institute of Historical Research*, XXX, 1957, 17–40

——, 'War and the Emergence of the English Parliament 1297–1360', *Journal of Medieval History*, II, 1976, 35–56

Harvey, I. M. W., *Jack Cade's Rebellion of 1450*, Oxford, 1991

Harvey, M., *England, Rome and the Papacy 1417–1464: The Study of a Relationship*, Manchester, 1993

——, *The English in Rome 1362–1420. Portrait of an Expatriate Community*, Cambridge, 1999

Hay, D., 'The Division of the Spoils of War in Fourteenth Century England', *Transactions of the Royal Historical Society*, 5th Series, IV, 1954, 91–109

Heal, F. M., *Of Prelates and Princes: A Study of the Economic and Social Position of the Tudor Episcopate*, Cambridge, 1980

Herbermann, C. G., ed., *The Catholic Encyclopedia*, 17 vols, New York, 1907–18

Herde, P., 'The Dispute between the Hospitallers and the Bishop of Worcester about the Church of Down Ampney. An Unpublished Letter of Justice of Pope John XXI (1276)', in *The Hospitallers, the Mediterranean and Europe. Festschrift for Anthony Luttrell*, ed. K. Borchardt, N. Jaspert and H. Nicholson, Aldershot, 2007, 47–55

Hewitt, H. J., *The Black Prince's Expeditions of 1355–57*, Manchester, 1958

——, *The Organization of War under Edward III, 1338–62*, Manchester, 1966

Hicks, M. A., 'Bastard Feudalism, Overmighty Subjects and Idols of the Multitude during the Wars of the Roses' *History*, LXXXV, 2000, 386–403

——, *English Political Culture in the Fifteenth Century*, London, 2002

——, *False Fleeting Perjur'd Clarence. George, Duke of Clarence 1449–78*, 2nd edn, Bangor, 1992

——, ed., *Profit, Piety and the Professions in Later Medieval England*, Gloucester, 1990

——, ed., *Revolution and Consumption in Late Medieval England*, Woodbridge, 2001

——, *Richard III as Duke of Gloucester: A Study in Character*, Borthwick Paper 70, York, 1986

——, *Richard III and his Rivals: Magnates and their Motives in the Wars of the Roses*, 2nd edn, Stroud, 2000

——, *Warwick the Kingmaker*, Oxford, 1998

Holmes, G. A., *The Estates of the Higher Nobility in Fourteenth Century England*, Cambridge, 1957

——, *The Good Parliament*, Oxford, 1975

——, 'The Rebellion of the Earl of Lancaster, 1318–19', *Bulletin of the Institute of Historical Research*, XXVIII, 1955, 84–9

Hooker, J. R., 'Notes on the Organization and Supply of the Tudor Military under Henry VII', *Huntington Library Quarterly*, XXIII, 1950, 19–31

Houlbrooke, R., 'The Decline of Ecclesiastical Jurisdiction under the Tudors', in *Continuity and Change: Personnel and Administration of the Church in England 1500–1642*, ed. R. O'Day and F. Heal, Leicester, 1976, 239–58

Housley, N., *The Avignon Papacy and the Crusades, 1305–1378*, Oxford, 1986

——, *The Later Crusades: From Lyons to Alcazar, 1274–1580*, Oxford, 1992

Hunt, E., *The Medieval Super-Companies: a Study of the Peruzzi Company of Florence*, Cambridge, 1994

Jacob, E. F., *The Fifteenth Century 1399–1485*, Oxford, 1961

James, M. E., 'English Politics and the Concept of Honour, 1485–1642', *Past and Present*, Supplement 3, 1978,

Johnson, P. A., *Duke Richard of York 1411–1460*, Oxford, 1988

Jones, M., *Ducal Brittany 1364–1399*, Oxford, 1970

Jones, M. C. E. and Vale, M. G. A., eds, *England and her Neighbours 1066–1453. Essays in Honour of Pierre Chaplais*, London, 1989

Jones, M. K., 'Somerset, York and the Wars of the Roses', *English Historical Review*, CIV, 1989, 285–307

Kaeuper, R. W., *Bankers to the Crown: The Riccardi of Lucca and Edward I*, Princeton, NJ, 1973

——, *War, Justice and Public Order: England and France in the Later Middle Ages*, Oxford, 1988

Keen, M. H., *England in the Later Middle Ages*, London, 1973

—— and Daniel, M. J., 'English Diplomacy and the Sack of Fougères in 1449', *History*, LIX, 1974, 375–91

King, E. J., *The Grand Priory of the Order of the Hospital of St John of Jerusalem in England*, London, 1924

——, *The Knights of St John in the British Empire*, London, 1934

—— and Luke, H., *The Knights of St John in the British Realm*, London, 1967

Kirby, J. L., *Henry IV of England*, London, 1970

Kitching, C. J., 'The Probate Jurisdiction of Thomas Cromwell as Vicegerent', *Bulletin of the Institute of Historical Research*, XLVI, 1973, 102–6

Knowles, D. and Hadcock, R. N., *Medieval Religious Houses, England and Wales*, 2nd edn, London, 1971

Koch, H. W., *Medieval Warfare*, London 1978

Laird, W., *The Royal Navy: A History from the Earliest Times to the Present*, I, London, 1897

Lander, J. R., *Crown and Nobility 1450–1509*, London, 1976

——, *Government and Community 1450–1509*, Cambridge, MA, 1980

Landi, A., *Il papa deposto, Pisa 1409: l'idea conciliare nel Grande Scisma*, Turin, 1985

Le Neve, J., *Fasti Ecclesiae Anglicanae, 1300–1541*, 12 vols, ed. H. King, London, 1962–7

Lehnberg, S., *The Reformation Parliament of 1529–1536*, Cambridge, 1970

Lewis, N. B., 'The "Continual Council" in the Early Years of Richard II, 1377–80', *English Historical Review*, XLI, 1926, 246–51

——, 'The Last Medieval Summons of the English Feudal Levy, 13 June 1385', *English Historical Review*, LXXIII, 1958, 1–26

——, 'The Recruitment and Organisation of a Contract Army, May to November 1337', *Bulletin of the Institute of Historical Research*, XXXVII, 1964, 1–19

Lloyd, S., *English Society and the Crusade, 1216–1307*, Oxford, 1988

Loades, D. M., *Politics and the Nation: England 1450–1660*, 5th edn, Oxford, 1999

Lord, E., *The Knights Templar in Britain*, Edinburgh, 2002

Lunt, W. M., *Financial Relations of the Papacy with England to 1327*, Cambridge, MA, 1939

——, *Financial Relations of the Papacy with England 1327–1534*, Cambridge, MA, 1962

——, *Papal Revenues in the Middle Ages*, 2 vols, New York, 1965

Luttrell, A., 'Change and Conflict Within the Hospitaller Province of Italy after 1291', in *Mendicants, Military Orders, and Regionalism in Medieval Europe*, ed. J. Sarnowsky, Aldershot, 1999, 185–99

——, 'English Contributions to the Hospitaller Castle at Bodrum in Turkey: 1407–1437', in *Studies on the Hospitallers after 1306*, Aldershot, 2007, 163–72

——, 'Hospitaller Birgu: 1530–1536', 121–150, *Crusades*, II, 2003, 121–50

——, 'The Hospitallers in Cyprus after 1386', in *The Hospitaller State on Rhodes and its Western Provinces, 1306–1462*, ed. A. Luttrell, Aldershot, 1999, V, 1–20

——, *The Hospitallers in Cyprus, Rhodes, Greece and the West (1291–1440)*, London, 1978

——, 'The Hospitallers at Rhodes, 1306–1421', in *A History of the Crusades*, III, ed. K. M. Setton, Madison, WI, and London, 1975, 278–339

——, *The Hospitallers of Rhodes and their Mediterranean World*, Aldershot, 1992

——, *The Hospitaller State on Rhodes and its Western Provinces, 1306–1462*, Aldershot, 1999

——, *Latin Greece, the Hospitallers and the Crusades, 1291–1440*, London, 1982

——, 'The Military Orders 1312–1798', in *The Oxford Illustrated History of the Crusades*, ed. J. Riley-Smith, Oxford, 1995, 326–64

——, 'The Military Orders: Further Definitions', *Sacra Militia: Rivista di storia degli Ordini militari*, I, 2000, 7–12

——, *Studies on the Hospitallers after 1306: Rhodes and the West*, Aldershot, 2007

——, *The Town of Rhodes 1306–1356*, Rhodes, 2003

—— and Nicholson, H., eds, *Hospitaller Women in the Middle Ages*, Aldershot, 2006

MacCulloch, D., ed., *The Reign of Henry VIII: Politics, Policy and Piety*, Basingstoke, 1995

Macdougall, N., *James III: A Political Study*, Edinburgh, 1982

——, *James IV*, 2nd edn, East Linton, 1997

McFarlane, K. B., *England in the Fifteenth Century: Collected Essays*, ed. G. L. Harriss, London, 1981

——, *Lancastrian Kings and Lollard Knights*, Oxford, 1972

——, *The Nobility of Later Medieval England*, Oxford, 1973

Mackie, J., *The Early Tudors 1485–1558*, Oxford, 1952

McKisack, M., *The Fourteenth Century 1307–1399*, Oxford, 1959

McNamee, C., *The Wars of the Bruces. Scotland, England and Ireland, 1306–1328*, East Linton, 1997

McNiven, P., 'Prince Henry and the English Political Crisis of 1412,' *History*, LXV, 1980

Macquarrie, A., *Scotland and the Crusades 1095–1560*, 2nd edn, Edinburgh, 1997

Maddicott, J. R., *Thomas of Lancaster*, Oxford, 1970

Madison, K. G., 'The Seating of the Barons in Parliament, December 1461', *Mediaeval Studies*, XXXVII, 1975, 494–503

Malament, B. C., ed., *After the Reformation: Essays in Honour of J. A. Hexter*, Manchester, 1980

Mallett, M., 'Diplomacy and War in Later Fifteenth Century Italy', *Proceedings of the British Academy*, LXVII, 1981, 268–88

——, *The Florentine Galleys in the Fifteenth Century*, Oxford, 1967

Mallia-Milanes, V., ed., *The Military Orders: History and Heritage*, Aldershot, 2008

Mayer, H. E., *The Crusades*, 2nd edn, Oxford, 1988

Mifsud, A., *Knights Hospitaller of the Venerable Tongue of England*, Malta, 1914

Miller, H., 'London and Parliament in the Reign of Henry VIII', in *Historical Studies of the English Parliament* II, ed. E. B. Fryde and E. Miller, Cambridge, 1970, 125–46

——, *Henry VIII and the English Nobility*, Oxford, 1986

Mitchell, J. and Moran, M., eds, *England and the Continent in the Middle Ages: Studies in Memory of Andrew Martindale. Proceedings of the 1996 Harlaxton Symposium*, Stamford, 2000

Mitchell, S. K., *Taxation in Medieval England*, New Haven, CT, 1951

Mizzi, J., ed., *Catalogue of the Records of the Order of St John of Jerusalem in the Royal Malta Library*, 13 vols, Malta, 1964–7

Mol, J. A., Militzer, K. and Nicholson, H., eds, *The Military Orders and the Reformation: Choices, State Building and the Weight of Tradition. Papers of the Utrecht Conference, 30 September–2 October 2004*, Hilversum, 2006

Morgan, D. A. L., 'The Political After-Life of Edward III: The Apotheosis of a Warmonger', *English Historical Review*, CXII, 1997, 856–881

Mueller, R. C., *The Venetian Money Market: Banks, Panics, and the Public Debt, 1200–1500*, Baltimore, MD, 1997

Murray, A. V., ed., *From Clermont to Jerusalem: The Crusades and Crusader Societies, 1095–1500. Selected Proceedings of the International Medieval Congress, University of Leeds, 10–13 July 1995*, Turnhout, 1998

Myers, A. R., 'A Parliamentary Debate of 1449', *Bulletin of the Institute of Historical Research*, LI, 1978, 78–83

——, 'A Parliamentary Debate of the Mid-Fifteenth Century', *Bulletin of the John Rylands Library*, XXII, 1938, 388–404

New Catholic Encyclopedia, 17 vols, Catholic University of America, New York, 1967–79

Newcourt, R., *Repertorium or an Ecclesiastical History of the Diocese of London*, 2 vols, London, 1708–10

Newhall, R. A., *The English Conquest of Normandy, 1416–1424*, New Haven, CT, and London, 1924

Newns, B., 'The Hospice of St Thomas and the English Crown 1474–1538', in *The English Hospice in Rome: The Venerabile*, XXI, Exeter, 1962, 145–92

Nicholson, H., 'The Hospitallers in England, the Kings of England and Relations with Rhodes in the Fourteenth Century', *Sacra Militia: Rivista di storia degli Ordini militari*, II, 2001, 25–45

Nicholson, H., *The Knights Hospitaller*, Woodbridge, 2001

——, 'The Military Orders and the Kings of England in the Twelfth and Thirteenth Centuries', in *From Clermont to Jerusalem: The Crusades and Crusader Societies 1095–1500: Select Proceedings of the International Medieval Congress, University of Leeds, 10–13 July 1995*, ed. A. V. Murray, Turnhout, 1998, 203–18

——, ed., *The Military Orders: Welfare and Warfare*, Aldershot, 1998

——, *Templars, Hospitallers and Teutonic Knights: Images of the Military Orders 1128–1291*, Leicester, 1993

Nicholson, R., *Edward III and the Scots*, Oxford, 1965

——, *Scotland, The Later Middle Ages*, Edinburgh, 1974

O'Day, R. and Heal, F., eds, *Continuity and Change: Personnel and Administration of the Church in England 1500–1642*, Leicester, 1976

O'Malley, G. J., *The Knights Hospitaller of the English Langue, 1460–1565*, Oxford, 2005

Oman, C., *The Great Revolt of 1381*, 2nd edn, Oxford, 1969

Ormrod, W. M., 'Edward III and the Recovery of Royal Authority in England, 1340–1360', *History*, LXXII, 1987, 4–19

——, ed., *England in the Fourteenth Century*, Woodbridge, 1986

——, 'On and Off the Record: The Rolls of Parliament, 1337–1377', *Parchment and People: Parliament in the Middle Ages*, ed. L. Clark, *Parliamentary History*, XXIII, Special Issue, 2004, 39–56

——, *The Reign of Edward III*, New Haven, CT, and London, 1990

Palmer, J. J. N., *England, France, and Christendom, 1377–99*, London, 1972

——, 'The Impeachment of Michael de la Pole in 1386', *Bulletin of the Institute of Historical Research*, XLII, 1969, 96–101

——, 'The Last Summons of the Feudal Army in England (1385)', *English Historical Review*, LXXXIII, 1968, 771–5

——, 'The Parliament of 1385 and the Constitutional Crisis of 1386', *Speculum*, XLVI, 1971, 477–90

Pastor, L., *The History of the Popes from the Close of the Middle Ages*, 6th edn, 40 vols, tr. F. I. Antrobus, R. F. Kerr, E. Graf and E. F. Peeler, Nendeln, 1968–9

Phillips, J. R. S., *Aymer de Valence Earl of Pembroke 1307–24*, Oxford, 1972

——, 'Edward II and the Prophets', in *England in the Fourteenth Century*, ed. W. M. Ormrod, Woodbridge, 1986, 189–201

Phillips, S. D., 'The Recycling of Monastic Wealth in Medieval Southern England,

1300–1530', *Southern History: A Review of the History of Southern England*, XXII, 2000, 45–71

Pinks, W., *The History of Clerkenwell*, ed. E. J. Wood, London, 1881

Plucknett, T. F. T., 'The Impeachments of 1376', *Transactions of the Royal Historical Society*, 5th Series, I, 1951, 153–64

Pocquet de Haut-Jussé, B. A., *François II, duc de Bretagne et l'Angleterre, 1458–88*, Paris, 1929

Poole, A. L., ed., *Medieval England*, Oxford and New York, 1958

Potter, D., 'Foreign Policy', in *The Reign of Henry VIII: Politics, Policy and Piety*, ed. D. MacCulloch, Basingstoke, 1995, 101–33

Potter, G. R., ed., *The New Cambridge Modern History*, I, Cambridge, 1957

Powell, J. E., and Wallis, K., *The House of Lords in the Middle Ages*, London, 1968

Powicke, M. R., *Military Obligation in Medieval England: A Study in Liberty and Duty*, Oxford, 1962

——, *The Thirteenth Century 1216–1307*, 2nd edn, Oxford, 1962

Prestwich, M. C., *Edward I*, London, 1988

——, *English Politics in the Thirteenth Century*, London, 1990

——, *The Three Edwards: War and State in England 1272–1377*, London, 1980

——, *War, Politics and Finance under Edward I*, London, 1972

——, Britnell, R. H. and Frame, R., eds, *Thirteenth Century England*, VI, Woodbridge, 1997

Prince, A. E., 'The Payment of Army Wages in Edward III's Reign', *Speculum*, XIX, 1944, 137–60

——, 'The Strength of English Armies in the Middle Ages', *English Historical Review*, XLVI, 1931, 353–71

Pugh, T. B., ed., *Henry V and the Southampton Plot*, Gloucester, 1988

Queller, D. E., *The Office of Ambassador in the Middle Ages*, Princeton, NJ, 1967

Ramsay, J. H., *A History of the Revenues of the Kings of England, 1066–1399*, 2 vols, Oxford, 1925

——, *Lancaster and York. A Century of English History (1399–1485)*, Oxford, 1892

Rees, W., *A History of the Order of St John of Jerusalem in Wales and on the Welsh Border*, Cardiff, 1947

Richardson, H. G. and Sayles, G. O., eds, *The English Parliament in the Middle Ages*, London, 1981

—— and Sayles, G. O., *The Governance of Medieval England*, Edinburgh, 1963

Riley-Smith, J., *The Atlas of the Crusades*, New York, 1991

——, *Hospitallers: The History of the Order of St John*, London, 1999

——, *The Knights of St John in Jerusalem and Cyprus, c. 1050–1310*, London, 1967

——, ed., *The Oxford Illustrated History of the Crusades*, Oxford, 1995

——, *What Were the Crusades?*, London, 1977

Rodger, N. A. M., *The Safeguard of the Sea: A Naval History of Great Britain*, I, London, 1997

Roncière, C. de la, *Histoire de la Marine Française*, II, Paris 1900

Roskell, J. S., *The Impeachment of Michael de la Pole, Earl of Suffolk, in 1386*, Manchester, 1984

——, *Parliament and Politics in Late Medieval England*, vol. I, London, 1981

——, 'The Problem of the Attendance of the Lords in Medieval Parliaments', *Bulletin of the Institute of Historical Research*, XXIX, 1956, 153–204

——, Clark, L., and Rawcliffe, C., eds, *The History of Parliament. The House of Commons 1386–1421*, I, Stroud, 1992

Ross, C. D., *Edward IV*, 2nd edn, New Haven, CT, and London, 1997

——, ed., *Patronage, Pedigree and Power in Later Medieval England*, Gloucester, 1979

Rowe, J. G., ed., *Aspects of Late Medieval Government and Society: Essays Presented to J. R. Lander*, Toronto and London, 1986

Runciman, J. C. S., *A History of the Crusades*, 3 vols, Cambridge, 1951–4

Russell, J. G., *Diplomats at Work: Three Renaissance Studies*, Stroud, 1992

——, *The Field of Cloth of Gold: Men and Manners in 1520*, London, 1969

——, *Peacemaking in the Renaissance*, Philadelphia, PA, 1986

Russell, P. E., *The English Intervention in Spain and Portugal*, Oxford, 1955

——, *Portugal, Spain and the African Atlantic, 1343–1490: Chivalry and Crusade from John of Gaunt to Henry the Navigator*, Aldershot, 1995

Sapori, A., *La Crisi delle Compagnie Mercantili dei Bardi e dei Peruzzi*, Florence, 1926

Sarnowsky, J., 'Kings and Priors: the Hospitaller Priory of England in the Later Fifteenth Century', in *Mendicants, Military Orders, and Regionalism in Medieval Europe*, ed. J. Sarnowsky, Aldershot, 1999, 83–102

——, ed., *Mendicants, Military Orders, and Regionalism in Medieval Europe*, Aldershot, 1999

Saul, N., 'The Despensers and the Downfall of Edward II', *English Historical Review*, XCIX, 1984, 1–33

——, *Richard II*, New Haven, CT, and London, 1997

Sayle, R. T. D., *A Brief History of the Worshipful Company of Merchant Taylors of the Fraternity of St John Baptist in the City of London*, London and Reading, 1945

Sayles, G. O., 'The Deposition of Richard II: Three Lancastrian Narratives', *Bulletin of the Institute of Historical Research*, LIV, 1981, 257–70

——, *The King's Parliament of England*, London, 1975

Scarisbrick, J. J., *Henry VIII*, 2nd edn, New Haven, CT, and London, 1997

——, *The Reformation of the English People*, Oxford, 1984

Schofield, A. N. E. D., 'The First English Delegation to the council of Basel', *Journal of Ecclesiastical History*, XII, 1961, 167–96

Scofield, C. L., *The Life and Reign of Edward the Fourth*, 2 vols, London, 1923

Seton-Watson, R. W., ed., *Tudor Studies*, London, 1924

Setton, K. M., ed., *A History of the Crusades*, 6 vols, Madison, WI, and London, 1969–90

——, *The Papacy and the Levant (1204–1571)*, 4 vols, Philadelphia, PA, 1976–84

Sherborne, J. W., 'Indentured Retinues and English Expeditions to France, 1369–1380', *English Historical Review*, LXXIX, 1964, 718–46

——, *War, Politics and Culture in Fourteenth Century England*, London, 1994

Sire, H. J. A., *The Knights of Malta*, New Haven, CT, and London, 1994

Sloane, B. and Malcolm, G., eds, *Excavations at the Priory of the Order of the Hospital of St John of Jerusalem, Clerkenwell, London*, Museum of London Archaeology Service Monograph XX, London, 2004.

Snape, R. H., *English Monastic Finances in the Later Middle Ages*, Cambridge, 1926

Somerville, R., *The Duchy of Lancaster: 1265–1603*, I, London, 1953

Steel, A. B., *The Receipt of the Exchequer, 1377–1485*, Cambridge, 1954

Storey, R. L., *The End of the House of Lancaster*, London, 1966

——, 'The Wardens of the Marches of England towards Scotland, 1377–1489', *English Historical Review*, LXXII, 1957, 593–615

Taylor, J. and Childs, W., eds, *Politics and Crisis in Fourteenth-Century England*, Gloucester, 1990

Thielemans, M. R., *Bourgogne et Angleterre, Rélations Politiques et Économiques Entre Les Pays-Bas Bourguignons et l'Angleterre, 1435–1467*, Brussels, 1966

Thornley, I. D., 'The Destruction of Sanctuary', in *Tudor Studies*, ed. R. W. Seton-Watson, London, 1924, 182–207

Thornton, T., 'The English King's French Islands: Jersey and Guernsey in English Politics and Administration, 1485–1642', in *Authority and Consent in Tudor England*, ed. G. W. Bernard and S. J. Gunn, Aldershot, 2002, 197–217

Thurley, S., 'The Domestic Building Works of Cardinal Wolsey', in *Cardinal Wolsey: Church, State and Art*, ed. S. J. Gunn and P. G. Lindley, Cambridge, 1991, 76–102

——, *The Royal Palaces of Tudor England: Architecture and Court Life 1460–1547*, New Haven, CT, and London, 1993

Tipton, C. L., 'The English Hospitallers during the Great Schism', *Studies in Medieval and Renaissance History*, IV, 1967, 91–124

——, 'The English and Scottish Hospitallers during the Great Schism', *Catholic Historical Review*, LII, 1966, 240–5

——, 'The Irish Hospitallers during the Great Schism', *Proceedings of the Royal Irish Academy*, LXIX, 1970, 33–43

Tout, T. F., *Chapters in the Administrative History of Medieval England*, III, Manchester, 1920

Triposkoupsi, A. and Tsitouri, A., eds, *Enetoi kai Ioannites Ippotes: Diktia Ochiromatikis Architektonikis (Venetians and the Knights of St John: Networks of Defence Architecture)*, Athens, 2001

Tristram, E. W., *English Medieval Wall Painting. The Thirteenth Century*, 2 vols, Oxford, 1950

——, *English Wall Painting of the Fourteenth Century*, London, 1955

Tuck, J. A., *Crown and Nobility: England 1272–1461*, 2nd edn, Oxford, 1999

——, *Richard II and the English Nobility*, London, 1973

—— and Goodman, A., eds, *War and Border Societies in the Middle Ages*, London, 1992

Tyerman, C., *England and the Crusades 1095–1588*, Chicago and London, 1988

Unwin, G., ed., *Finance and Trade under Edward III*, Manchester, 1918

Vale, M. G. A., *The Angevin Legacy and the Hundred Years War*, Oxford, 1990

——, *English Gascony 1399–1453*, Oxford, 1970

Valentini, R., 'Un capitolo generale degli Ospitalieri di S. Giovanni tenuto in Vaticano nel 1446', *Archivio Storico di Malta*, VII, Rome, 1935–6, 133–68

Vaughan, R., *Charles the Bold*, London, 1973

——, *Philip the Good*, London, 1970

The Venerabile, *The English Hospice in Rome*, XXI, Sexcentenary Issue, Exeter, 1962

The Victoria History of the Counties of England, 200+ vols, London, 1899–

Virgoe, R. L., 'The Composition of the King's Council, 1437–61', *Bulletin of the Institute of Historical Research*, XLIII, 1970, 134–160

——, 'The Death of William de la Pole Duke of Suffolk', *Bulletin of the John Rylands Library*, XLVII, 1964–5, 489–502

——, 'A New Fragment of the Lords' Journal of 1461', *Bulletin of the Institute of Historical Research*, XXXII, 1959, 83–7

Walker, S. K., *The Lancastrian Affinity 1361–1399*, Oxford, 1990

Watts, J. L., *Henry VI and the Politics of Kingship*, Cambridge, 1996

Waugh, S. L., *England in the Reign of Edward III*, Cambridge, 1991

Wedgwood, J. C. and Holt, A. D., *History of Parliament: Register of the Ministers and of the Members of Both Houses 1439–1509. Biographies of the Members of the Commons House*, 2 vols, London, 1936–8

Weir, A., *Henry VIII: King and Court*, London, 2001

Willard, J. F. and Morris, W. A., eds, *The English Government at Work, 1327–1336*, I, Cambridge, MA, 1940

Wolffe, B. P., *The Crown Lands 1461 to 1536*, London, 1970

——, *Henry VI*, 2nd edn, London, 2001

Wylie, J. H., *History of England under Henry the Fourth*, 4 vols, London, 1884–98

——, *The Reign of Henry V*, 3 vols, London, 1914–22

Youings, J., *The Dissolution of the Monasteries*, London, 1971

Unpublished theses

Beard, F., 'The Cartulary of Godsfield and Baddesley Preceptory', M.Phil. thesis, King Alfred's College, Winchester, 1999

Brown, R., 'Bastard Feudalism and the Bishopric of Winchester, 1282–1530', Ph.D. thesis, King Alfred's College, Winchester, 2002

Index